THE EXPANSION OF EUROPE

Motives, Methods, and Meanings

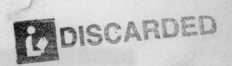

PROBLEMS IN EUROPEAN CIVILIZATION

THE
EXPANSION OF EUROPE

Motives, Methods, and Meanings

EDITED WITH AN INTRODUCTION BY

De Lamar Jensen

BRIGHAM YOUNG UNIVERSITY

D. C. HEATH AND COMPANY · BOSTON

Englewood · *Indianapolis* · *Dallas* · *Burlingame* · *Atlanta*

Library of Congress Catalog Card Number 67–16809

COPYRIGHT © 1967 BY D. C. HEATH AND COMPANY

Printed March 1967

Table of Contents

Introduction

A PROMINENT SCHOLAR recently remarked that if the history of Western civilization is still studied a thousand years from now, and if college curricula allow only a single lecture for it, that lecture will probably be devoted to the topic, "The Expansion of Europe." Although judgments differ sharply as to the moral justification of European penetration into Asia, Africa, and America, and opinions still diverge as to its political and economic consequences, very few will deny that this Europeanization of much of the earth's surface is one of the most significant features of modern history.

The European expansion of the fifteenth and sixteenth centuries had the profoundest effect upon the civilizations of the New World, where languages, religion, and politico-economic institutions were transplanted with comparatively little change. The social and cultural impact was only slightly less pronounced than the political, and, if we consider the European intellectual and economic domination of the nineteenth century to be a later phase of this same expansion, we can recognize some of its extent and profundity. Indeed, even the dynamic elements of today's anti-imperialism (nationalism, industrialism, Marxism) stem largely from ideas spawned in Western Europe. For better or for worse, the world we live in is to a very great extent a product of the expansion of Europe, with all of its accompanying repercussions.

For obvious reasons this volume will be directed toward only a few of the innumerable problems of that expansion, principally those related to its initial motivation, to the responsibility for discovering America, to the Spanish methods of conquest and colonization, and finally to the general meaning and effects of the expansion. This of course does not "cover" the expansion of Europe, even in a limited sense, but it does deal with certain problems of interpretation, evaluation, and judgment; problems which students of history will encounter almost daily.

Few episodes in the saga of man's continuing struggle with nature demonstrate more vividly his unconquerable will, and his almost limitless physical endurance. But the age of discovery and conquest reminds us that men are also cruel, deceitful, and despotic. The period was one of vigorous life and violent death, a time when a man might sacrifice everything he possessed, even himself, for an idea (or a minute point of doctrine), but would be just as apt to take the life of another for the slightest variation from his own belief. The student should not be surprised at the superhuman strengths and the inhuman brutalities of Renaissance men, yet he ought not be insensitive to the lessons that can be drawn from them.

It is little wonder that any age of such sharp contrasts has given birth to an equally controversial historical literature. Some of the disagreement can be attributed to writing from a nationalistic bias, and some to religious zeal; but much of the literary conflict stems from differences of analysis and interpretation that are more profound and in most cases more meaningful. It will be for the student to decide which are the most significant for him, and which arguments are the most cogent for the questions asked.

The first selection, by the best-known writer of philosophical history in our day, approaches the problem of the motivation of European expansion from the wider context of oriental and early medieval civilizations. Professor Arnold Toynbee's answer to the problem is simpler than the involved rhetoric he employs to arrive at it. For him, challenge and response, as in other examples of cultural movements, account for the expansive energy of Portugal and Castile in the fifteenth century and for the failure of neighboring Aragon to keep pace with her peninsular partners. The stimulus for expansion was provided by rival Islam, which for centuries had exerted continuing pressure on Western frontiers. Although his answer gives rise to many questions, it is suggestive and has itself stimulated many responses.

Among the most fruitful of these responses, although it was not written as such, is that given by Myron Gilmore, who believes that it was not so much the external challenge to Latin Christendom which accounts for its sudden expansion in the fifteenth century as its own unique attitudes and institutions. Whereas Toynbee dwells on the similarities of Western culture with those of the East, Gilmore emphasizes their differences and demonstrates how some of these contrasts — particularly the difference in attitude toward technology and wealth — help to explain why it was Europe rather than the more prosperous and apparently more dynamic societies of China and the Middle East that first broke the geographic barrier and followed up with continued expansion and exploitation.

Our third selection, an eloquent essay on Prince Henry the Navigator by Garrett Mattingly, takes us from the general to the particular and shows how the political-religious views and aspirations of this Renaissance prince actually opened the era of expansion and determined the lines it was to follow for more than a century. Filling in a corner of Toynbee's challenge and response thesis, Mattingly places unusually heavy emphasis on Prince Henry's hope of reaching the mysterious Prester John and using his aid (since he was also a Christian) in the vital fight against Islam. The legend (or legends) of Prester John was well known in fourteenth- and fifteenth-century Europe but its significance in the Portuguese expansion did not emerge until Prince Henry envisioned the advantages afforded by an alliance with this elusive African ruler. This interpretation seems to illustrate again that fiction is sometimes more meaningful than fact as historical causation. Men are motivated by their beliefs. Whether or not we accept this explanation as part of Henry's motivation, we must admit that the Henrician voyages opened the Age of Discovery and pointed the way not only toward future Portuguese explorations of Africa and the opening of direct commercial relations with India and the Far East, but also helped stimulate initial Spanish ventures in the West.

The discovery of a New World gave an additional direction and interest to European expansion and introduced Spain into the world arena. There are perhaps more myths connected with the discovery of America than with any phase of the expansion, and most of them concern Christopher Columbus in one way or another. The exact nature and intent of Columbus' first voyage is still not certain, and violent arguments still continue as to whether or not it was he who made the discovery in the first place. It seems evident from the general outline of his "Plan of the Indies," that he hoped to reach China, or at least off-shore islands within reach of the mainland. He was not unique in believing the world was round — this had been known since Hellenic times — but he did think it was much smaller than most geographers maintained, and therefore accepted the feasibility of crossing the Atlantic with the type of ships and navigational equipment then available. In this case, his error was more a cause of the discovery than was the truth. When he reached San Salvador, at the approximate location (according to his calculations) of the outlying islands of Asia, a new era of expansion began.

The controversial Mexican historian-philosopher, Edmundo O'Gorman, opens this second section with a drastic revision of the whole idea of the discovery of America. The student may find this essay difficult to follow through the first few pages, but as he proceeds he will be successively shocked, amazed, and fascinated by O'Gorman's systematic exposé of the "myth" of the discovery of America. Columbus could not possibly have discovered America, he argues, because America as such did not exist. What did exist in the "discoverer's" mind was a conception entirely foreign to what we have come to identify as America. But since Columbus's conception of Asia turned out to be erroneous, and America was non-existent, it cannot be said that he discovered either one. What did happen, O'Gorman asserts, is that the concept, and thereafter the reality, of America was "invented" rather than discovered, and for that process of exposition Amerigo Vespucci was more responsible than was Columbus. America "did not suddenly emerge full-blown as the result of the chance discovery by Columbus of a small island on October 12, 1492," he concludes; "it developed [was invented] from a complex, living process of exploration and interpretation which ended by endowing the newly-found lands with a proper and peculiar meaning of their own."

O'Gorman's thesis, developed in several articles and books but most elaborately in his *La idea del descubrimiento de América* (1951), has caused a considerable reverberation both north and south of the Rio Grande and on both sides of the Atlantic. One of O'Gorman's frequent and most perceptive antagonists is the well-known French historian Marcel Bataillon. Pleased at O'Gorman's endeavor to penetrate beyond the outward events of history and delve into their meaning, both past and present, Bataillon praises the Mexican scholar's initiative and courage, but sharply criticizes his thesis and also his method. Most of all he takes him to task for his careless reading of the sources and for creating something of a scapegoat to make his extravagant thesis more plausible. Still,

there is much to be said for a more philosophical approach to the problems of the discovery, and Bataillon suggests a few fruitful avenues in that direction himself.

O'Gorman is not alone in his attempts to reappraise the contributions of Amerigo Vespucci. Many historians now agree that the Florentine seaman has been misunderstood and misrepresented for several centuries. There is less agreement, however, over Vespucci's exact contributions and how they should be weighed in the total balance of credits. The most influential Vespucci revisionist was the Argentine historian Roberto Levillier, whose book *América la bien llamada,* published in 1948, began a new trend in the Columbus-Vespucci controversy. By demonstrating the authenticity of two of Vespucci's letters which had long been considered forgeries (or at best apocryphal), Levillier argued that Vespucci merits recognition not only as the first popularizer of the concept of America, but also as an important contributor to a systematic (scientific) study of New World geography. In the Levillier tradition, Germán Arciniegas eloquently defends Vespucci while counterattacking his detractors, from Father Las Casas to Duarte Leite and Alberto Magnaghi. The Amerigo Vespucci who emerges from Arciniegas' book, a chapter of which is included here as our sixth selection, is the kind of man who would make anyone proud to bear the name American.

But the Columbus-Vespucci controversy does not end there; it still goes on and it continues to arouse excitement and occasionally serious scholarship. The most effective recent opponent of O'Gorman, Levillier, and Arciniegas is the American, Wilcomb E. Washburn, scholar, of the Smithsonian Institution. By exposing and examining some of the principal terms of the Age of Discovery — such as "tierra firma," "discover," "continent," "Indies," and "New World," — and showing that they were no better understood by Vespucci than they were by Columbus, Washburn effectively undermines O'Gorman's argument against the "discoverer," and repudiates Arciniegas' rehabilitation of Vespucci.

Another dimension to the argument was added by the 1956 discovery of the John Day letter, a document which suggests that Bristol seamen reached the coast of the New World several years before Columbus' voyage was undertaken. David Quinn carefully examines the internal evidence of this letter and concludes, cautiously yet positively, that the English probably did discover America at least ten years before Columbus. It is too soon to measure the full impact of this development on geographical and historical thought, but it will certainly have its effect in the future, if for no other reason than by stimulating, modifying, and adding fuel to the controversies. Of course, the argument that there were previous discoveries is not new. The recent Yale University disclosure of the so-called Vinland map, which gave new and positive evidence of the eleventh-century Viking explorations, and the immediate violent reaction of the Italian Historical Society and others against this announcement, shows that the issue is far from dead.

Section three is devoted to some of the problems of the conquest and settlement of the New World. Here the arguments have been bitter and deep, based on nationalistic jingoism, sometimes on religious emotionalism, and occasionally on more solid differences of opinion. Very early in the era of expansion, French, English, and Dutch writers dwelt upon the brutality of Spanish conquistadores and upon the atrocities of settlement and colonization. There was much truth in their charges, but it was mostly buried beneath an avalanche of meaningless and distorted invective.

But the so-called "Black Legend" of Spanish atrocities did not begin in an enemy nation nor among rival religious sects; it began with a pious and literate Spanish colonist turned priest and reformer. Bartolomé de Las Casas was once an *encomendero* (holder of Indian laborers by government grant) himself, but, shocked by the evil effects of Spanish conquest upon the Indian populations, he set out to become their champion. Armed with an unusually caustic pen, even for an age when polemical invective was at an all-time high (or low), Las Casas began his self-appointed crusade in earnest. He attacked many aspects of the Spanish system (if the incongruous process of colonization could be called a system), and not a few of the colonial personalities, in a stream of letters and advices to the Emperor Charles V. On several occasions he appeared at court in person to plead his case for the Indians, and participated in the notorious Valladolid debate with some of the leading divines and scholars of the day. But the most effective of all Las Casas' efforts was his publication of a small book, called the *Brevissima relación de la destruición de las Indias Occidentales,* bluntly depicting the cruelty of the early conquest. A competent and perceptive historian in his own right, and author of several outstanding books, Las Casas, like Machiavelli, is not nearly so well-known for these better works as he is for this shorter, less meritorious but more influential broadside.

In his crusading zeal, Las Casas stepped on many people's feet. But this was not an age of quiet suffering; anyone injured by the zealous priest was sure to have a ready reply and a passionate counterattack. Not only did the colonists and encomenderos resent his accusations, many clerics believed he was doing more harm than good with his crusade. One of the most outspoken of these missionaries was Friar Toribio de Motolinía, of the rival Franciscans, who considered Las Casas an enemy of truth and justice. The excerpt which follows the Las Casas polemic is from Motolinía's famous letter to the Emperor Charles V, in which he answers many of the Dominican's charges with counter-charges of his own, and presumes to set the Emperor straight on the real conditions in the Indies.

Modern historians have been equally unable to agree on the merits or faults of the perplexing Las Casas. He has been variously depicted as an inspired saint, and an obsessed demon, as well as most of the categories in between. The most comprehensive examination to appear in many years has come from the pen of the renowned dean of Spanish historians, Don Ramón Menéndez Pidal. At the age of ninety-three, Menéndez Pidal published *El Padre Las Casas: su doble personalidad* (1963), arguing that the reason scholars have experienced such difficulty in reaching an agreement about Las Casas is that the friar was a paranoiac, suffering from serious mental derangement. This psychosis, according to Menéndez Pidal, accounts for the extreme divergences in biographies of Las Casas. The most active Las Casian scholar, Lewis Hanke, is not at all impressed with Menéndez Pidal's thesis, nor with his scholarship. In the next selection, Hanke denounces the venerable Spaniard's book as narrow, biased, and completely unreliable.

Salvador de Madariaga, another well-known Spanish historian and diplomat, enters the controversy from a different direction. Concentrating on institutions rather than personalities, he demonstrates that there were tremendous cruelties and hardships inflicted upon the Indians, especially in the Peruvian mines under the *Mita* system, but argues that these injustices were inflicted primarily by the settlers rather than by order or desire of the Spanish government, which consistently acted as protector of the natives. This view comes closer to Hanke's position which is that, through the insistence and devoted labor of Las Casas and others who saw the problems and dangers of the conquest, Spain became the leader in defense of the rights of the Indians and the great innovator in their legal protection. To the Spaniards, he points out, justice was as important in the colonization as was the more famous trilogy of gold, glory, and gospel. Hanke's stand is summarized in the concluding article of this section.

Finally we return again to a more gen-eral problem, to the important question of meaning and significance. What overall effect did the European expansion have on the nations and peoples of the modern world? What impact, if any, did the New World have on Europe? How soon was the impact felt, and how was it manifested? The articles in section three dealt primarily with the effects of Spanish colonizing on the New World. Silvio Zavala, however, takes the position of William R. Shepherd that the impact of America on the Old World was even more profound. The article selected here from the writings of this respected Latin American historian summarizes the principal areas and nature of New World influence on Europe and Asia during the sixteenth, seventeenth and eighteenth centuries, and declares that "For the first time in history there had been formed the genuinely world-wide network of relationships that characterizes the modern era and differentiates it from all preceding times."

Most writers on the subject have been content to talk about the influence of European expansion within these general assumptions. But the American historian Walter Prescott Webb became obsessed with a much more inclusive notion of expansion, which applied the type of analysis made by Frederick Jackson Turner of the American frontier to the broader frontier of European expansion after 1492. The principal thesis of his *The Great Frontier* (Boston, 1952) is that the discovery of the New World, with its rich and almost uninhabited lands, precipitated an enormous economic boom which lasted over 400 years. This boom, according to Webb, in turn gave rise to many of the institutional and individual characteristics of Western society, such as democracy, capitalism, individualism, and the idea of progress. He further suggests that by 1900 the Great Frontier began to close, as the ratio of land to population gradually returned to its pre-1492 base, and sees the post-1914 era as a time of frustration and failure due to the closing of the world frontier. Webb's summary of this boom hypothesis of the European expansion is presented here, along with a thought-provoking answer from the distinguished British historian of ideas, Geoffrey Barraclough.

Barraclough, who delights in Toynbeean types of historical syntheses, is complimentary to Webb's book and believes it deserves recognition as an original and meaningful interpretation. But he also considers its methodology crude and its presentation careless. His criticism focuses on Webb's exaggeration and distortion of the influence of frontier institutions, and on his failure to recognize and include other frontiers, such as the Russian, in his thesis. Barraclough rejects *The Great Frontier* as presented, but not the idea behind it. Many historians have not been so kind to Webb, however. One refers to the book as "an astonishing work, the product of an alert, uncritical and obsessed mind;" another calls it the reduction of the frontier conception "to its ultimate absurdity;" and another dismisses it as a complete waste of time. But these opinions must still be placed alongside those who believe that "except for Mr. Toynbee, it is hard to think of any modern author likely to have a greater effect on future thinking about the historical process." And so it goes. History is controversy, and the expansion of Europe remains one of the most excitingly controversial problems in European civilization.

[NOTE: Footnotes have generally been omitted except where needed to explain the text.]

The Conflict of Opinion

I. MOTIVES OF EUROPEAN EXPANSION

"It was the spirit aroused in these Western Christian frontiersmen by their triumphant response to Muslim pressure that nerved them to hazard their lives on the apparently illimitable ocean; and it was the impetus acquired in their victorious counter-attack that carried them not only out into the great deep but right across it into new worlds beyond."

— Arnold J. Toynbee

"The opportunity for expansion occurred for both China and Europe; . . . Yet the European society whose rulers were far less wealthy than the Chinese emperor was in reality in a much better position to seize that opportunity. In the absence of comprehensive monolithic government control the European system allowed for a greater measure of individual incentive and broader basis of participation."

— Myron P. Gilmore

"The monkish ardor of a medieval prince, his long quest for a mythical kingdom, made inevitable the modern world."

— Garrett Mattingly

II. DISCOVERY OF A NEW WORLD

"The fault that lies at the root of the entire history of the idea of the discovery of America consists in assuming that the lump of cosmic matter which we now know as the American continent has always been that, when actually it only became that when such a meaning was given to it."

— Edmundo O'Gorman

"What O'Gorman fails to do is to carry his theory to its logical conclusion. Certainly Columbus did not discover "America" in a strictly logical sense. But if America is not what Columbus found, neither does it make sense to call America the lands in which our forefathers were born, in which we were born, or in which our children will be born."

— Wilcomb E. Washburn

"Nevertheless, with all its limitations, it [the John Day letter] does provide a rational case for placing the English discovery of America in the decade before Columbus sailed in 1492, and possibly as early as 1481."

— David B. Quinn

III. THE SPANISH CONQUEST

"We are sure that on the mainland our Spaniards, through their cruelties and infamous works, have depopulated and desolated more than ten king-

doms larger than all of Spain, including Aragon and Portugal, all filled
with rational men, and have left a desert of more land than twice the distance
from Seville to Jerusalem."

— BARTOLOMÉ DE LAS CASAS

"The virtuous Las Casas is not at the same time the defamer; the studious
Las Casas is not at the same time the malicious distorter of facts. Las Casas
was a mental case, a paranoiac who, of necessity and involuntarily, falsified
the true facts."

— RAMÓN MENÉNDEZ PIDAL

"In presenting his version of Las Casas, Don Ramón reminds one both of
a Royal Canadian mounted policeman stalking a criminal in the wasteland
of the north and of a prosecuting attorney rather than of a historian at
work."

— LEWIS HANKE

"Without unduly straining the point, or closing one's eyes to the heavy
responsibilities of the Crown itself in such matters as taxation of destitute
natives, sale of offices and often poor choice of officials, it is possible to conclude that through the three centuries of Spanish rule in the Indies, the
tendency to order, lawfulness, fair dealing to all, good government and
protection of the natives came chiefly from the Crown."

— SALVADOR DE MADARIAGA

IV. THE MEANING OF EUROPEAN EXPANSION

"It is clear that, as a consequence of the expansion that followed the
great discoveries, Europe passed through a series of significant new experiences. The modern life of that continent was extended to far-flung territories overseas, extracted from its ancient channels, and spread over a vast
new world."

— SILVIO ZAVALA

"The Great Frontier precipitated a boom on the Metropolis [Europe], a
boom of gigantic proportions which began when Columbus returned from
his first voyage and accelerated until all the new lands had been appropri-
ated. The boom . . . attended the birth of a set of new institutions and
ideas designed to service a booming society, chief among them modern
democracy and capitalism and the idea of progress."

— WALTER PRESCOTT WEBB

"Webb illuminates part of the scene, but does not illuminate the whole
scene because his vision — though wider than that of the average western
European historian — is still not world-wide."

— GEOFFREY BARRACLOUGH

I. MOTIVES OF EUROPEAN EXPANSION

Stimulus and Response

ARNOLD J. TOYNBEE

Arnold Toynbee, born in 1889, is one of the best-known historians in the world today. Now Professor Emeritus of the London School of Economics, he has served as research professor of international history there, as director of studies at the Royal Institute of International Affairs (1924–58), during which time he published many volumes of the *Survey of International Affairs*. During World War II he was also director of research at the British Foreign Office. His greatest fame, however, is derived from the publication of his monumental *A Study of History*, 12 vols. (1934–61), which examines with insight and erudition the causes and significance of the rise and fall of civilizations. Among his scores of other challenging books are *Civilization on Trial* (1948); *The World and the West* (1953); *Christianity Among the Religions of the World* (1957); and *The Present Day Experiment in Western Civilization* (1962).

T HE LAST FRONTIER of Western Christendom that calls for consideration here is the land-frontier in the Iberian Peninsula *vis-à-vis* the Syriac Society in its latest phase — a phase which began when the Arabs reintegrated the Syriac universal state in the seventh century of the Christian Era. In the history of this frontier there are two outstanding features. In the first place, Western Christendom came under pressure from an alien civilization at a far earlier stage in this quarter than in any other. In the second place, the Powers which came into being, in response to this pressure, on the Iberian marches of Western Christendom eventually came to play a leading role, which was all their own, in the propagation of the Western Civilization.

As regards the first of these two points, we have seen that on the North European continental land-frontier Western Christendom was confronted at the outset solely by barbarians. In that quarter, the Western World did not become subject to pressure from the main body of Orthodox Christendom before the Ottoman impact upon Hungary in the fifteenth century of the Christian Era, while it was not until the sixteenth century that the Russian offshoot of Orthodox Christendom exerted pressure upon the West in the form of a Muscovite impact upon Lithuania. On the other hand, on the Iberian land-frontier, Western Christendom found itself under pressure from the Syriac Civilization at the dawn of Western history. Indeed, this Syriac menace to the existence of Western Christendom in its infancy was still more formidable than the contemporary menace from the North European barbarians; and our Western Society was awakened to its first glimmer of self-consciousness by the ordeal of wrestling simultaneously with these two deadly foes — like the infant Hêraklês when he rose in his cradle to wrestle with the two serpents that had been sent by a malevolent goddess to take

From *A Study of History*, Volume II, pp. 202–206, by Arnold J. Toynbee. Oxford University Press, 1935. Reprinted by permission.

1

his life, and saved himself alive by strangling both monsters, each single-handed.

The Arab onslaught upon the infant civilization of the West was an incident in the final Syriac reaction against the long Hellenic intrusion upon the Syriac domain; for when the Arabs, in the strength of Islam, took up and completed the task which had proved to be beyond the strength of Zoroastrians and Jews and Nestorians and Monophysites, they did not rest until they had recovered for the Syriac Society the whole of its former domain at its widest extension. Not content with reconstituting as an Arab Empire the Syriac universal state which had originally been embodied in the Persian Empire of the Achaemenidae, the Arabs went on to reconquer the ancient Phoenician colonial domain in the Western Mediterranean which, in the Achaemenian age, had been welded into a unity of its own — an overseas counterpart of the Persian Empire — under the hegemony of Carthage. For a moment in the eighth century of the Christian Era an Arab Caliph fulfilled the ambition which a Persian King of Kings had found himself unable to fulfil in the sixth century B.C. The last Umayyad who reigned at Damascus was at least nominally master of the whole compass of the Syriac World, from the farthest limits ever attained by the Achaemenian Empire in the east to the farthest attained by the Carthaginian Empire in the west. In the latter direction, the Arab commanders had crossed not only the straits of Gibraltar but the Pyrenees in the footsteps of Hannibal in A.D. 713; and thereafter, though they had not emulated their great Carthaginian predecessor's passage of the Rhône and the Alps, they had broken ground which Hannibal never trod when they carried their arms to the Loire in A.D. 732. At the Battle of Tours, the Arabs were attacking Western Christendom in its cradle.

The discomfiture of the Arabs by the Franks on this occasion has assuredly been one of the decisive events in history; for the Western reaction to Syriac pressure

which declared itself on the battle-field of Tours in A.D. 732 continued in force and increased in momentum on this front until, some eight centuries later, its impetus was carrying the Portuguese vanguard of Western Christendom right out of the Iberian Peninsula and onward overseas round Africa to Goa and Malacca and Macao, and the Castilian vanguard onward across the Atlantic to Mexico and thence across the Pacific to Manila. These Iberian pioneers of Western Christendom performed an unparalleled service for the civilization which they represented. They expanded the horizon, and thereby potentially the domain, of our Western Society from an obscure corner of the Old World until it came to embrace all the habitable lands and navigable seas on the surface of the planet. It is owing to this Iberian energy and enterprise that Western Christendom has grown, like the grain of mustard seed in the parable, until it has become "the Great Society:" a tree in whose branches all the nations of the Earth have come and lodged. This latter-day Westernized World is the peculiar achievement of Western Christendom's Iberian pioneers; and the Western energy which performed this feat was evoked and sustained and wrought up to its high intensity by the challenge of Syriac pressure on the Iberian front.

The Portuguese and Castilian seafarers who made their presence felt throughout the World in the first century of our modern age (circa A.D. 1475–1575) were the heirs of frontiersmen whose spirit had been tempered by thirty generations of strenuous border warfare against the Moors on the Iberian marches. On this frontier, the Franks first turned back the tide of Arab conquest from the heart of Gaul; thereafter, under Charlemagne's leadership, they carried their counter-offensive to the Iberian side of the Pyrenees, where they joined forces with the remnant of the Visigoths in the fastness of Asturia; and eventually, during the post-Syriac interregnum (circa A.D. 975–1275), when the Umayyad Caliphate in Andalusia broke up, these Christian barbarians of the Pyrenaean hinterland contended victoriously for the possession of the Umayyads' Peninsular heritage with the Muslim Berbers from the opposite hinterlands in Africa: the wild Murābit Nomads from the Sahara and the still wilder Muwahhid highlanders from the Atlas.

The dependence of Iberian Christian energy upon the stimulus administered by pressure from the Moors is demonstrated by the fact that this energy gave out as soon as the Moorish pressure ceased to be exerted. In the seventeenth century of the Christian Era the Portuguese and Castilians were supplanted in the new world which they had called into existence overseas by interlopers from the Transpyrenaean parts of Western Christendom — the Dutch and the English and the French — and this discomfiture overseas coincided in date with the removal of the historic stimulus at home through the extirpation (by massacre, expulsion, or forcible conversion) of the remaining "Moriscos" in the Peninsula.

Again, if we look farther back, we shall observe that Portugal and Castile were only two out of the three Christian "successor-states" of the Umayyad Caliphate which had divided the Iberian Peninsula between them. Why did not Aragon take her part, side by side with Castile and Portugal, in the vaster enterprises of discovery and commerce and conquest on which the two sister kingdoms embarked at the turn of the fifteenth and the sixteenth century? In the immediate past, during the later "Middle Ages," Aragon had played a more brilliant role than either Castile or Portugal in the life of the Western Society. She had shared in the brilliance of the North Italian city-states and had made certain original contributions of her own — in the fields of cartography and of international law — to the North Italian medieval culture. Why was it, then, that, just when Portugal and Castile both entered upon the brilliant phase of their careers, Aragon allowed

herself to be dominated and effaced by her Castilian neighbour? The explanation perhaps lies in the fact that the stimulus of Moorish pressure had been lost by Aragon several centuries before it was lost by either of the other two Peninsular kingdoms. In the days of da Gama and Columbus, both Portugal and Castile were still serving as marches of Western Christendom against the Moors. Castile then still marched in the Peninsula with the surviving Moorish kingdom of Granada, while Portugal marched with Morocco in her Tangerine province on the African side of the Straits of Gibraltar; and the Portuguese and Castilian exploits overseas, which began in that age, were simply diversions, to a new and wider field, of energies which had hitherto been employed assiduously against the Moors at home. On the other hand, Aragon had been relegated to the interior of Western Christendom since A.D. 1235, when the overthrow of the Muwahhid Berbers by the Iberian Christians at the Battle of Las Navas had confined the Moors in the Peninsula to the Granadan enclave. Since that time, Aragon had been insulated from the Moors on land by the intervening Castilian province of Murcia, while in the Mediterranean her Moorish warfare had been brought to an end in A.D. 1229–32 by her conquest of the Balearic Islands. Thus the stimulus which was the common source of Iberian Christian energies had ceased to play upon the Aragonese at least two-and-a-half centuries before it ceased to play upon their Castilian and Portuguese neighbours; and this may partly explain why it was that Aragon fell out of the running before the great opportunity of overseas expansion offered itself to the Peninsular Powers, while Castile and Portugal did not finally succeed in cutting off the source of their own energies by extirpating the "Moriscos" in their midst until the stimulus of Moorish pressure at home had carried the Portuguese and Castilian pioneers to the four corners of the World.

The Creative Surge of Latin Christendom

MYRON P. GILMORE

Myron Gilmore is a highly respected professor of history at Harvard University. He is a dedicated New Englander, born in Walpole, Massachusetts in 1910, educated in the primary and secondary schools of Massachusetts, and graduated from Amherst College. He received his A.M. degree from Harvard in 1933 and the Ph.D. in 1937 from the same university, immediately joining the Harvard staff as an instructor of history. In 1962 he received the L.H.D. from Amherst. Active in the field of Renaissance studies and early modern history and law, he has published many articles and books, including *Argument from Roman Law in Political Thought, 1200–1600* (1941); *The World of Humanism, 1453–1517* (1952); and *Humanists and Jurists in the Renaissance* (1964).

SEEN in the perspective of world history, Latin Christendom occupied in the fifteenth century a territory relatively small and insignificant in comparison with the habitable areas of the earth's surface. It amounted in fact to no more than a western peninsula jutting out from the great Asiatic land mass. From time to time, and especially in the thirteenth and early fourteenth centuries, vistas had been opened toward the east. These vistas provided glimpses of societies whose territorial extent, population, material wealth, and political stability were superior to anything in recent European experience, and whose achievements in arts and letters bore at the very least a favorable comparison with the Latin west. This knowledge had never been shared by many and was now in the fifteenth century blurred and overlaid with a mass of legend. The most optimistic calculation taken in the middle of that century might have concluded that a society that had occupied western Europe for so long a time, with occasional if ephemeral bursts of outward expansion, might continue to survive and hold its own.

No one, however, in this general situation could have foreseen that before the fifteenth century was finished western Europeans would have discovered the vast lands of the western hemisphere that now lay open to exploitation, or would have established the new sea routes to the civilizations of the east, which this time were to be regular and permanent. By 1500 the greatest steps in this unique and dramatic expansion had been taken, and within two more decades — by the time the religious revolution was beginning in Germany — the Portuguese Empire had been established in India and southeast Asia; European Christians traded in Malacca and Canton, and in the New World the Aztec Empire was about to fall to a small band of Spanish adventurers. A man who remembered the fall of Constantinople as a boy could easily have lived to hear the news of the circumnavigation of the globe. Within the space of hardly more than a generation the horizon of Latin Christendom had lifted; Europe was in a position to take a view of the world, and this perspective was not again to be closed.

It is natural that history should have endowed the men and events associated with this achievement with a transcendent significance. Adam Smith in the eighteenth century declared that the discovery of America and of a passage to the East Indies by the Cape of Good Hope were the two greatest and most important events recorded in the history of mankind, and at least half of this judgment is enshrined in the memory of every American schoolboy. Succeeding generations, recalling these names and dates, have celebrated not only the triumphs of individual genius and persistence; they have also and more importantly registered a conviction that here began a new epoch in the history of Europe and the world. We are dealing here with the kind of events that become symbolic of dramatic and revolutionary change. What is often minimized or forgotten is the extent to which the voyages of Columbus and Da Gama rested upon the labors of countless predecessors in the European past, but what is never forgotten is the fact that they were succeeded by increasing numbers of followers who finally carried the civilization of Europe to the remotest parts of the earth. In this sense their historical significance depends upon the belief that they mark the beginning of a continuous process. It may seem unnecessarily obvious to suggest that if Columbus had returned from his first voyage and reported his results to a society absolutely indifferent whether the east was reached or not — if in other words there had been no encouragement, no response, no imitation — then the date 1492 would hardly occupy its present sacred place in the historical calendar. When we celebrate this date the emotional focus is on Columbus with all the drama justified by history and enriched by legend. We forget the extent to which we presuppose or imply the existence in fifteenth-century Europe of a society ready and eager to follow the paths which had been opened. So strongly do we feel that it was natural, indeed inevitable, to seize all the advantages that followed from the great voyages of the fifteenth century that we cannot imagine a condition of affairs in which the achieve-

ments of a Columbus or a Da Gama would have remained without consequences. Yet there have been other societies and other times in the history of Europe itself in which comparable achievements appear as isolated phenomena, irrelevant happenings, promising beginnings that led to nothing. The voyages of the Norsemen to North America left no perceptible mark except in literature either on the lands which they reached or on the society from which they came. The successes of the Polos inaugurated no permanent routes between Europe and the east.

If examples from the history of Europe are not convincing on this point, consider the case of China. The same fifteenth century in which the western Europeans began their successful expansion by sea to the east was the century in which the tribute fleets of the Chinese emperors accomplished their most remarkable voyages in the south and west. In the years between 1405 and 1433 seven great expeditions ordered by the Ming emperors sailed to the western seas under the command of the eunuch, Cheng Ho. Their purpose seems to have been the establishment of diplomatic relations and the collection of tribute from the barbarian kingdoms. They were official undertakings of formidable size. Typically each expedition consisted of over 27,000 men embarked in fifty or more huge ocean-going junks. These great fleets visited the East Indies, Malacca, Siam, Ceylon, India, Ormuz in the Persian Gulf, the Red Sea and the eastern coast of Africa. Aden and other Red Sea ports were reached several times and a delegation from at least one of the expeditions was sent to Mecca. The fleets touched at various places on the African coast at least as far south as Melinda and perhaps beyond.

During the years when the China Sea, the Indian Ocean, the Red Sea, and the Persian Gulf were thus being swept by Chinese fleets, the Portuguese were inching along the western coast of Africa and, in 1434, the year after the last great recorded expedition of the Ming, Gil Eannes in the service of Prince Henry rounded Cape Bojeador, only a little more than eight hundred miles from Lisbon. In the long history of the relations between east and west there are few contrasts more dramatic than that presented by these two voyages, the Portuguese with its *barca* of twenty-five tons carrying a handful of men, and the Chinese fleet manned by thousands. Yet the Chinese voyages had no revolutionary consequences in the society from which they came, and in the end it was the west that conquered. Cheng Ho's ships visited over twenty countries and brought back many rare and costly things, but these results failed to stimulate in China the same aggressive impulse to expansion that was produced in the west by a handful of gold dust and a few slaves brought back from the Guinea coast.

The contrast between the achievements and attitudes of the Chinese and those of the Europeans in the fifteenth century is one of the striking coincidences of history, but the Chinese were of course not alone in failing to exploit possibilities of cultural and commercial expansion in the way that became characteristic of Europeans after the fifteenth century. Throughout the medieval and early modern period the civilization of Islam was in some ways in a uniquely favored position to undertake a program of further military, political or cultural conquests until its influence should circle the globe. The far-flung commerce of the Arabs stretched from China to western Europe. Their geographers knew more about the world than those of any other society. Their merchants were in direct contact with the greatest number and variety of religious and political systems. Yet with all this the Arab civilization failed to produce the same kind of thinking and action that developed in Europe. So it has been with others. The expansion of Latin Christendom, with all its fateful consequences, has been a unique phenomenon in the history of the world.

The question that forces itself upon us is: Why was this expansion successful in Europe and not elsewhere? Why did the voyages of discovery "take" in Europe and not in China? Mr. Toynbee has drawn us a picture of a "pre-Da Gaman belt" of civilizations stretching from Europe through the Ottoman Empire and the Mongol states of India to China and Japan. He points out that all these civilizations had certain common social and cultural characteristics. All were essentially peasant societies in which a large mass of agricultural laborers supported a minority of rulers. In each case the ruling class was maintained by religious sanctions as well as by secular political controls. Each of these societies believed it had received the revealed truth and that its way of life was uniquely civilized. Mr. Toynbee considers that of all these particular parochial societies Latin Christendom was the most unlikely candidate to undertake expansion on a world-wide scale and to carry that expansion through to a successful conclusion.

There are many features of the situation that appear to support this view. We might agree with Mr. Toynbee that both the Arabs and the Chinese seem to have been more favorably situated in the fifteenth century than the Europeans. Even in the field of technology the European superiority was far from clear. For, if the Europeans had developed the technical skills to make possible the voyages of Prince Henry, the Chinese, as we have seen, were able to perform navigational feats of incomparably greater magnitude. Clearly, also, the mere existence and availability of any particular technology is less important than what is done with it. Professor Panofsky has reminded us that although Roger Bacon had an optic tube which anticipated the telescope, it was used to see whether names could be read on a gravestone from a distance, whereas Galileo's telescope was directed to the exploration of the secrets of the universe. The particular technological revolution in fifteenth-century Europe that permitted the development of sea communications must therefore be understood in relation to the total complex of ideas and institutions in which it appeared.

Seen from this point of view, Latin Christendom, far from being the least likely candidate for expansion, emerges as the candidate most likely to succeed. Behind those appearances on which Mr. Toynbee dwells we can discern specific characteristics in the European intellectual inheritance and in the European institutional structure that help us to understand the energies behind the voyages of discovery and the overseas conquests. In one sense the remaining chapters of this book may be regarded as an exploration of those characteristics and their manifestations in various kinds of human activity. However, it is necessary to consider here, if only briefly, some of those which were most closely related to the process of expansion.

In the first place, although the western world was indeed assured of its possession of Christian revelation, it was never completely convinced that its own institutions were the most perfect embodiment of that revelation. A golden age lay in the past; the kingdom of Prester John existed in the east; the lost isles of Atlantis and Saint Brendan were to be discovered in the west. The vision of a mythical "better place," a Utopia that existed somewhere else, fitfully haunted the mind of Latin Christendom and was a spur to curiosity. Perfection was not here, not now; it had existed long ago in time; it might be found again surviving far away in space. Thus the attitude of the European world toward the barbarians and the infidel beyond its horizons was never so completely closed and assured as that which appears to have been characteristic of the Chinese.

In the long run this curiosity was closely connected with Christian missionary zeal. Yet the impulse to proselytize was as intense among the Moslems as among the Christians; in this respect the Christian religion was not unique. What was shared, however, by no other society of the "pre-Da Gaman belt" was the complex of traditions, doubts, and hopes that seemed to promise the existence of a center of civilization outside and beyond the horizon with which the Christian world might eventually hope to be in contact. Intertwined with the persistent drive for conversion, this other inheritance of curiosity is of critical importance in the intellectual background that prepared the way for European expansion.

Turning from ideas to institutions it is equally clear that there were fundamental characteristics in the organization of western society that favored the success of expansion. This was nowhere more apparent than in the structure of property relationships and in the provision of financial support for the voyages of discovery.

The contrast between the Chinese and the Portuguese expeditions of the fifteenth century is as striking in this respect as it is in others. The emperor of China, ruling all things, had only to command in order that the wealth of the imperial treasury might be expended on the magnificent expeditions he had ordered. In the west, however, the sovereigns, who could never find sufficient revenue for their ordinary expenses and whose chancellors exhausted themselves in pleading with estates and diets for grants of money, had little capital to put into the financing of hazardous adventures overseas. On the whole, therefore, there were many cases in Europe in which the governments contributed the authority and private individuals the property that made possible these voyages.

The sharp separation between the rights of authority and the rights of property was a fundamental part of the western inheritance. Medieval theory, and to a large extent medieval practice, had insisted that the king should "live of his own"; that is, his expenses should be met by the revenues of his own domain. Only emergencies of a recognized kind justified a demand for a wider levy, and in such circumstances the consent of the estates was requested. The widening scope of action by government conflicted with these ideas, with the result that, almost universally, early modern governments in Europe found themselves hard up. The "ordinary" revenues had ceased to be in any degree sufficient to meet the needs of government, and there was everywhere a resort to those "extraordinary" revenues that had originally been the recourse of emergency, but were now needed all the time as the regular basis of the government's support. In this situation it is understandable that governments had little available capital to invest in exploring expeditions.

Isabella did not have to pawn her jewels to finance Columbus, but the money was secured partly by borrowing on the authority of a royal official and partly by contributions from what we call "private" sources. Columbus himself raised about an eighth of the required capital. There were many examples of authorizations by governments where no funds at all were supplied. In England the charter of Henry VII to Cabot conferred authority to establish in the name of the king of England dominion over such territories as might be discovered, but it explicitly left to Cabot himself and to the faithful merchants of Bristol the provision of the necessary capital. In an earlier period . . . individuals like Cadamosto had been attracted to the service of Prince Henry by the prospect of turning "one soldo into six or ten." Later, when the kings of Portugal found it impossible to continue as a government what Prince Henry had achieved as a private individual, the rights to the Guinea trade, with the obligation to continue exploration, were leased out to a Lisbon merchant in return for an annual payment. Although there are certainly examples of expeditions in which the governments concerned footed the entire bill, it is clear that the incentives created by the structure of property relationships were already of decisive importance in this early period.

In the conquest of the Spanish Empire in the New World the most important of all the early acquired territories were obtained at no direct cost to the crown. Individual leaders from many walks of life were allowed to participate in the process of conquest on their own initiative. In the name of the sovereign, or by virtue of royal patents, they conquered territory at their own expense, hoping they would be assigned rights that would make their fortune when they had finished. Mexico, Peru, Yucatan, and Guatemala are all examples of territories brought to the Spanish crown in this way.

Similar incentives were largely absent in the case of the Chinese. The great expeditions of the Ming in the fifteenth century were characteristically enterprises financed by the government and staffed by the bureaucracy. Even where merchants were permitted to participate for their own gain, institutional guarantees for private property did not exist on the same scale as in Europe. The opportunity for expansion occurred for both China and Europe; indeed, from the point of view of technological achievement as measured by the size and range of expeditions, the opportunity presented to China was far greater. Yet the European society whose rulers were far less wealthy than the Chinese emperor was in reality in a much better position to seize that opportunity. In the absence of comprehensive monolithic government control the European system allowed for a greater measure of individual incentive and broader basis of participation.

The success of the expansion of Latin Christendom must thus be viewed against the general background of the pluralism of the European intellectual inheritance and institutional structure. Competing ideas and competing interests sustained a great creative effort. At the same time expansion had its price. The altered situation of Europe in the world, the very opportunities that were increasingly opened by the voyages of exploration and discovery accentuated the divergences within the Christian community.

The Lure of Prester John

GARRETT MATTINGLY

Few American historians have been so respected and admired, both at home and abroad, as has Garrett Mattingly (1900–1962). His career as a teacher and historian touched the lives of thousands at Northwestern University (1924–28), Long Island University (1928–42), and Columbia University (1948–62). In 1959 he was made William R. Shepherd Professor of European History at Columbia, and at the time of his death was George Eastman Visiting Professor at Oxford. Mattingly's primary scholarly interests were early modern diplomatic history and the expansion of Europe. As can be seen from the article below, he was not only a great teacher but also a master of English prose, artistically and colorfully transforming years of meticulous research into a literary saga of men's struggle with nature and themselves. This skill won him a coveted Pulitzer citation in 1960 for his *Armada*.

FIVE HUNDRED YEARS ago there died in a storm-battered little castle, perched on a cliff at the extreme southwestern corner of Europe, a medieval prince who was the father of the modern world. We have come to call him "Henry the Navigator," although he never sailed farther than the coast of Morocco just across from Portugal, and probably never navigated anything. He gave his father's house and the cheerful, comfortable, slightly backward little nation his father ruled, one of the most far-flung empires and one of the richest overseas trades the world had ever seen; but no progeny of his succeeded to that empire, and it seems doubtful whether trade or empire had much place in his plans. We can only guess at what those plans were, and what forces drove him to change the whole picture of the world.

We find him baffling, inscrutable. So did his contemporaries. The face which looks out from the "panel of Prince Henry" in the famous reredos at Lisbon is different from all the surrounding faces, not just because it is swarthier, not because the eyes are more brooding and the forehead

more lined with thought, but because the whole countenance is marked by a deliberate stillness; withdrawn, aloof, it looks as if no one else existed, as if there was nothing at all except the vision or puzzle on which his attentive eyes are fixed. All we can be sure of is that he is seeing something no one else can see.

What it was he saw, he never said. His was a voluble, mercurial, self-dramatizing family, given to noisy quarrels and tearful reconciliations, to violence and rhetoric (after all, he and his brothers were half Plantagenets), to childishly magnificent display and childishly cunning political charades. Amidst all this uproar, Prince Henry moved like an abstracted adult through the noisy play of children. Even his generosity had something absent-minded about it, so that while men respected him and served him gladly, it seems unlikely that many loved him. His family was literate, even literary, and for men of their time, unusually self-explanatory, but Henry wrote nothing, except perhaps a few prayers, that was not strictly utilitarian. His letters, for the most part, are as dry and businesslike as if he were

Garrett Mattingly, "Navigator to the Modern Age," *Horizon*, III (© November 1960 by American Heritage Publishing Company, Inc.), pp. 73–83. Reprinted by permission of the publisher.

9

the bailiff of his own estates. Nowhere is there a line to tell us what he hoped and dreamed. The clues to that are in what happened.

What happened began like a tale in a romance of chivalry. The three eldest sons of King John I of Portugal — Duarte, Pedro, and Henrique (Edward, Peter, and Henry) — had grown up during an uneasy truce with Castile which only the year before had been converted into a permanent peace. Now, in 1411, they were, respectively, twenty, nineteen, and seventeen, and it was high time they should be knighted. But there was no enemy against whom they might win their spurs; so their father planned a series of magnificent tournaments to which all the best knights of Europe would be invited and where the three princes might exhibit their prowess at the risk of nothing more than a few bumps and bruises. The king had no more than begun his plans when his sons sought an audience and knelt at his feet. Let not the wealth of the kingdom, they implored, be squandered on vain displays and mock battles. Let them, instead, flesh their swords on the enemies of Portugal and of the Christian faith. Portugal had been born of the Crusade. With their new dynasty, let the Crusade begin again. And since the lands of Castile lay athwart the way to the nearest infidels, the Moors of Granada, let them requite the old insults of past invasions and strike at the paynims, this time on their own African soil. Let them attempt the conquest of Ceuta.

It was a surprising suggestion. People still talked about the Crusade but seldom did anything about it. Crusading had gone out of fashion. The princes' uncle, Henry IV of England, said often enough that he hoped one day to lead an army to liberate the Holy Land and lay his bones at last somewhere near the sepulcher of his Saviour, but the nearest he got to doing so was to die amidst his ill-gotten gains in the Jerusalem Chamber at Westminster. As for his son, the future Henry V, he found a nearer and richer enemy more attractive, and would soon be setting out to demonstrate his superior claim to the crown of France by burning the wretched villages of his prospective subjects. In general, throughout Europe, Christian princes preferred to pursue their vendettas with one another while they wrangled over which of the three current popes best deserved their allegiance. Christendom seemed to be shrinking and breaking up. The Ottoman Turks, quickly recovering from the awful blow dealt them by Tamerlane, pressed forward again on its eastern flank. Even in Portugal, which from one end to the other had been carved out of Moslem territory by the swords of crusaders, nobody had done any serious crusading for a hundred and fifty years.

Nevertheless, when he came to think of it, King John could see merits in his sons' suggestion. Ceuta, lying just across the straits from Gibraltar, was the chief port of the Barbary corsairs. It could watch all the shipping that went to and fro in the strait. From Ceuta swooped the swift galleys to seize Italian merchantmen making for Lisbon or to raid the little villages of the Portuguese Algarve and carry off men, women, and children to the slave markets of Africa. Moreover, Ceuta was the favorite staging area and jumping-off-place for the hordes of desert fanatics who from time to time had swept into Spain. To hold it was to hold one of the chief keys to the whole peninsula. Finally, Ceuta was the chief terminus west of Algiers for the caravan trails which came up across the great desert from the wealthy Negro kingdoms of the south. The bazaars and warehouses would be stuffed with monkeys and parakeets, ostrich plumes and elephants' tusks, rare woods and Guinea pepper, and there would be leather bags of gold dust and wedges of reddish-yellow gold tucked away in the strong rooms of every prosperous merchant. At the very least there would be rich spoil, and if the caravans would keep coming, the trade of Africa might fill the coffers of Portugal. When his spies reported that Ceuta might prove vulnerable to determined assault, King John began to make his preparations.

There was a great deal to do. Portugal had to buy cannon and gunpowder abroad, and even ordinary arms and armor. It had to hire ships. And it was impossible in a poor little kingdom to keep these expensive preparations secret; so all of Portugal's neighbors got justifiably nervous. There was grave danger that Castile might take alarm and, thinking these preparations were meant against her, strike first. There was even graver danger that Ceuta might smell the threat and strengthen her defenses. A properly prepared Ceuta would be, against any possible Portuguese effort, impregnable. But by an elaborate comedy of misdirection, King John actually succeeded in persuading observers that what he was preparing was an invasion of — of all places — Holland, so that when the Portuguese armada turned south from Lisbon, the watchful Moors were astonished and dismayed. Even though a tempest blew the invasion fleet off station before a surprise attack could be mounted, Moorish vigilance and Moorish valor could not stop the wild rush of the Portuguese who came boiling off their little ships and splashing through the shallows with Prince Henry at their head. There was savage fighting in the narrow, twisty streets, but before nightfall the last Moorish defenders had fled, and King John was able to knight his three sons in the first city, outside Europe, taken from the infidels in almost three hundred years.

The loot of Ceuta was richer even than had been anticipated. This was a city as stuffed with treasure as Venice, and though most of the gold and precious stones seem to have vanished into the pockets of seamen and archers and men-at-arms, the immediate profit to the crown made the venture a success. But for the long pull, Ceuta was a liability. No more caravans brought the wealth of Ghana across the Sahara to its bazaars. No more merchants from Cairo came with the silks and spices of the East. The wooded hills behind Ceuta were full of Moorish partisans, and the place was under virtual siege except when its former ruler found enough allies to make the siege close and actual. In either case, a strong Portuguese garrison had to be maintained, and the whole town, Christians and Moors alike, had to be fed by sea by convoys escorted by war galleys. For a little country like Portugal, the drain of such an outpost was heavy and the advantage doubtful. No one expected in 1415, when the eyes of Europe were fixed on Agincourt and Constance and on all the internal squabbles which were weakening Christendom against the advancing Turk, that the capture of Ceuta marked the reversal of a trend and that, henceforward, instead of contracting, as it had done for the past two hundred years, Europe would begin to expand again until its civilization circled and dominated and began to unite the globe. It was for no such reason that the Portuguese hung on to Ceuta; they did so simply because it seemed shameful to abandon a city won from the infidels.

The burden of its defense was laid on Prince Henry. Some months after the taking of the city, when he was only twenty-two, his father appointed him Governor of Ceuta and, a little later, Lieutenant-General of the Kingdom of the Algarve, the southernmost province of Portugal, and Grand Master of the crusading Order of Christ. Entrusting the actual command of the garrison at Ceuta to a deputy, the prince himself undertook the harder task of maintaining the line of supply. At first he lived mostly near the sleepy little port of Lagos on the south coast. Later he spent more and more time on the wind-swept headlands of Cape St. Vincent looking out south and west over the tumbling Atlantic. And sometime in those years he saw the vision and accepted the mission to which, with monklike dedication, he devoted the rest of his life. In an ominous waxing crescent, the great world of Islam, stretching from the Russian steppes to the Atlantic coast of Morocco, hemmed in and threatened the smaller Christian world. But beyond the barrier of Islam to the east and south were non-Islamic peoples, some of them (nobody knew how many) Christians. If Islam could be outflanked, the old enemy could be taken in the rear and the Crusade resumed. There was only one way to do it — by sea.

The thing to do was to sail south down the African coast. Henry's earliest chronicler, Zurara, sets forth the prince's objectives as if they had been analyzed by a staff for a command decision. The date, he implies, was about 1419, when Henry was first setting up his court at Sagres. A scientific objective: to explore the coast of Africa beyond the Canary Islands and Cape Bojador because at that time nothing was known by experience, or from the memories of men, or from books, of the land beyond that cape. An economic objective: to seek beyond the cape countries with whom it would be possible to trade. A military objective: to find out by reconnaissance how far south the country of the Moors extended, since a prudent man tries to learn the strength of his enemy. A political objective: to seek a Christian kingdom as an ally. A religious objective: to extend the faith. More than thirty years later, Duarte Pacheco told a somewhat different story. "One night," he said, "as the Prince lay in bed it was revealed to him that he would render a great service to our Lord by the discovery of the Ethiopians . . . that many of them could be saved by baptism . . . and that in their lands so much gold and other riches would be found as would maintain the king and people of Portugal in plenty and enable them to wage war on the enemies of our holy Catholic Faith." There is at least a poetic truth in Pacheco's version, for what turned out to be the greatest series of scientific experiments ever conducted up to that time by Western man, a series which changed the face of the globe and introduced the modern age, began in the haze of a medieval dream. The dream is explicit in the fourth of Zurara's dryly stated objectives: to seek a Christian kingdom as an ally. That could only be the kingdom of Prester John.

Probably the first Prester John heard of in Europe was some Turkish chieftain of the Eastern steppes, some sort of Buddhist or, perhaps, Nestorian Christian, a priest and king at enmity with neighboring Moslems. Later, Prester John became identified with the Coptic Christian overlord of the Abyssinian highland, some of whose priests had chapels at Jerusalem and Bethlehem and some of whose envoys, or persons representing themselves as his envoys, occasionally found their way to Rome and the courts of the West. Medieval Europe was able to transfer the same king, with the same legend, from central Asia to northeast Africa with a minimum of trouble, for both lands lay "somewhere toward the Indies" on the borders of myth and fable. Here unicorns strayed and griffins guarded gold. Here were cannibals, and men whose heads did grow beneath their shoulders, and other men who hopped about on one leg with an enormous foot which, when they took a noonday siesta, they used as an umbrella. Here was a nation of giants who hunted dragons, using lions as hunting dogs. In the midst of these wonders, Prester John dwelt in a high-perched impregnable castle, its moat a constantly flowing river, not of water but of precious stones, and in its throne room a magic mirror in which the Priest King could see at will any part of the world. Seven kings served at his court, sixty dukes, and three hundred and sixty counts. Seventy-two kings obeyed him. Thousands of war elephants marched at his command and hundreds of thousands of horsemen, to say nothing of a special division mounted on ostriches and another on camelopards. His foot soldiers were as innumerable as the sands of the sea. The legends of Prester John vary. In one he was John, the Beloved Disciple, who could not die before the Second Coming and so sat, meditating on his mountain, guarded by hosts of the faithful, awaiting the day of the Last Judgment. But however the legends vary, there is one common factor: in all, the Priest King is very wealthy and very powerful, a reputation which, one may be sure, such subjects of the Ethiopian emperor as reached the West did nothing to diminish. To reconnoiter the Moorish left flank, and perhaps to divert to Portugal the trade which the Moors had diverted from Ceuta, to increase knowledge and convert the heathen, these were all worthy objectives, but the grand objective was to find Prester John and reunite the broken halves of Christendom in a renewal of the Crusade.

The only way to get in touch with Prester John was by sea. And by sea there were, geographically, two possibilities. Either Africa was a peninsula, almost an island, or it was not. Herodotus said it was and that a bold crew of Punic seamen had once sailed down its west coast and emerged, after three years, at the head of the Red Sea. Nobody was known to have repeated their feat since, and certainly not all of Herodotus's geographical information was thoroughly reliable; but some Greek, some Arabic, and some Western geographers spoke of Africa as a peninsula, though they differed about how far it might extend to the south. The contrary opinion, however, was sustained by the great authority of Ptolemy, an authority never greater than in the first years of Prince Henry's mission, for the first complete Latin translation of Ptolemy's geography had just been published in 1410. Ptolemy was sure that the land masses north and south of the equator must be roughly equal, otherwise the globe would be overbalanced. So the great world map constructed from his gazetteer shows Africa curving round until it joins with Asia, making the Indian Ocean a vaster Mediterranean.

Nevertheless, Prince Henry thought the best chance of reaching Prester John was to sail south past Cape Bojador. For even if Ptolemy were right, and the way by sea was blocked, there might be another way to the fabled kingdom. Some Arab sages said that the Nile which flowed through Egypt rose in a great lake amidst the Mountains of the Moon. And out of that same lake, they said, flowed another mighty river, the Western Nile, which took its course through the land of the Negroes and emptied into the Atlantic. At least one fourteenth-century map showed both rivers with, right between them and near the shores of the lake in the Mountains of the Moon, the magic castle of Prester John. Now it was well known that through wealthy Ghana flowed a great river (the Niger, really) with rich cities on its banks. It was not unreasonable to assume that the kings of these cities, like the Ethiopians farther east, were the subjects and vassals of the Priest King, and that the ascent of their River of Gold might lead directly to the Priest King's court. So Prince Henry said to his captains, "Go south!"

Nevertheless, for fourteen years none of them got south of Cape Bojador. Their resources were somewhat limited. Most years, there were at sea in the prince's service not more than two or three *barcas,* the kind of ships the Portuguese used in fishing for tunny or hauling wine and grain along the coast — half-decked vessels shaped like butter tubs with one stubby mast and one clumsy great square sail amidships, commanded by daring, impecunious *fidalgos* and manned by fishermen from the neighborhood of Lagos. They were not afraid of blue water, however, and they knocked about a good deal in the Atlantic, perhaps looking for the islands, real or imaginary, with which all medieval maps dotted the Ocean Sea, perhaps testing Ptolemy's hypothesis that India was, after all, not very far west of Spain. In the course of their voyages they touched the Canaries and discovered, or rediscovered, the Madeiras and the Azores. And every year one or more of them went down to Cape Bojador, took a good look, and came away again. In spite of Prince Henry's repeated exhortations to go farther south, that was as far as any of them went.

It is not that it is so hard to round Cape Bojador. It's an insignificant little bump on the coast of Africa, and once you have reached it, the difficulty is *not* to round it. Most of the time a wind blows steadily from the northeast — the wind Yankee sailors called, hundreds of years later, "the Portygee Trades" — a wind capable of shoving even a tubby Portuguese *barca* along at a stiff clip while the current tugs at her keel with a force of another knot and a half. But out to seaward, as far as the eye can see, there is brown shoal water with here and there a tumble of breakers. Once past this cape, with no sea room to maneuver and the wind and current against you, how would you ever get back? Rounding Cape Bojador was like entering the mouth of a trap. That is what men were convinced it was, a death trap, for the wind and current would be thrusting you on into the Green Sea of Darkness.

The legend of the Green Sea of Darkness begins with the theories of the Greek geographers. Basically, they said, the globe was divided into five zones. At either pole there was a Frigid Zone, where men could not live because it was too cold. Its outer ring was merely inhospitable, gradually becoming incapable of supporting life. Nearer the pole, the air was so mixed with frozen water that it was opaque and unbreathable. One Greek traveler actually claimed to have seen this interesting phenomenon. Then there was the Temperate Zone, with the best climate, of course, in Greece, getting gradually too hot in Egypt and too cold in Scythia. In the Southern Hemisphere there was another Temperate Zone, the Antipodes, where, some said, everything in the north Temperate Zone was exactly reproduced. But it would be impossible to find out because between the two lay the Torrid Zone. In it the heat of the sun grew so fierce that no man could hope to cross the Torrid Zone and live.

To this symmetrical Greek picture, the Arabs added horrors of th·n own to describe the sea beyond Cape Bojador. As the sun grew hotter, the steaming sea became a thickening broth coated with a scum of green weed and infested with loathsome monsters. Near the equator the sea boiled, the tar would boil in a ship's seams, and the brains would boil in a man's skull. But it was unlikely that any ship could get that far. Long before, it would have been dragged to the bottom by the huge sea serpents which abounded in the region, or crunched up like a biscuit by a crocodile bigger than the biggest whale. Allah had placed the Green Sea for a barrier across the southern ocean. Even to attempt to enter it was blasphemy.

Only the most ignorant believed that the world was flat and that men who sailed too far would fall off the edge, but geographers, Arab and Latin, took the Green Sea of Darkness seriously. Nobody knew just where it began, and many must have rejected its more spectacular terrors, but there was considerable agreement that the ocean south of Cape Bojador was dangerous. At least no one had sailed it and returned. In 1291 two Genoese brothers had rounded Bojador, making for India by sea. They were never heard of again. Half a century later, an adventurous Catalan expedition on the same course, looking this time for the River of Gold (the Western Nile?), also disappeared without a trace. Understandably, even brave Portuguese *fidalgos* hung back. But Prince Henry still said, "Go farther south."

Then, in 1434, after these probes into the vast spaces of the ocean had gone on for fourteen years, one of the prince's captains, Gil Eannes, rounded Cape Bojador and returned. The sea and the wind and the sandy desert shore seemed much the same on one side of the cape as on the other, and the next year Eannes went farther, and the next year one of his companions went farther still, four hundred miles into an unexplored ocean along an unexplored coast. Then came a pause. A disastrous campaign in Morocco and serious domestic disorders distracted Henry's attention, and without the prince's driving will nobody went exploring.

In that interval a great step forward must have been taken in the development of the vessel which made possible the conquest of the ocean. According to Zurara, Gil Eannes rounded Bojador in a *barca.* Nobody says what ships made the next two voyages, and no record survives of how the new type was developed; but when exploration was resumed in 1441, only caravels were used, caravels built in Prince Henry's port of Lagos, expressly, one assumes, for the prince's captains. Caravels continued to carry the explorers until almost the end of the century. They were longer, narrower, more graceful ships than *barcas,* with lateen sails — the primitive form of the fore and aft rig — on two or three masts. They could lie close to the wind and were capital for inshore work. "The best ships in the world and able to sail anywhere," wrote the Venetian Cadamosto after he had commanded one for Prince Henry. For some years, only the Portuguese built caravels, and they sedulously cultivated the legend that no other type of ship could make the African voyage.

We know nothing, except by inference, of Prince Henry's role in the development of the caravel. And we know almost as little of the famous "school" which he set up at his villa at Sagres. He early drew there Jaime of Majorca, prince of cartographers and instrument makers, a man learned in everything that concerned the stars and the sea, the son of the great Abraham Cresques who designed the Catalan Atlas, and possessor, probably, of his father's books and maps. But Henry was always drawing learned men to Sagres, and experienced pilots and far-wandering travelers. It was not so much a school, really, as a sort of scientific congress in continuous session, working out for the first time the problems of navigating the trackless ocean and of charting unknown coasts by using what the northerners knew of tides and the lead line, what the Italians knew of stars and compass piloting, what could be learned from the Arabs, and what from the ancient Greeks — all to be tested by continuous experiment at sea.

Henry died in 1460, just as his captains began reporting that the African coast was trending to the east. He must have died hoping that Prester John and the fabulous Indies were now not far off. They were more than a generation off, actually, but the back of the problem was broken. By compass and quadrant, Portuguese pilots were finding their way across the trackless ocean, standing boldly out from the Cape Verdes to make a landfall at the Azores, harnessing the great wind systems of the Atlantic — the trades and the westerlies — confidently to their purpose. The African coast was mapped as far as the beginning of the Gulf of Guinea. So were the islands. And sugar from Madeira and cargoes of slaves from Negroland were helping to finance the exploring voyages. Men had seen a new heaven and a new earth, the lush green land beyond the Sahara and the rising constellations of the Southern Hemisphere. And, best of all, the superstitious terrors of the Sea of Darkness, the scientific terrors of the Torrid Zone had been dispersed forever. The ocean south of Cape Bojador was like the ocean north of it. There were no clinging weeds, no horrendous monsters, and a man on the deck of a ship off Sierra Leone, less than ten degrees from the equator, was no more uncomfortably hot than he might have been on a July day in the streets of Lagos. To the south, anyway, there were no unnavigable seas, no uninhabitable lands.

More than forty years of patient, probing experiment had at last made Europeans free of the ocean. From this the voyages of Vasco da Gama and Columbus and Magellan, the European settlement of the Americas, the European commercial dominance of Asia and Africa necessarily followed, and with these things followed too the revolutions, in men's ways of thinking and of making a living, which ended the Middle Ages. The monkish ardor of a medieval prince, his long quest for a mythical kingdom, made inevitable the modern world.

II. DISCOVERY OF A NEW WORLD

The Invention of America

EDMUNDO O'GORMAN

One of the most active and controversial Latin American historians of the present day is Edmundo O'Gorman, professor of history at the University of Mexico. O'Gorman, born in 1906 in Mexico City — where he studied, then practiced, law — is interested in the philosophy of history and in the nature and meaning of the concepts that underlie historical events. He has written many articles and several books dealing with various aspects of this subject, including *Fundamentos de la historia de América* (1942); *Crisis y porvenir de la ciencia histórica* (1947); and *La idea del descubrimiento de América* (1951). For many years he was historian and assistant director of the Archivo General de la Nación in Mexico City, and co-founder of the publishing house Alcancia. He has traveled widely outside of Mexico, and taught in the United States at Brown University and the University of Indiana.

T HE MOST IMPORTANT problem concerning the history of America is the need of giving a satisfactory explanation of the way in which America appeared as such on the historical scene. Our conception of America's nature and of the meaning of its history depends on how this problem is stated and solved.

This highly significant question has been given full attention by historians in the past, and the unanimous answer today is that America appeared as the result of its having been "discovered" on October 12, 1492, when Christopher Columbus arrived at a small island which he believed to be one of a group in the neighborhood of Japan. The truth of this way of describing the event of October 12 is now held to be self-evident. But the object of our inquiry is to test the scientific validity of the idea that what Columbus really did was to "discover" America.

A. We must bear in mind, first, that we are dealing with an *idea* about what Co-lumbus did, not with a description of the facts as they appear in contemporary evidence. The statement that Columbus "discovered" America the moment he reached that island in 1492 is only a statement by historians about what they think Columbus did, not what the evidence tells them that he actually did. It is merely an interpretation of that evidence.

B. But if it is only an interpretation it may not be the only possible one or necessarily the best one. Hence we are at liberty to challenge it if we suspect that it does not explain the facts adequately.

The point is of such importance that it may be well to clarify it by an example. Many centuries ago St. Augustine voiced the opinion that the ecumenical unity achieved by the Roman Empire could be explained only by God's design to prepare the world for the advent of the Savior. At that time and for many centuries afterward believers accepted this interpretation of history not merely as one of several possible

From Edmundo O'Gorman, *The Invention of America* (Bloomington: Indiana University Press, 1961), pp. 9–11, 35–47. Reprinted by permission of Indiana University Press.

interpretations but as the only possible one; it was regarded, indeed, not as an interpretation at all but as a statement of fact. They could not see that it was in reality no more than an opinion, based not on empirical evidence but on faith in God and His providential guidance of human history. In time, not without a fierce struggle on the part of traditional scholars who had the backing of both Church and State, a few historians, inspired by modern currents of philosophical thought, began to see that the facts regarding the political achievement of the Romans could be interpreted in a different and more rational way; the old providential conception of history lost ground and finally gave way to new interpretations.

In the same way we have now reached the point where the traditional interpretation of the facts concerning the appearance of America can reasonably be challenged on the ground that its philosophical foundations are no longer tenable. . . .

Since we now intend to subject an interpretation to a test, it is well to have a clear idea of just what an interpretation is.

Any act considered in itself is a mere happening that lacks meaning; we cannot say what it *is;* it has no particular being. In order that it may possess a being, that we may be able to say just what it is, it is necessary to assign to it some intention or purpose. The moment we do this, the act takes on a meaning and we can then state what it is; we endow it with a specific being chosen from various possibilities. This operation is what is known as an interpretation. To interpret an act is to endow it with a specific being by granting it a particular intention.

Let us take an example. We see a man leave his house and walk toward a near-by forest. The act, considered in itself, is a pure happening, a *factum.* But what is the act? Obviously it can be any one of many different things: a stroll, an escape, a survey aimed at lucrative ends, a scientific exploration, the beginning of a long journey, or as many other things as imagina-

tion can provide, always depending on the intention which the man may be supposed to entertain.

Our capacity for granting a specific being to an act by interpreting it is, however, subject to limits. Whatever intention is assumed, it must be attributed to an agent, not necessarily capable of carrying it out, since he may use another agent for that purpose, but capable of having intentions, since otherwise we should have an absurdity. There are all sorts of entities which can be and have been conceived as capable of volition and of carrying out their intentions, such as God, the angels, man, spirits from the outer world, and even animals, whereas others are capable of volition, but not of action, such as certain metaphysical entities, Nature, or Universal History, depending on the way in which some philosophical doctrines understand them. But what may not be conceived in such a way are all inanimate entities, such as geometric figures, numbers, or material things: a triangle, the number two, a table, the sun, or the sea. Should we conceive of them as capable of having intentions, it is in a metaphorical sense only; otherwise we go beyond the bounds of reason and arrive at a logical absurdity.

Thus an interpretation of an act can be admissible even though the agent carrying it out may be incapable of having intentions, provided that the purpose which gives the act its significance derives from an entity capable of having them. The opposite case, though, would be absurd, even if we assume that the agent carrying out the act has this capacity.

In the light of these considerations, let us examine the historical evolution of the idea of the discovery of America as we know it. We are dealing with three different ways of interpreting the same act, namely, Columbus' voyage of 1492.

In the first stage, the interpretation consists in affirming that Columbus showed that the lands which he found in 1492 were an unknown continent, since it was with that intention that he undertook the voyage. Here we have an admissible interpretation, since the intention which endows the act under interpretation with the meaning of being a venture of discovery is placed on a person, that is, on someone capable of having intentions and of carrying them out. We know, however, that this interpretation had to be discarded, because documentary evidence rendered its empirical basis untenable.

In the second stage, the interpretation consists in affirming that Columbus showed that the lands which he found in 1492 were an unknown continent for, although this was not the intention with which he undertook the voyage, and although he had no idea of what he had accomplished, in carrying out this act he fulfilled the designs of history, which required that humanity be made aware of the existence and being of that continent.

In this second case the interpretation is still admissible, since the intention which gives the act under interpretation the meaning of a venture of discovery is placed on the act itself; that is, it is conceived as immanent in history, an entity previously understood as capable of embracing intentions, though without the capacity of carrying them out, so that it makes use of Columbus as an instrument for that purpose. We know, however, that this interpretation also had to be discarded, not through the failure of its empirical basis, but because the theoretical premise became untenable.

In the third stage, the interpretation consists in affirming that Columbus showed that the lands which he found in 1492 were an unknown continent purely by chance, that is, with no intention whatever being involved in the process.

In this case it is clear that, from the point of view of the requisites of any interpretation, the thesis offers a serious difficulty, because in spite of its denying the intention, the act is endowed with the same meaning as in the previous cases. Since this is impossible, because without that requisite the act could not assume the meaning which is assigned to it, it is necessary to assume that the intention exists in spite of its having been denied. The problem therefore appears in a twofold aspect: first, how to reconcile that contradiction, and second, to find out the whereabouts of the intention which must be assumed in order that the act may have the meaning which it has been given.

The contradiction can be got around if we bear in mind that it is not necessary for the agent who is carrying out the act to have the intention which gives it its meaning, since we know that he may be acting as a mere instrument of some design that is not his own. In this way Columbus could have revealed the being of the lands which he found without having the intention of doing so, so that from Columbus' point of view it would be legitimate to assert that the act was not intentional. Only by assuming that Columbus acted as an instrument of a design which was not his own can we avoid the contradiction that we have pointed out. On this score the thesis under consideration may be salvaged.

But where are we to find this concealed and mysterious intention which gives the 1492 voyage its meaning as a "discovery"? The answer leaves no room for doubt. Since any act can in this respect offer only three possibilities, namely, (1) the agent or subject of the act, (2) the act itself, and (3) the thing or object of the act, and since in this case the first two have already been tested and discarded, we can only conclude that in this third stage the intention is placed on the object which is said to have been discovered as something immanent in it. But it then seems obvious that the thesis ends in an absurdity, since the continent which we call America is clearly one of those inanimate entities incapable of conceiving intentions.

Thus we have disclosed the basic logical absurdity of this thesis and have arrived, at long last, at an explanation of what seemed to us so very suspicious from the beginning, that is, to have held a man historically responsible for something that it is known he did not do. When it is affirmed that Columbus discovered the American continent by chance when he hit upon some lands which he believed were part of Asia, that is, when we are told that Columbus revealed the being of an object entirely different from the one with which he had endowed it, we are actually being asked to believe that that object itself revealed its secret and hidden being at the moment when Columbus perceived it and by virtue only of that perception, for otherwise there is no other possible way to explain the revelation which we are told took place.

The logical absurdity in this thesis becomes even more patent as soon as we draw the inevitable consequences, for it is now clear that the idea of a chance discovery of the American continent not only cancels Columbus' personal purposes and opinions as inoperative, but also turns him into a docile and blind instrument, no longer of some assumed designs of historical progress, but of some intentions absurdly supposed to be immanent in a mere physical object. When we admit this, however, we have turned history upside down and deprived man of even the questionable liberty which was granted to him by philosophical idealism. Instead of conceiving history as the result of decisions taken by men and carried out by men, it is now conceived as the result of designs that are immanent in objects, blindly and inexorably fulfilled by men. Thus man is no longer the serf of historical development, conceived as a rational process according to idealism — which in itself was bad enough; he is now the slave of nobody knows what mechanical blind process pertaining to inanimate material objects.

The history of the idea of the "discovery" of America has shown that we are dealing with a process of interpretation which, as it successively exhausted its only three logical possibilities, necessarily arrived at a logical absurdity. History itself provides the best possible argument for the definite and final refutation of this way of explaining the appearance of America within the sphere of Western culture. Before proceeding to draw the pertinent conclusions, it will be necessary to consider one last problem, which enables us to seek out the roots of the evil that afflicts the whole structure.

Our analysis would be lame if we failed to take account of three fundamental questions that arise from it. First, what is the reason for the very idea that America was "discovered"; that is, what is the condition of the possibility of the interpretation itself? Second, how can we explain the insistence on maintaining this interpretation against all empirical evidence; that is, why was it not abandoned as soon as the true purposes and opinions of Columbus were made patent? Third, how is it possible to assume such a flagrant logical absurdity as the one implied in the final thesis of the process; that is, in what way can it be conceived that the American continent harbored the purpose of revealing its own being?

We do not naïvely maintain, of course, that the fault may be traced to some mental deficiency in the historians who developed the process, or in any diabolical machinations that confused and misled them. Rather it springs from a previous assumption in their way of thinking, which as an *a priori* principle conditions all of their reasoning and which, at least since the time of the Greeks, has been one of the foundations of Western philosophical thought. We allude to the ancient and venerable idea that all things are something in themselves, *per se;* that all things are ready-made according to one and only one possible type, or to state it more technically, that all things are endowed for all time, for anyone and anywhere, with a set being, predetermined and unalterable.

According to this way of understanding reality, what one thinks a thing is, at a given moment, *is* what it has always been and what it will always be, something already made, endowed with a definite structure, which cannot cease to be what it is in order to become something else. The being — not the existence — of things appears thereby as something substantial, something mysteriously and intimately lodged within things, their very nature, that which makes things be what they are. For example, it is usually thought that the sun and the moon are a star and a satellite, respectively, because the former partakes of the nature of a star and the latter partakes of the nature of a satellite; thus, it is believed, the sun has always been a star and the moon a satellite, and they always will be until they disappear.

But the great scientific and philosophical revolution of our time has shown us that this old substantialist way of conceiving reality is untenable, for we have come to understand that the being — not the existence — of things is nothing but the meaning or significance which they are given within the over-all framework of the picture of reality accepted as true at some given historical moment. In other words, the being of things is not something that they contain within themselves, but something that is assigned or granted to them.

A fuller exposition of this change of philosophical perspective and the way in which it affects our manner of conceiving man and his world would lead us too far from our immediate purpose. It will suffice to expand briefly on the example we have just given. If we put ourselves in the historical period that accepted a geocentric view of the universe, the sun and the moon are two planets, and not a star and a satellite as in the heliocentric system. In both cases they are heavenly bodies, but in a mythical concept of the universe they would be gods or spirits. Thus the being of those two existent bodies, those two lumps of cosmic matter, does not belong intimately to them, it is not lodged within them; rather it is the meaning assigned to them according to the prevailing idea of truth and reality. The sun and the moon have successively been gods and planets, and are now a star and a satellite, respectively; but there is no legitimate ground for concluding that endowing a thing with a given being in reference to a given view of reality constitutes an error merely because such a view is no longer in use. On the contrary, it is obvious that the error would be to endow the sun and the moon with the being of a star and a satellite, respectively, if we were considering a period in which the geocentric view of the universe was held, in the same way as it would be an error to consider them two planets today.

The answer to our problem now becomes clear: the fault that lies at the root of the entire history of the idea of the discovery of America consists in assuming that the lump of cosmic matter which we now know as the American continent has always been that, when actually it only became that when such a meaning was given to it, and will cease to be that when, by virtue of some change in the current world concept, that meaning will no longer be assigned to it. We can now see why it has seemed necessary to conceive the appearance of America as the result of a discovery, why this notion has been upheld in spite of all the difficulties arising from the historical evidence, and how it has been possible to maintain the obvious logical absurdity implied in placing the intention that the act of discovery requires on the object which was supposed to have been discovered. Let us examine these three aspects of the problem separately.

A. If we assume that the lump of cosmic matter that is known today as the American continent has always been that, or rather, if we suppose that it is that in itself and of itself, it becomes clear that an act which establishes the existence of that lump of matter must be conceived as the revelation, or "discovery," of its hidden being, because the existence and the being of that entity have been previously identified one with the other. Thus we have an entity which, like a chest containing a treasure, is endowed with a "discoverable" being, so that its first appearance can and must be explained as the result of a "discovery."

B. But if it is assumed that that lump of matter is endowed with a discoverable being, it is also necessary to assume that such a revelation may well take place by the mere physical perception of the object, and hence independently of any idea held on that score by the "discoverer," since what he, or anyone else, may think in this regard can produce no effect on this predetermined and unalterable being. We are dealing with an assumption that the act which reveals the being is an act in itself, endowed with a predetermined meaning, since irrespectively of any opinion or intention held by the person who carries it out, the act must necessarily be the discovery of that discoverable being. And thus, at long last, we arrive at an understanding of a point that allows no other plausible explanation, the insistence on maintaining that the true meaning of Columbus' 1492 voyage was the "discovery" of the American continent, after it was known and proved that what Columbus actually did was something quite different.

C. Finally, if we assume that the discovery of the object's being is fulfilled merely by physical perception, it follows that the revelation is realized independently of the personal intentions of the agent, and also that the object has the capacity, or, we might say, the intention to reveal the being that lies immanent within it. In no other way can we explain how the discovery could be effected. We can now understand how it is possible to assume the logical absurdity that the American continent entertained the desire of discovering itself when Columbus established physical contact with it. If instead of thinking that that lump of matter was endowed at a given moment with a being in order to explain its existence within a given geographical picture, we think that it has always had that being as something intimately its own and quite independent of us, we must recognize that it has the capacity to impose its being on us as we establish relationship or contact with it. It thus becomes possible

for us to concur in the absurdity which we have found at the bottom of the thesis of the chance discovery of America. This may explain the emotional language used by historians in describing the event of October 12, 1492. Morison's account, for example, concludes by saying that "never again may mortal men hope to recapture the amazement, the wonder, the delight of those October days in 1492 when the New World gracefully yielded her virginity to the conquering Castilians." What does this metaphysical rape really imply save the idea that, fully constituted in its being, the American continent had always been there patiently waiting throughout the centuries to reveal itself to the first man who, as in a fairy tale, would come to touch it?

I should like to end with a little story which may help to clarify matters. As I was leaving the lecture room after explaining the foregoing ideas, someone in the audience said to me: "Do you seriously mean that it is impossible for a man to discover by chance a piece of gold, for instance, without its being necessary to assume that that piece of gold was there, inclined and, let us say, desiring to be discovered?"

"I leave the answer to you," I replied, "but you must consider that if that man has no idea of what we call gold so that he may endow that piece of matter which he found by chance with the meaning belonging to that idea, it is absolutely impossible for him to make the discovery for which you make him responsible. And that," I added, "is precisely Columbus' case."

The time has now come to answer the question with which our inquiry began. We asked whether or not the idea that the American continent was "discovered" was acceptable as a satisfactory way of explaining its appearance on the historical scene of Western culture. We may now answer that it is not satisfactory, because this interpretation does not account adequately for the facts that it interprets; it reduces itself to an absurdity when it reaches the limits of its logical possibilities. The reason for this absurdity is the substantialistic concept of America as a thing in itself. We must conclude that it is necessary to discard both this obsolete notion and the interpretation that depends on it, in order to seek a more adequate way to explain the phenomenon.

Our conclusions have, moreover, laid open to criticism the foundations of American historiography as conceived up to now. The traditional idea of America as a thing in itself, and the no less traditional idea that because of this previous notion we are dealing with an entity endowed with a "discoverable" being, which in fact was discovered, are, respectively, the ontological and hermeneutical premises on which the truth of that historiography depends. If one ceases to conceive of America as a ready-made thing that had always been there and that one day miraculously revealed its hidden, unknown, and unforeseeable being to an awe-struck world, then the event which is thus interpreted (the finding by Columbus of unknown oceanic lands) takes on an entirely different meaning, and so, of course, does the long series of events that followed. All those happenings which are now known as the exploration, the conquest, and the colonization of America; the establishment of colonial systems in all their diversity and complexity; the gradual formation of nationalities; the movement toward political independence and economic autonomy; in a word, the sum total of all American history, both Latin and Anglo-American, will assume a new and surprising significance. Thus it will be possible to see that the fundamental issue in the understanding of that history is the ontological understanding of America, which will no longer be conceived as an unalterable and predetermined substance, unconsciously postulated *a priori*, but rather as the result of a unique and peculiar historical process, which is of course intimately linked with the process of universal history. Historical events will

no longer appear as something external and accidental that in no way alters the supposed essence of an America ready-made since the time of Creation, but as something internal which constitutes its ever-changing, mobile, and perishable being, as is the being of all that partakes of life; and its history will no longer be that which *has happened* to America, but that which *it has been, is, and is in the act of being*.

We may conclude that our analysis means the bankruptcy of the old essentialistic concept of American history, and that the way is now open toward a new way of understanding it as something dynamic and alive. If this is the case, we must bear in mind that we can no longer rest on any *a priori* idea as to what America is, since that notion may be derived only from historical research and not, as is commonly supposed, from some substantialist logically previous premise. This means that if we pretend to tackle the great American historical problem — to explain how the idea of America arose in the consciousness of Western culture — we are committed to a procedure which is diametrically opposed to the one which has traditionally been followed. *Instead of starting from a preconceived idea of America in order to explain how Columbus revealed the being of that entity, we should start with what Columbus did in order to explain how such a being was conceived*. This new road implies full acceptance of the historical meaning of Columbus' enterprise as it appears from the evidence, from the viewpoint of his personal intentions and convictions, instead of ignoring their significance as it has been traditional to do. Our purpose, then, may be considered as a fourth stage of the same process, in which, finally abandoning the idea that America was the object of a "discovery," we shall seek a new concept by which the facts may be explained more adequately. This new concept, if we may anticipate, is that of America not discovered but invented. . . .

O'Gorman's "Idea" of the Discovery

MARCEL BATAILLON

Born at Dijon in 1895, Marcel Bataillon has dedicated a lifetime to precise scholarship and inspired teaching, primarily in the field of Spanish and Latin American studies. After rising through the exacting Lycées of Dijon and Louis-le-Grand in Paris, Bataillon graduated from the École Normale Supérieure, and then the École des Hautes Études Hispaniques, with a Doctor of Letters degree. Since 1945 he has been professor of Iberian and Latin American languages and literature at the Collège de France, and, since 1949, vice-president of the Conseil Supérieur de l'Éducation Nationale. He also has been a professor of French at the University of Lisbon, of Spanish at the Lycée de Bordeaux, director of the Institut d'Études Hispaniques at the University of Paris, and director of both the *Bulletin Hispanique* and the *Revue de Littérature Comparée*. His most valuable historical work is the two-volume *Erasme et l'Espagne*, published in 1937.

EDMUNDO O'GORMAN's latest book [*La idea del descubrimiento de América*] will be avidly read by all those who wish, as he does, to go beyond dryly objective history, those who do not believe that the events of the past can be recaptured by finding one by one the details of fact, but who are more concerned with knowing what *significance* an event had for the men who lived it, and what different *significance* it took on for the men of following epochs.

For a long time the author has wondered what it meant, in the history of the human mind, to "discover America." The little book entitled *Fundamentos de la historia de América* (Mexico, 1942) already bore on its cover a large question mark superimposed on a picture of the American continent. Since that time, philosophizing on what he calls *Crisis y porvenir de la ciencia histórica* (Mexico, 1947), O'Gorman has taken for his starting point the question: "Do we really know what we mean by the discovery of America?" "History [says the author, thinking about the history of culture], if considered abstractly, can only appear as a long series of errors; which amounts to saying that in history the idea of error, as the physical sciences understand it, is not valid unless it is decreed that all history is itself an error — an acknowledged absurdity. Everything in history that is presented to us as an error in interpretation — for example, 'Columbus discovered America' — is not an error, but a wandering (*un errar*), in other words the living proof (*mostración*) that the past saw, and lived, things differently than we see and live them. . . . Therefore it is not a question of something susceptible to correction. It could be said that the historian

These pages constitute part (pp. 23–28, 53–55) of a study published in the *Bulletin Hispanique*, vol. LV (1953), 23–55, "L'idée de la découverte de l'Amérique chez les Espagnols du XVIᵉ siècle." That article evoked a response from O'Gorman, entitled "Marcel Bataillon et l'idée de la découverte de l'Amérique," *Bulletin Hispanique*, LVI (1954), 345–363, followed on pp. 364–365 by a brief commentary by M. Bataillon. These articles (with the exception of the last two pages), augmented by an exchange of correspondence between the two authors, have been republished by the Universidad Autónoma de México, Centro de Estudios Filosóficos, under the title *Dos concepciones de la tarea historica — Con motivo de la idea del descubrimiento de América*, de Marcel Bataillon y Edmundo O'Gorman (Mexico: Imprenata Universitaria, 1955), 117 pp. Reprinted here by permission of the Directeur du *Bulletin Hispanique*. [Editor's translation] is the man on whom falls the task of justifying to his contemporaries the way of life of past generations. *His mission is to give explanations for the dead, not to pick a quarrel with them.*" A fine motto for the historian of ideas. And O'Gorman blames all modern historiography of the discovery for "its lack of perspectivism or historicism," meaning by these wicked abstract words "the generous attitude of man which understands all to understand something."

The new book could be an illustration of chapter I of the preceding one. In it O'Gorman passes in review the successive interpretations of the discovery of the New World since the sixteenth century (unfortunately not since the fifteenth) up until the year 1942 when the books by Morison and Enrique de Gandia and the clarification of Emiliano Jos appeared. From all this a total view is revealed which satisfies the mind. It might be summed up by saying that the sixteenth century, eminently expressed by Las Casas and continued in the seventeenth, interpreted Columbus' undertaking in the providentialist perspective of a universal history which was still a theology of history. During the eighteenth century, the transcendental finalism of the divine government gives way to the imminent finalism of human progress, the discovery of America thus becoming, for Humboldt, a decisive moment in the "science of the Cosmos" by which humanity took possession of its universe. Finally, recent historiography, as far as it affirms the fortuitous character of the discovery and the disproportion between the initial act and what followed it, accentuates rather the contingency of history and at the same time a certain determinism, and detaches itself from all finalism, explicit or implicit.

But, if such is the lesson to be drawn from O'Gorman's book, I confess, for my part, that I am irritated (giving to the word all its force) by the way he presents the "ancient stage" of the interpretation of the discovery. And since I suppose that others concerned with the sixteenth century will also be bothered, I would like to point out what does not satisfy me. It will be seen that it is his way of treating the old historians which seems to me too unconstrained. But why this liberty? It is necessary to read attentively what is presented to us as the "Genesis" of the history of the discovery.

O'Gorman has the notion that, intellectually speaking, the discovery of the New World did not date from the year 1492, when Columbus landed on the islands which are the vanguard of the American continent, because, in the mind of the discoverer, these islands were the vanguard of Asia. It dates rather from the moment when it was recognized that this was a question of *new* land, unsuspected by ancient and medieval geography. Now, was it not as far back as 1503 that a short account entitled *Mundus Novus* by the navigator Amerigo Vespucci appeared? There indeed is the revelation of the newness of what was to be called America! Of little importance were the interminable discussions, recently revived again by Roberto Levillier (*América la bien llamada,* Buenos Aires, 1948) about the authenticity, the date, and the extent of Vespucci's explorations on the shores of the continent. America was not ill-named if Vespucci was the first to have "understood" it as a new continent in relation to the known world. This revelation seems to O'Gorman clear enough, obvious enough to gain credence as far back as the first decade of the sixteenth century, at least in the minds of the learned, and to efface the "Asiatic project" of Columbus just as the day replaces the night.

But this is not all. The Mexican historian-philosopher was impressed to find everywhere — at least beginning in 1535 — the tradition, or the legend, of the unknown pilot. A navigator, whose name the story does not give, was supposed to have been carried along by a storm as far as one of the Greater Antilles, where he took a bearing on at least the approximate position and, upon his return, seriously ill, was taken in by Christopher Columbus, to whom he disclosed his secret before he died. After all is said and done, the *New World* would therefore have been discovered by chance, and Columbus would have done nothing but definitively find the sea route. The chroniclers who lived in America a short time after Columbus do not mention the tradition of the anonymous pilot as a truth established by witnesses worthy of belief. Las Casas, in his old age, presents it as an explanation which was held among the Spanish in the islands during the first decade of the sixteenth century. What did this *vox populi* signify? O'Gorman does not stop at the overly simple idea that it might be the daughter of resentment or envy, that it might be, in short, a means of taking away from Columbus the glory of having encountered a new world while failing in his daring project to reach Asia by the west. Preoccupied by his problem, which is that of the intellectual comprehension of the discovery of the new world, the historian-philosopher thinks that he sees there a simple solution to this problem, a kind of popular "ersatz" of the "revelation" of the learned Amerigo Vespucci. What the legend effaces, according to him, is not the merit of Columbus the discoverer, but his Asiatic error. If Columbus had really thought to reach the shores of Asia, from which he remained so distant, by way of the Atlantic, this foolish project does not count for more than a dream of a sick man, compared with what he actually found. It was better for his glory, as well as for good sense, that he went to find Atlantic lands, knowledge of which had been revealed to him by another, who had been cast upon them by a "chance of the sea." This other, postulated by popular good sense, is the anonymous pilot.

Vespuccian revelation, legend of the unknown pilot; O'Gorman believed that here he was in the presence of a double genesis of the idea of the discovery. A scholarly genesis, a popular genesis, both of them fatal to the "Asiatic project" of Columbus. How he could henceforth make fun of

the endless controversies between the Harrisses, the Vignauds, and the Carbias, who all deny the Asiatic project, and the erudite classical historiography, which denied the unknown pilot! "Let us no longer say," he proposes, "that the story of the unknown pilot is 'a falsehood' (*una falsedad*); let us say that it is the 'truth' (*la verdad*) of our ancestors, and let us therefore open wide the doors to the historical comprehension of the first event of our American existence."

It remained, after that, to interpret the literature of the sixteenth century using the double directing thread which had been adopted. It is here that the respectful reader of *texts* is dismayed. O'Gorman, who formulated with such bliss the rule for historical comprehension: "to give explanations for the dead, not to pick a quarrel with them," finds himself led to trying to pick a quarrel (and what nasty quarrels!) with Oviedo, Fernando Colón, and Las Casas; to accuse the first of paralogism, the second of bad faith, and to blame the third for wishing to be something other than what he was. Only perhaps Gómara acquits himself, because it is he who officially "consecrates" the legend of the unknown pilot by giving it as the truth, pure and simple. He has the right, therefore, to ignore the Vespuccian revelation. The others see their thoughts brought to light by an inquisitor who flatters himself that he can see clearer than they themselves. They are forced to "confess" their stretching of the truth as opposed to the O'Gormanian logic. But who is the guilty one? The old authors or the logician? Is it not true, for a historian careful to read the texts with the objective of searching for what they *meant* and not of summoning them to answer ready-made questions by a *yes* or a *no,* that the fact that their answers are beside the point the sign of a poorly conducted interrogation? One thinks he hears the old authors protesting against the mistreatment of this accuser who tortures them: "Strike, but listen!" We would like to call upon them again, and to make them

judges, in turn, of the worth of O'Gorman's postulates. Is it true that the "Asiatic" idea which animated Columbus died
from one day to the next? Is it on the
threshold of the sixteenth century, and
thanks to Vespucci, that the Spanish his-
torian-geographers conceived of America as
a new continent independent from Asia?
Did the legend of the unknown pilot appear in the works of these historians in a
context of serene explanation or in one
of impassioned disputation? The ground
thus cleared, we will be better able to understand that they shared at the same time,
without being inconvenienced, two conceptions which O'Gorman wishes to make
into contradictory "theses": the discovery
conceived as the fruit of human knowledge
and calculations, and the discovery conceived as a providential event. Perhaps this
syncretism, illogical in the eyes of an exis-
tential philosopher of today, is that which
best characterizes the understanding of the
discovery in the sixteenth century. But this
goes infinitely beyond the problem formulated by O'Gorman. And it is one of the
most fascinating subjects that an existen-
tialist or a phenomenologist can give himself. . . .

Such speculations put the finger on the
profound difference which separates the
ancient history and the recent history of
the discovery. For a man of today, accustomed to a disassociating geography and
history, it is not absurd, at first glance, to
wish to bring to light what the navigator
Columbus accomplished objectively, technically, an abstraction made of his ideas
about what he wanted to do and about
what he did. In looking more closely, this
pretension is illusory. Let us thank O'Gorman for having said this in his somewhat
overly caustic criticism of the good naviga-
tor-historian Herbert S. Morison. But let
us also object that, obsessed by the supposed "Vespuccian revelation," he himself
curtailed his analysis of the old historians
by interrogating them only on the question
of the spatial dependence or independence
of the discovered lands in relation to the
known world — especially in relation to
Asia. Is not that still a point of view of the
specialists in navigation? During the sixteenth century, and certainly for the pilots
and for the sovereigns who bore the costs
of the expeditionary discoveries, it was a
very important point of view. But it was
not only a question of a discovery of lands
better located on the maps. It was a discovery of gold and other precious things. It
was above all a discovery of man. And, if
to the blind *codicia* of the conquerors for
gold, the men were nothing but cheap
manpower, to those who thought according
to Christian theology — the evangelizers
and the rulers who listened to their opinions, and all the clergymen in general —
this gigantic discovery of men was an event
full of meaning in providential history.
Geography, history and metahistory were
indissolubly bound together. Taking again
the image of Las Casas, the New World,
the key to which had been given by God to
Christopher Columbus, was a world
swarming with men. For what mysterious
design had it been locked up until then?
From this stemmed so many problems
about the origin of these men and about
the intentions of Providence regarding
them. Had they been touched or not, on
the morrow of the death of Christ, by "the
evangelization of Saint Thomas"? Were
they destined to furnish the elect of the
City of God or were they definitively
abandoned to the Devil? Was it principally the gold and the silver of these countries that Providence had wished to have
passed into the hands of the Spaniards?
Were not the West Indies but a stopping-
place on the way to China, the land where
Christianity would finally conquer men of
"great capacity," on the last stage of its trip
around the world and through history?
All these questions were asked with insistence during the entire sixteenth century
and beyond. The temporal horizon which
imposed itself upon everyone is that, when
the discovery begun by Columbus reached

its end with the promulgation of the Gospel to all the non-Christians, the world would end.

The idea of the discovery of the New World is all this, at least for the Spaniards, for whom this discovery was the principal interest [*la grande affaire*]. If, instead of wasting a subtlety worthy of a better use in formulating "theses," falsified in advance by the postulates of the formulator, O'Gorman had set forth the cosmological, geographical, historical (and metahistorical) concepts implied in the diverse ancient explanations of the discovery, he would have given his work a portico far greater and stronger and would have greatly improved our understanding of the mutation of the idea of the discovery during the time of Humboldt. He would not have toyed with a series of "theses" as with a kaleidoscope presenting curious and irritating solutions to a claimed "logical difficulty." He would have taken the old authors as they are. He would have taken into account the *development of the discovery* after Columbus, and even after Magellan, to explain the *development of the idea of the discovery* during the sixteenth century. He would certainly have thus gained more partisans for philosophical history, for which he battles. O'Gorman, by his talent, is one of the most effective men among those today who are awakening strictly erudite and "factual" history from its dogmatic sleep. One does not like to believe that he loves to scandalize more than to convert. Truly, the good erudites, whose horizon is often limited, may gain a taste for wider perspectives, may perceive that in such perspectives they renew their comprehension of the old authors whom they were approaching without enough perspective. But it is good, in order to attract them to vast panoramas, not to blur their "foregrounds" at will, to appeal to their respect for texts instead of wounding it. The pages which precede would like to contribute to the defense of O'Gorman philosopher of history against O'Gorman magician of historical criticism. If, in reading the first two parts of his book, honest erudites are stopped by too many arbitrary affirmations, by the overlooking of too many essential facts, let them pass beyond, let them catch the intention of the whole, let them recognize the fecundity of it. Going back then and rereading the texts better than O'Gorman read them, they will be grateful to him for having made them reread them; they will perceive that the *facts* themselves of the history of the discovery in the fifteenth and sixteenth centuries become more intelligible if one brings to light *the ideas* of those who have successively recounted it and given it a meaning.

Amerigo Vespucci and the New World

GERMÁN ARCINIEGAS

An illustrious teacher, writer, diplomat, and educational administrator, Germán Arciniegas has become a familiar figure in inter-American relations. He was born in Bogotá, Colombia, in 1900, and educated there, receiving the LL.D. from the University of Bogotá in 1925. In 1930 he was vice-consul in London, served as chargé d'affaires in Buenos Aires from 1939 to 1941, and in 1959 became Colombian ambassador to Italy. From 1941 to 1946 he served as Minister of Education in his native country, and since 1948 has been professor of Spanish American literature at Columbia University in New York. In 1963 he also became director of the outstanding Latin American review, Cuadernos, published in Paris. Among his most important works in English are: The Knight of El Dorado (1943); The Green Continent (1944); Caribbean, Sea of the New World (1946); and The State of Latin America (1952).

FOR CENTURIES a controversy has raged around Amerigo Vespucci. He has been presented as a sly thief who cunningly robbed Columbus of his rightful glory. This defamation of Amerigo is almost coextensive with the history of America; scholars have repeated it; the textbooks of twenty nations have carried it.

Father Las Casas started this second black legend. In his pen he had a magnificent tool for the fabrication of such legends, abetted by a verbal intemperance in which he has had few equals. He wrote: "And it is well to give thought here to the injustice and offense that that Amerigo Vespucci seems to have done the Admiral, or those who first printed his four voyages, attributing to himself, or alluding only to him, the discovery of this mainland."

As a matter of fact, Las Casas had no knowledge of how the edition of the four voyages came to be published in Saint-Dié. But when he got started on an argument he lost his self-control. What had at first been a vague, tentative suggestion later became an article of faith. "It amazes me," he subsequently wrote, "that Don Ferdinand Columbus, the son of the Admiral

himself, and a person of goodly wit and prudence, and who had in his possession those very relations of Amerigo, as I know for a fact, did not realize this theft and usurpation Amerigo Vespucci had committed against his father."

Las Casas, who in many aspects had not emerged from the Middle Ages, felt much closer to Columbus than to Amerigo. Columbus had received his training in the thought of the Renaissance, and had utilized the theories of Toscanelli and the humanists, but his experiences in Castile had turned him into a renegade from the Renaissance. The opposition he encountered among the friars of Salamanca, the intolerance that was mounting under Cardinal Cisneros, and, perhaps, his Jewish ancestry taught him that it was better to hold fast to the texts of the Church Fathers, to take a prophetic, miraculous line, than to range himself on the side of science. He went so far as to state, in a famous phrase, that the mappemondes had been of no use to him, but that he had been the instrument Divine Providence had used to fulfill its prophecies. The stubbornness with which he insisted on this in his later days gave him a completely medieval stamp. And in this he and Las Casas stood shoulder to shoulder.

To be sure, there are gleams of modern thought in Las Casas. Volumes have been written to show that his ardent crusade on behalf of justice put him well in advance of his day in the field of human rights. But one has only to read his treatise on magic to realize how medieval his learning was. It is an encyclopedia of witchcraft. The Devil becomes a being so real that he can carry men through the air over mountains and valleys. Opposed to the Devil is the power of the miracle. If the Friar's books were not so voluminous, if his sermons did not lose themselves in a tedious labyrinth of endless erudite meanders, they would be a delightful source of shivery entertainment. The part of his writing that has remained alive is his diatribes against the conquistadors and Amerigo, the themes of the two black legends.

In contrast with Columbus, Amerigo represented, in Father Las Casas's eyes, the living culture of the Renaissance. Amerigo was the one who put all his faith in maps. His subtle, ironic, balanced, rational spirit stood in sharp contrast with the violent chiaroscuro in which Las Casas and Columbus moved.

All this explains the strong likes and dislikes that conditioned the thinking of a man of Father Las Casas's impassioned temperament. But there was still another factor. Las Casas's concepts, like those of all his contemporaries, were imperial. He looked upon the Indian as a childlike being deserving paternal solicitude, but he saw the New World as nothing but a colony. And Amerigo had set afoot a concept that was a forerunner of the idea of independence. These are the hidden seeds that take root in the subconscious. The term *New World* diminished the force of empire. *America* was a word that meant rebellion against the vocabulary the Crown was minting. It ran counter to imperial objectives. It never occurred to anyone that the new continent should be called Co-lonia, or Colombia, or Columbia. Las Casas never suggested such a thing. Spain wanted to keep the denomination *Indies,* which Columbus had given to his discovery. In line with this the Laws of the Indies were promulgated, the Indian Code was drawn up, the natives were called Indians, there was a profusion of histories of the Indies, an Indian policy was worked out, and so on. It was not a question of defending Columbus's glory, but of treating the New World as an appanage of Asia.

The gifted Crown historian Antonio de Herrera (1559–1625) followed in Las Casas's footsteps. In one passage of his *Décadas* he alludes to a suit instituted by the heirs of Columbus over the discoveries on the mainland. In the testimony of the witnesses, which he compares, there is no mention of any discovery by Amerigo. This was to be expected. Amerigo had been second in command on voyages that were not his, but King Ferdinand's. But, says Herrera: "By [the omission of his name] Amerigo Vespucci's slyness in appropriating to himself another's glory becomes more patent." And in another passage: "With great cunning Amerigo Vespucci transposes things that happened on one voyage to another to conceal the fact that the admiral, Don Christopher Columbus, discovered the mainland. . . . The invention of Amerigo is clearly proved."

As the tendency grew to dramatize Columbus's life, Spain was made to seem more and more culpable. A series of unfortunate incidents, caused as much by the Admiral's maladroitness as by the overzealousness of officials like Bishop Fonseca and Francisco de Bobadilla, made Columbus suffer hell in this life. Already a reproachful finger was being pointed at Spain for not having spared the Genoese so much bitterness. This interpretation was coloring not only history, but drama, poetry, ballads, legend. And to men like Las Casas and Herrera, the simple, obvious answer was to find a scapegoat, invent a villain to bear all the guilt. For this Amerigo was made to order.

From that moment the river of adjectives insulting the thief of Columbus's glory began to swell and rage. Nobody had new facts to adduce; they simply repeated Las Casas's pronouncements, the shaky foundation of which are evidenced by the passages quoted from his own work.

Between 1825 and 1837 Martín Fernández de Navarrete published one of the most famous collections of documents relating to the discovery of America. It has been a source-book for scholars ever since. Fernández de Navarrete (1765–1844) was a distinguished researcher. Washington Irving, William Prescott, and Alexander von Humboldt were lavish with praise of him.

Columbus's sufferings, his poverty, the fetters with which he was bound in Santo Domingo, all of which were played up in the biographies that circulated in all lands and all languages, naturally weighed more heavily on Navarrete than on Las Casas or Herrera, and he was more eager to put the blame on Amerigo than to get at the facts. His "accurate" notes for Amerigo's biography afford abundant proof of this. But even more revealing is his correspondence at the time he was preparing his work. A letter to another notable scholar, Manuel González, is a case in point:

I am assembling materials for Volume III, which I plan to send to press in April. I would particularly ask you to bear in mind information concerning Amerigo Vespucci. . . . If you can find information about him from 1496 to 1505, particularly, it would be very useful to follow his movements and know whether he really accompanied Alonso Hojeda on his two voyages, because he certainly did not go as captain or by order of the King, as he gives to understand and pretends in his Latin relations, which he gave out everywhere to usurp Columbus's glory of discovering the continent to which, through his slyness, he managed to give his own name. To prove this truth clearly I need the support of such documents and information as you may come by, for these are in the historical fields the proofs and demonstration of geometricians' theorems.

The irresponsible way Navarrete states as a fact that Amerigo had said in his letters that he had sailed as commander of the fleet (a thing he never said); that he wrote his relations in Latin (which he never did); and that he was the inventor of the name *America* (which he was not), for the ends Navarrete attributes to him (which never existed) is the result of a passion not confined to the intimate field of Navarrete's private correspondence, but carried into his books to the extent of altering documents. To show, for example, that Amerigo had not made the voyage of exploration of the coast of Mexico, Navarrete wrote that from December 1495, when Gianetto Berardi died, to 1498 Vespucci could not have set foot outside Spain because he was in charge of outfitting the fleets. He based his assertion on an entry in the Ledger of Fleet Expenses, he said, compiled by the scholar Juan Bautista Muñoz. But Muñoz's book said nothing of the sort.

So unequivocal was Navarrete's statement that Humboldt fell into the snare. "The falsity of the sailing date — May 10–20, 1497 — given by Amerigo," he writes, "becomes evident. Preparations for the voyage of Columbus to Haiti and Parias . . . kept Vespucci busy in Seville and in Sanlúcar from April–May 1497 until the departure of Columbus on May 30, 1498."

Navarrete's fabrication, shored up by Humboldt's doubt, gave an Italian investigator, Alberto Magnaghi, his grounds for saying before a Congress of Americanists meeting in Rome in 1926: "Among the most powerful arguments of a chronological nature against this first voyage of Vespucci is the evidence to the contrary pointed out by Humboldt."

Once the belief that Amerigo had robbed Columbus of the glory of the discovery, and that his first voyage was a lie was accepted, it was easy to doubt everything. "Is it conceivable," Navarrete asked himself, "that a monarch as cautious and circumspect as Ferdinand would have entrusted the command of a Spanish expedition of such importance to an adventurer who was not yet even a naturalized Spaniard?" Navarrete harped once more on the command of the expedition — something Amerigo had never claimed — and overlooked the fact that Columbus, Cabot, and Díaz de Solís were as much foreigners as Amerigo in 1497. But his statement established a pattern, and in 1926 Magnaghi said: "Even if we were to grant that Amerigo's voyage had been tacitly permitted, the matter is not clear, for from June 14, 1496 until May 30, 1498 Columbus was in Spain at the peak of his glory and prestige, and his credit was ace-high not only at court, but also with businessmen. . . . If the ships hired in 1495 (those which Amerigo outfitted) were not to be used in Columbus's third voyage, at any rate they were intended for it, as supporting and auxiliary vessels."

The situation invented by Magnaghi shows Columbus at the height of his triumph when, as a matter of fact, his reputation was being subjected to careful scrutiny. His prestige on his return from the second voyage was low. Ferdinand, his son, says that he suffered jeers and mockery at court because of the adverse reports about him sent back from Hispaniola. The ships of 1495 were being readied for the very purpose of doing away with Columbus's privileges. As a result of the highly unfavorable reports he was receiving, the King was becoming aware of the need to investigate his activities and those of his brother Bartholomew in the governing of Hispaniola.

Nevertheless, Navarrete's asseveration, repeated by Humboldt, according to which Amerigo was occupied in Spain in 1497 and could not have been on a voyage, went unchallenged. Not until the scholar Henry Harrisse examined all the documentation on which Navarrete based his statement was the point cleared up. This is his conclusion:

. . . we must declare that there is no entry in the archives of the Trade Council for the Indies which refers directly or indirectly to these activities of Vespucci on any date subsequent to January 12, 1496. Nor is any such record in the 127 volumes containing the extracts and notes compiled by Muñoz in 1779 when he was commissioned by Charles III to write the History of America. As for the fleet mentioned by Navarrete, which consisted of twelve ships engaged by Berardi in 1495, it was dispatched from San Lúcar before the end of that year. All that Vespucci did in connection with the expedition was to supervise its outfitting from April to November of 1495. He entered in Berardi's account the expenditures made in his name, which were reimbursed by the royal treasurer on January 12, 1496. Following this date, Vespucci's name disappears completely from the Spanish documents, and does not reappear until February 5, 1505. There is not a shred of evidence, therefore, that Vespucci was in Seville or in Spain from 1496 until after 1498, and no proof, therefore, that he could not have been at sea from May 1497 until October 1499, as he states in the relation of his first voyages of discovery.

If Spanish historians of the school of Las Casas, Herrera, and Navarrete altered basic facts in the foregoing manner to render Amerigo's voyages impossible or to put in doubt the truth of his relations, it is not to be wondered at that others outside Spain should have followed in their footsteps. As eminent a scholar as William Robertson in his *History of America* called Amerigo "a lucky imposter," and Ralph Waldo Emerson said: "Strange. . . that broad America must wear the name of a thief. Amerigo Vespucci, the pickle-dealer at Seville . . . whose highest naval rank was boatswain's mate in an expedition that never sailed, managed in this lying world to supplant Columbus and baptize half of the earth with his own dishonest name. . . ."

This mountain of adjectives heaped on Amerigo's memory had as its result that nobody believed his letters. He was not only a thief, but also a liar. Few documents in history have undergone so searching an analysis as Amerigo's letters. It was a fertile field for the scholar's amusement. The original manuscript texts had disappeared. They left the hands of Lorenzo di

Pier Francesco de' Medici and Piero Soderini and began to circulate in copy or translation, in editions their author never heard
about, and over which he never had control. Slight or important changes, altered
words, have made them a scholar's jigsaw
puzzle for more than a century. It should
be mentioned in passing that the fate of
Amerigo's documents was not unique. The
diary of Columbus underwent the same
treatment at the hands of Las Casas, who
altered it to suit himself. Most of the relations of the conquistadors do not stand
up under careful analysis. But as they
either aroused little animus or were heroes
who became the object of worship after
meeting an untimely end, the documents
they left have been accepted at face value,
even with a generous margin of good will.
The inherent charm of Amerigo's writings,
their immediate fame throughout the
world, did him harm. Erudite studies have
been written on the Spanish words he
employed, on his literary shortcomings, on
coincidence of expression with Marco Polo
or Michele de Cuneo. Errors that well may
have been those of a secretary, a copyist,
or the translator who put the relations into
Latin, or of another translator who turned
them back into Italian, or an editor who
wished to flatter a Mæcenas have all been
laid at Amerigo's door.

To avoid problems, the Italian scholar
Alberto Magnaghi, the last to establish a
school, who has contributed penetrating
observations and important studies on
Amerigo, proposed at the Congress of
Americanists in Rome in 1923 that the
two most famous letters of Amerigo — the
Mundus Novus and that to Soderini — be
discounted and only those which are preserved in copy in the archives of Florence
be accepted as authentic. That is to say,
throw out the two most important letters,
those which became famous in the sight
and presence of Amerigo's family. With
this Magnaghi would eliminate from
Amerigo's history two voyages — one the
most important of all. As the idea was pre-

sented with great trappings of lexicograph-
ical research, his book, though basically a
work of sophistry, produced an effect.

What disturbed Magnaghi was the idea
that Amerigo was guilty of improper literary conduct, and he took the stand that
neither would he have written letters containing such outspoken sexual observations,
nor would any distinguished humanist
have been a party to their translation. His
profound distaste is evident from the following lines, taken from the article he
wrote to deny the authenticity of the last
letter found in Italian archives, which remained unpublished until 1937: "If the
letter were authentic it would upset everything once more, and would plunge us into
that endless, tedious, fruitless, exhausting
discussion that has gone on for four centuries. . . . For that reason I, at least, cannot share the satisfaction the discoverer of
the letter evinces."

On the other hand, the school of affirma-
tive criticism which has attempted to explain Amerigo's history as a natural process
has labored under the difficulties of trying
to combat a legend cultivated with malice
aforethought since the sixteenth century.
The first of these was the Florentine abbot
Angelo Maria Bandini. In 1745 he wrote
*Vita e lettere di Amerigo Vespucci genti-
luomo florentino* and published for the
first time Amerigo's letter to Lorenzo di
Pier Francesco de' Medici, dated in the
year 1500 in Seville. It had been forgotten
for two hundred and forty-five years. A
second edition of Bandini's book was
brought out fifty-three years later by Gus-
tavo Uzielli, with copious notes. Uzielli
was a painstaking, dedicated investigator
devoted to the cult of Toscanelli. His study
of the great cosmographer is a model in its
field. Carried away by his enthusiasm, he
took the position that the New World
should not have been called America or
Colombia, but some variant of Toscanelli.
The suggestion came late, and the name
hardly lends itself to the purpose.

In 1879 Francesco Bartolozzi discovered

and published the letter on the third voyage, dated in 1502 in Lisbon. It had been buried in the archives of Florence for three hundred and seventy-seven years. Baron Alexander von Humboldt was the first to make a scientific study of the voyages of Amerigo, in the second volume of his *Examen critique de l'histoire de la Géographie du Nouveau Continent aux XV et XVI siècles*. His book and that of Bandini set a new trend in the history of Amerigo. It was followed by many studies, including those of Armand-Pascal d'Avezac (1858), Francisco Adolpho de Varnhagen (1858–1872), Henry Harrisse (1892), and John Fiske (1892). Uzielli in 1892 compiled a bibliographical list of 280 titles, and this was incomplete.

Amerigo's polemic letter in defense of those he had written to Lorenzo the Popolano was published by Roberto Ridolfi in 1937 — that is to say, four hundred and thirty-five years after it was written — and Amerigo's early correspondence was brought out by Ida Masetti-Bencini and Mary Howard Smith in 1902, some four centuries after it was written. This consists of seventy-one letters, which have never been collected in book form, and which appeared in a journal of history. Amerigo's composition book has not yet been published.

As scholars have concentrated their efforts on a study of the letters of Amerigo pertaining to his voyages, his life has come in for little attention. Up to the present there has been no biography of him as a person. There are a number of good biographies of Columbus and of nearly all the most important participants in the discovery and conquest, but we have only the raw materials for a life of the Florentine under whose name we live. A reading of George Northup's critical edition of Amerigo's letters (1916), Henri Vignaud's *Améric Vespuce* (1917), and, above all, the study of American cartography in Roberto Levillier's *América le bien llamada* (1948) give one the feeling that Amerigo is at last being discovered. After four centuries of wrangling about whether it was a good thing or a bad thing for the New World to bear his name, the simple reality of his life is beginning to come to light. And we find ourselves in the presence of a man who became famous without aspiring to be a hero and who without pursuing glory received it in full measure.

When Amerigo was born, five hundred years ago, Florence sang its babes to rest with enchanted lullabies. Many things about the Renaissance were in the nature of miracles. The government showed equal interest in politics and painters. Everything was an art. The year that Amerigo and Poliziano were born, refugees from Constantinople arrived in Florence bringing the gift of Plato. The Republic could give thought to the alliance with Venice and Milan as well as to the paintings Benozzo Gozzoli and Fra Angelico were working on; and a man like Lorenzo Ghiberti, who after many years' work had just finished the cathedral doors known as the Gates of Paradise, laid aside his burins to take up the pen and write a treatise on painting. Bookbinders gathered in the workshop to discuss Aristotle or Dante. At night the philosophers wandered into the streets to sing love songs. On a smaller scale, the banks were like those of today, with Florentine capital circulating throughout two continents in letters of exchange, and the ships of the Republic sailing all the seas. There were wars, but at the Battle of Anghiari, which has become famous, the only casualty left on the field was a single soldier who smothered in his armor, as Machiavelli points out. Yet to commemorate the battle Pedro Soderini, the gonfalonier, sent for Leonardo da Vinci to paint the picture designed for the hall of the palace.

In such an atmosphere the New World first came into being in the imagination. Globes and planispheres were designed before the ships set out on the Atlantic. Geography showed its gratitude by making these dreams come true. Spain opened the transatlantic routes. Her ships, which history had hardly taken account of until the day before, became the most famous. They were little wooden castles out of which sallied heroes such as the world had never before known: Balboa, Cortés, Pizarro, Jiménez de Quesada, Hernando de Soto, Ponce de León, Orellana, Valdivia. In fifty years the world sphere had emerged from between their hands.

Amerigo followed the process of these events with wide eyes, alert mind, a light heart, and a youthful soul. He was the most interested spectator and the most timely chronicler of this appearance of the New World. He saw it all: the broad gulf of Mexico, verdant Florida, the Pearl Coast, Venezuela reflected in the waters, Brazil with its cinnamon trees and its popinjays, the headland of Montevideo, Argentina, whose plains were then empty, and desolate Patagonia. But nothing so captured his imagination as the new stars, the skies of the south. Nobody equaled him in the freshness and enthusiasm with which he announced the news of the unknown quarter of the world that he was the first to see. He was a citizen of Florence and a citizen of León and Castile. With María Cerezo he was a Sevillian; and he was a transient, favored resident of Lisbon. His words threw a beam of light upon the assembly of poets and scholars of Saint-Dié. A representative man of the fifteenth century, a navigator formed by his own inquiring mind. Miracles were wrought in Florence, or in Seville, or in the Caribbean. The Mediterranean carried its fire as far as its restless waves spread. The Old World overflowed its bed, poured through the Pillars of Hercules, and found a larger world.

The Meaning of "Discovery" in the Fifteenth and Sixteenth Centuries

WILCOMB E. WASHBURN

Wilcomb Washburn belongs to a younger generation of scholars, but has already contributed greatly to the discovery and dissemination of historical knowledge. He was born in Kansas in 1925, educated at Dartmouth and Harvard, and in 1955 received his Ph.D. in American Civilization from Harvard University. In 1958 he became Curator of Political History at the Smithsonian Institution, and since 1961 has also lectured at the American University in Washington, D.C. In addition to writing articles in national journals, Washburn is author of *The Government and the Rebel: A History of Bacon's Rebellion in Virginia* (1957); *The Effects of Bacon's Rebellion on Government in England and Virginia* (1962); *The Indian and the White Man* (1964); and is co-author of *Bibliography of Indian-White Relations in America*.

COLUMBUS discovered America." Seemingly this statement, learned by every schoolboy, leaves no room for doubt as to its validity. Yet, examined critically, the statement can immediately be challenged and has been. What do we mean by "America"? The Mexican historian, Edmundo O'Gorman, has written books to uphold the thesis that Columbus did not discover America, because the concept as we know it today did not exist in his mind. Amerigo Vespucci should gain the credit, in O'Gorman's mind, since he allegedly first thought of the newly discovered lands as separate and distinct from Asia, and as forming a new continent, a concept which Columbus, a firm believer in the Asiatic concept, could never accept. Others would challenge the word "discover." The Norsemen discovered America, they will point out, or they may say that an unknown pilot told Columbus beforehand of the lands he later discovered. The least controversial word in the sentence is the name "Columbus." All agree that there was such a man, although we are treated to all the racial varieties when it comes to determining whether he was Italian, or Spanish, or Jewish, or Greek.

Why is there such confusion on such a simple subject? Perhaps, because the event was such an extraordinary one, the epistemological problem is fundamental. If so, then it behooves all writers on the subject to start from the beginning with a careful analysis of the terms of the debate and proceed from that point to the events themselves. This is what I propose to do in this essay. I do not hope to exhaust the possibilities of the subject. It is too vast. Hence my essay is suggestive rather than comprehensive. It ventures a series of hypotheses rather than expounds a point of view. I hope it will suggest further study of the problem by specialists in the cartographic, linguistic, literary, nautical, and historical fields. Perhaps such research will reveal elementary aspects of the problem which I have overlooked. Perhaps it will show new approaches which I have not followed.

My concern with the subject derives from a personal feeling of uncertainty as to just what was meant by the early writers when they used terms like "terra firma,"

Wilcomb E. Washburn, "The Meaning of 'Discovery' in the Fifteenth and Sixteenth Centuries," *American Historical Review*, LXVIII (October, 1962), pp. 1–21. Reprinted by permission of the author and the American Historical Association.

"discover," "new world," "Asia," "continent," and all the other phrases that blossomed forth in the Age of Discovery. We look at these phrases with the backward vision of those who know what the globe actually looks like, but has not this subsequent knowledge screened rather than illuminated our view of the mental situation in which the early explorers found themselves?

Not the smallest stumbling block to our understanding has been the development of a geographical organization of the world's land masses into "continents." The geographers of the eighteenth, nineteenth, and twentieth centuries never fully agreed on what should be called a continent and what an island or peninsula, but they did give prominence to the word "continent" that it never had before. The European peninsula was given continental status (surely from ethnocentric pride as well as from the traditional classification of Europe as one "part" of the world) as were the attached land masses of Asia and Africa, and the detached but connected land masses of North and South America. Australia was sometimes admitted to the inner circle, sometimes not. No geographer ever had enough authority to say without fear of contradiction that Australia's coastline was large enough to be a continent or small enough to be an island.

If one examines the earlier conception of continental status, one finds that medieval geographers and thinkers were blessedly free of this "scientific" category. Immersed in their dark ignorance, they tended merely to contrast land with sea, zone with zone, part with part, West with East, the known world with the unknown. Those who did organize the world on maps normally saw a central land mass, an *orbis terrarum*, surrounded by an enveloping water mass. The various inlets into this land mass, such as the Mediterranean and Baltic, were not understood to have created the present category of "continents" for the lands they washed.

I leave for others the task of explaining the long history of the Latin word "continents." But, even as used in the early postdiscovery years the word, I believe, refers to continuing, connected land, extensive, not insular, but not necessarily to our several twentieth-century continents, although it was used to describe lands within the central *orbis terrarum*.

The concept of the globe divided into "parts" rather than into "continents" is expressed in most geographical studies of the fifteenth and early sixteenth centuries. It is used, for example, in Martin Waldseemüller's famous *Cosmographiae Introductio* of 1507, in a passage which is traditionally conceived of as laying the basis for a new continent, distinct from Asia, to be called America, after Amerigo Vespucci whose travel account Waldseemüller reprinted in the volume. But while the maps accompanying the text seem to suggest a new hemisphere and a new continent (although in one case they separate North and South America and in another not), actually the western extension of the "new world" is problematical and undefined, and the text speaks of the lands described by Vespucci as a fourth "part" of the world which it specifically terms an "island."

It is, therefore, not a little disturbing to hear repeated over and over again the claim that Vespucci discovered, and Waldseemüller gave his blessing to, a fourth "continent," particularly when all reference to the specific word "island" is omitted, and the word "part" is admitted only as a synonym of "continent."

May it not well be that the later creation of artificial geographical distinctions more rigid than those used in earlier times (for example, "continent" instead of "part") encouraged later historians such as Roberto Levillier, Henry Vignaud, and Edmundo O'Gorman to conceive of the Age of Discovery in new and rigid terms? Is not the French historian Marcel Bataillon right when he says that the "problem" which O'Gorman sees in the Age of Discovery is a problem which is O'Gorman's own personal problem, not necessarily that of one who wants to see the period in terms of what happened at the time, rather than in terms of what was conceived about it later?

Most fascinating of all the special terms associated with the history of discoveries is the Latin "terra firma" and its various Romance equivalents such as "terra firme" in Portuguese and "tierra firme" in Spanish. As used in the fifteenth and sixteenth centuries, the term is found in both singular and plural form, with and without the definite article, capitalized and uncapitalized, hyphenated and unhyphenated. It is normally translated as "continent" or "mainland." I think the meaning more complex etymologically and less extensive geographically than we are accustomed to think, and in the following paragraphs I will suggest some of the varied significance I find in the term.

The term "terra ferma" appears in Italian portolanos of the fifteenth century primarily as a means of contrasting the islands off the coast of the European and African land masses with the "main land" itself. The phrase seems designed to contrast the main shore- or coast-land with the minor offshore lands, whether islands or mere sand bars. The phrase seems designed for the practical Mediterranean sailor, as were the portolanos in which the term appears, and does not, in my opinion, express a geographical conception of the continental land mass of Europe, Asia, and Africa, whether viewed as separate continents or as a single continent.

The term appears in Portuguese in the letters patent of July 24, 1486, given by King John II to Fernão Dulmo to discover the fabulous island of the Seven Cities, normally called Antilia. Antilia is drawn on numerous maps of the period as a comparatively large but obviously insular block of land in the Western Ocean. Indeed, the term Antilles, used by the Portuguese to denote certain West Indian islands, remains a memorial to the belief that the island did exist and was discovered by Columbus. The most significant aspect of the letters patent, however, is the descrip-

tion which is given of this "gramde ylha ou ylhas ou terra firme per costa, que se presume seer a ylha das Sete Çidades" that Dulmo was to attempt to discover at his own cost. The phrase "ylha ou ylhas ou terra firme" continues to be used throughout the document, changing at one point to "as ditas ylhas e terra."

Do we not have here evidence of the term "terra firme" used before the Age of Discovery in a way that is consistent with an insular land mass? If otherwise, does it not require the island of the Seven Cities to be equated with the great tripartite land mass of the *orbis terrarum* or else with an entirely new "continent"?

Perhaps the rarest form of the phrase is the plural form which, nevertheless, is one of the earliest. It appears in the Capitulations made with Columbus by Ferdinand and Isabella on April 17, 1492. In this agreement, Columbus is granted hereditary rights in "todas aquellas islas é tierras-firmes" that he may discover and gain in the "mares Océanas" claimed by the sovereigns. The form reappears occasionally, particularly in various claims of Columbus, such as his Majorat or Entail of His Estates and Titles, February 22, 1498. Nevertheless, in the Title issued two weeks after the Capitulations, on April 30, and covering the same ground, the plural phraseology is reduced to the singular, and Columbus is granted rights to "ciertas Islas, é Tierra-firme en la mar Océana" which he may discover and gain. Is the change of any significance? Is the meaning the same? Are there stylistic conventions which explain the alteration?

In Alexander VI's bull of concession of May 3, 1493, Spain is granted rights to "certas Insulas remotissimas, et etiam terras firmas" found by Columbus "per partes occidentales, ut dicitur, versùs Indos, in mari Oceano" while in the bull of May 4, creating the line of demarcation between Spain and Portugal, the language is repeated. In the papal bulls, the phrase "terras firmas" is not hyphenated (that is, joined together as a compound word), and the word "firmas" is occasionally dropped when the phrase is repeated, as in the phrase "in the said islands and lands" (for example, "in quibus quidem insulis et terris") closely following the complete phrase.

I have seen few scholarly comments on the plural form of the term. Indeed, the singular form in the Title of April 30 causes sufficient consternation and dispute as to whether the tripartite land mass of Europe, Asia, and Africa is meant, or a new unsuspected continent, or even an antipodean southern continent. Cecil Jane, in his introduction to the *Select Documents of Columbus,* championed the southern continent explanation, equating *Terra Australis* with the "tierra firme" Columbus had in mind. E. G. R. Taylor, who finished Volume II of the *Documents* when Jane died, had to indicate her entire disagreement with Jane's theory and had to insist that the Eurasian land mass was meant instead, even though Professor Taylor felt that Columbus could hardly have expected to become viceroy of the dominions of the Grand Khan.

The Columbian field is littered with the problems of explaining the phrase "tierra firme" in Columbus' Title. How much more difficult to explain the plural form! I would suggest, subject to more detailed study, that the term "tierras firmes" in the text of the royal agreement was designed more for legalistic completeness in describing land masses of varying sizes rather than for signifying major geographical distinctions in the minds of Columbus or of the sovereigns.

I would go beyond this statement and say that the term "tierra firme," in either its singular or plural form, in an age when the *orbis terrarum* was conceived of as *the* land mass of the world, frequently implied a relationship between the insular and non-insular areas of the same general portion of the globe, a relationship that is not inherent in later uses of the term. I do not rule out its use, particularly with the definite article, as a description of the central *orbis terrarum,* but I do suggest that even when used with this meaning the concept in the mind of the user is not normally of the whole tripartite land mass of Europe, Asia, and Africa, but of that portion of it with which he is directly concerned.

In all the documents of authorization and the like issued in 1493 following Columbus' return from his first voyage, and before his second voyage, the phrase "tierra firme" is invariably in the singular, without the definite or indefinite article, in contexts which make it doubtful that the reference is to the Asiatic land mass geographically conceived of as "a continent" or "the mainland."

For example, in the Confirmation of the title given to Columbus as admiral, viceroy, and governor of "las islas y tierra-firme" that have been and will be discovered, May 18, 1493, the original title of April 30, 1492 (which is also in the singular), is repeated, and the statement added that the sovereigns hope that Columbus will find "otras islas é tierra-firme en el dicho mar Océano á la dicha parte de las Indias" and that they confirm his titles of admiral, viceroy, and governor of the said Ocean Sea, "é islas é tierra-firme" that he has and will discover.

Document after document in this period repeats the title of Columbus as "Almirante de las Islas é Tierra firme, descubiertas é por descubrir en el mar Océano a la parte de las Indias." It is, of course, possible to interpret the phrase as encouraging Columbus to discover, along with other islands, other parts of a single continent assumed to have been discovered. Similarly, it is possible to interpret the phrase as encouraging Columbus to find for the first time a continent assumed to be yet undiscovered. But these, along with other possible explanations, do not seem to be adequate explanations of the language so frequently repeated in the documents of this period.

Can we solve the difficulty by translating "terra firma" as "lands," as Henry

Vignaud usually does? Vignaud was not consistent and occasionally translated the phrase as "continent" or "mainland," while at the same time not hesitating to speak of Antilia as "a large continental island." Since Vignaud was trying to prove that Columbus was not really looking for Asia, but for new lands that he knew to exist, it is important for him to deny that "terra firma" could refer to the Asiatic continent. Nor does he interpret the phrase to mean an America of continental proportions since evidence to prove Columbus' prior knowledge of the existence of such a land mass would be equally difficult to demonstrate. Vignaud, therefore, steered a cautious middle ground by avoiding the problem of precise definition of the term, neither identifying it with one continental land mass or the other, careful only to make its definition serve his thesis that Columbus had prior knowledge of lands of unspecified extent to which his enterprise was directed. Vignaud thus hit on a usage — I cannot say he formulated a definition since he is inconsistent — which is closer to the truth than is the usage of many of his opponents, but he does so for the wrong reason, and hence it does not serve to salvage his misguided theory of Columbus' intentions.

It is sometimes asserted that European monarchs expected to sail to Asiatic shores and immediately "take over." I cannot accept this assumption, although it is true enough that Europeans expected to take possession of minor offshore islands. That the Europeans did not conceive of appropriating the sovereignty of the great mainland kingdoms of Asia is suggested by the experience of Vasco da Gama, the first European to reach by sea the sought for India of the East, who came with cautious respect and regard for the diplomatic niceties.

The observance of similar diplomatic niceties in the preparation for Columbus' voyage reinforces my view that the "tierra firme" of the Capitulations could not have meant the Asiatic continent with its rich and powerful kingdoms described by Polo.

The diplomatic mission carried by Columbus, headed by Luis de Torres, a converted Jew "who knew Hebrew and Aramaic and even some Arabic," carrying a Latin passport, Latin letter of credence from Ferdinand and Isabella, and a royal gift, was actually dispatched in Cuba to find the court of the Grand Khan and pay the respects of the Spanish monarchs. When it proved impossible to find any but naked people and simple huts, the facts of power began to assert themselves even while the land remained in theory Asiatic.

Columbus' belief that Cuba was the mainland of Asia was re-enforced in the course of his second voyage, after sailing for more than a month along its southern shore. Before turning back late in June 1494, Columbus required his crew members to declare whether they believed Cuba to be in fact "la tierra-firme" (note the article). In the testimony, the arguments involve the assertion that this land must be part of the Eurasian land mass. The mariners asserted that they had never heard or seen an island 335 leagues long on one coast from East to West which still continued even further. All declared that the land must be "la tierra-firme y no isla." Some affirmed that in not too many leagues further on there "must be" highly cultivated people.

It was not until Columbus' third voyage that he actually arrived at what we consider continental lands in the Western Hemisphere. For a long time Columbus considered the lands he encountered on this voyage islands, and so named them. Finally, just before leaving the coast for Hispaniola, Columbus, in the words of Las Casas, became "conscious that so great a land was not an island, but a continent." In his journal for August 14–15, he recorded his belief that "this is a very great continent, which until today has been unknown." Morison cites this passage as a typical example of how Columbus' mind worked, noting as extraordinary that despite a two-weeks' sail along this land mass, it "failed to meet his mental specifications of how a continent should appear." What were Columbus' specifications for a continent? Did the concept, as we know it, exist in his mind? The fact that Columbus considered not only that this was "tierra firme," but that it was an "Otro Mundo," or "Other World," unknown to the ancients, did not alter his conviction that it was both part of Asia and an island between which and China a passage could be found back to Europe. Are we not again, perhaps, being swayed by our later conception of "continent"?

In Amerigo Vespucci's first letter on his voyages to Piero Soderini, the original of which we do not have, we read that Vespucci left Cadiz May 10, 1497, crossed the Ocean Sea, and discovered "molta terra ferma & infinite isole." In the description of the second voyage Vespucci's narrative also notes that he arrived at "una nuoua terra" which he deemed to be "terra ferma & continua con" the land previously found. Note the lack of articles and the obviously adjectival form of the words modifying "terra." To translate "terra firma" as "continent" in the twentieth century requires an identification with presently defined continents and is not, I suggest, necessarily valid for the Age of Discovery.

As further exploration of the vast lands originally discovered by Columbus was carried on by others, and as doubts that Columbus had reached Asia piled up, the term "tierra firme" tended to be applied more and more to a restricted portion of the northern coast of South America. The two volumes of testimony concerning Columbus' son's rights and his father's achievements, the famous *Pleitos*, give abundant evidence of this meaning. Increasingly the term is capitalized in both its members, and often hyphenated, and takes on the character of a proper name for a specific area rather than serving as a geographical description of a type of land area.

One is hampered by the grandiose character of all suitable translations for "tierra firme." In the Spanish and Portuguese one finds the term often used without the article while English translations almost invariably have to say "the mainland." I suggest that the English translation may be one reason for the assumption that "tierra firme" must refer to continental land masses in the sense in which we know them now.

Most revealing of all usages is "tierra firme" not as the antonym of "island," but as a synonym. In one of the documents concerning the privileges that were to accrue to Columbus we read:

And if it should be argued that the third part granted to the Admiral of Castile is to be understood as relating to moveables, which he might acquire by sea; whereas the said islands being mainland [e que por ser las dichas yslas tierra firme], although acquired by sea, the third part of them cannot belong to the Admiral in consequence of their being unmoveable. . . .

We need the type of collecting of examples which the Romance philologists have done for the polite literature of the period. Unfortunately, few of their dictionaries of early Spanish pay much attention to the historical documents in which these uses occur.

In the midst of these shifting uses of basic terms, is it any wonder that historians have found different answers to the Columbian problem? It is as though someone kept changing the ingredients in a scientist's experiment. He could hardly be expected to come out with consistent results. Yet historians have been trying to solve a problem without first knowing what they were talking about.

It is too easy for us to conceive of "terra firma" in terms of well-defined, well-known land masses. As a result we are inclined to define "terra firma" in conceptual terms of a geographically theoretical sort. I believe the men of affairs of the fifteenth and sixteenth centuries saw "terra firma" in terms of ill-defined, little-known land masses, or as one part of a geographical relationship, and as a result defined the phrase in practical terms of a geographically descriptive sort.

What is meant by "discovery"? Can lands known by reputation and past visitation be said to be "discovered" by later visitors? Can an Italian in the fifteenth century "discover" China? Or had Marco Polo performed that operation several centuries earlier? Can Japan be "discovered" by a fifteenth- or sixteenth-century European who had read Polo's description of the kingdom gained not by personal visit but by knowledge acquired in China? Cecil Jane felt that it would be "impossible" for Columbus to claim he had discovered China, while it would be "hardly possible" for him to allege that he had discovered Japan. Yet I think a good case can be made for asserting in each instance that these Oriental countries could be discovered by fifteenth-century Europeans. Indeed, one might say that discovery is a personal accomplishment. Nothing can be discovered for us; we must discover it. How many Americans "discovered" Japan for the first time after World War II?

But what do we mean by the verb "to discover" in the time of Columbus? Do we mean uncovering land that was "hidden" to us, but known to exist? Or does it mean reaching, by calculation or by chance, lands never known before? Columbus persisted in referring to his discoveries under the first heading. In his letter to the Catholic King, around October 18, 1498, he listed the lands that had come under the Spanish crown as a result of his effort, among which he included a large portion "of terra-firma, well known to the ancients and not unknown, as the envious and ignorant would have it."

Is Columbus' "discovery" any less valid because he insisted on giving Oriental names to what he, in behalf of Europe, "uncovered" physically for the first time instead of "discovering" without worrying about theory? Theory, even false theory, is necessary for the person taking an utterly new step, as Columbus did. No theory is necessary for those who merely followed his course and then went a little beyond. As Las Casas put it, in measuring Columbus' achievement: "It was he that put the thread into the hands of the rest, by which they found the clew to more distant parts." Should the others, Vespucci, for example, be dignified by the word "discoverer" in the same sense in which it is applied to Columbus? It seems hardly less reasonable to call Columbus' unruly crew "discoverers" because they followed his commands as the others followed his routes.

The most extensive analysis of the term "discovery" has been made by the Mexican historian Edmundo O'Gorman. In O'Gorman's concept " 'Discovery' implies that the nature of the thing found was previously known to the finder, i.e., that he knows that objects such as the one he has found can and do exist, although the existence of that particular one was wholly unknown." O'Gorman reserves the word "invent" for the person who first conceives that what has been discovered is of a new order of reality and unlike the class of discovered objects expected. Hence the historian's statement that "Columbus discovered America October 12, 1492," is only an interpretation, inadequate to O'Gorman, and not a statement of fact. To O'Gorman, "In order to maintain that Columbus had revealed the existence of such a continent [one hitherto unknown], it was necessary to establish that he was previously aware of its existence; otherwise there would be no justification in attributing the 'discovery' to him." O'Gorman insists that Columbus make his belief that he has arrived in Asia "fit empirical data." To do so Columbus must prove "that part of the coast line explored by him belonged to a continental mass, as he thought, or that, not far to the west, such a mass of land existed." It is not enough, O'Gorman believes, for Columbus to show that what had been found was merely "an archipelago located somewhere in midocean, as Peter Martyr [the contemporary chronicler of Columbus' voyages] was inclined to believe." Of course this begs the question. Martyr's "new world" is consistent not only with a location near Asia, but can even be argued to be consistent with a portion of the *orbis terrarum* not hitherto known in Europe. In what does O'Gorman think the "empirical evidence" about Asia consists? Does the account of Marco Polo and a few others exhaust the knowledge that is needed for a European to "know" Asia? The notion is absurd, particularly when applied to places like Japan and the myriad islands thought to be southeast of China which Polo had never visited.

O'Gorman, like his fellow Latin Americans, Germán Arciniegas and Roberto Levillier, prefers to honor Amerigo Vespucci as the true "discoverer" of the Americas, on the assumption that it was he who first conceived of the new lands as a continental land mass separate and distinct from Asia. The intricate yet essentially simplistic arguments in which one must be involved to consider this proposition are too sterile to bear lengthy restatement here.

Among the specific problems involved in the dispute is the meaning of the verb used by Waldseemüller, in his *Cosmographiae Introductio,* to describe Vespucci's "discovery." In this book Waldseemüller speaks of the fourth part of the world which, by Vespucci "inventa est. . . ." O'Gorman points out that the word is normally translated as "discover" and has led to the charge that Vespucci (or Waldseemüller for him) usurped the honor that rightly belonged to Columbus. O'Gorman insists that the translation read "conceive" and that it merely recognizes that Vespucci conceived of the existence of this fourth part of the world as a separate entity. Do we not see here the twisting of the meaning both of the word "part" and of the words "inventa est"? Vespucci's exploring mission along an extended coastline to which his name is applied is elevated to the enunciation of a modern conceptual scheme of the world.

How does one categorize the voyages of fishermen who may well have preceded the "discoverers" to the New World? As David Quinn has put it, "The history of the Newfoundland fishery, from the time it emerges in the early sixteenth century, demonstrates how incidental and casual was the attention of the fishermen of four nations to the land which bordered the fishing grounds." Can we say that where there is no interest in the geographical aspects of the discovery there is no discovery? Or would we be falling into the same trap into which O'Gorman has enmeshed himself? I think we can say that it is important to recognize that the eye with which the historian looks at the discoveries is one oriented to modern maps, modern conceptions of continents, islands, and the historical development that followed the discoveries. The professor's hands are not dirtied by the baskets of fish that motivated the fisherman. And is not the "discovery" of the formally commissioned explorer — the Cabots and the Columbuses — something else again? The royal commissions that such discoverers carried with them were normally to "discover and gain," and the phrase is perhaps more instructive of the meaning of their voyages of "discovery" than is the professor's geographical "discovery" or the fisherman's new-found "fishing grounds."

What has been said about discovery illustrates the complexity of the simple little term. Yet few historians have gone deeply into the subject. Samuel Eliot Morison's brief essay on the meaning of the verb "descobrir" in his *Portuguese Voyages to America in the Fifteenth Century* is one of the few such disquisitions. Morison aptly selects a quotation illustrating most of the varied meanings of the term. These meanings, whether emphasizing the sense of "finding by chance," "uncovering," or "exploring," are basically similar in Spanish and, indeed, in French and English. Would that the historical profession had members willing to compile the word lists which form the grist of the philologists' mill.

As Professor Charles E. Nowell has pointed out: "The word India in the Middle Ages had no exact geographical meaning to Europeans; it was a convenient expression denoting the East beyond the Mohammedan world." But what of "the Indies"? The phrase "Las Indias" in the plural rather than the singular is so common to us today that we do not stop to consider the special circumstances of its origin. As Admiral Morison has put it: "*La Empresa de las Indias,* the Enterprise of the Indies, as Columbus called his undertaking in after years, was simply to reach 'The Indies,' that is, Asia, by sailing westward." Yet I would like to ask when one finds the first use of the phrase "The Indies"? The phrase appears in almost all official Spanish documents relating to Columbus following his return from his first voyage in March 1493.

How frequently does it appear before that time? The famous letter of Paolo Toscanelli of June 25, 1474, uses the term in its Spanish version made by Las Casas in the sixteenth century, but not in its earlier Latin or Italian versions. I do not question its use by Toscanelli; nor do I assert that the term was not used before 1492. It did not, however, as many assume, refer to the islands off the mainland of Asia, even though Polo had written of 12,700 in the Sea of India. Rather the expression seems to have derived from the habit of dividing India into various parts, usually "India the Greater," "India the Lesser," and the "Indian Islands." The plural form, therefore, could cover, indiscriminately, all parts of the world known as "India," just as it eventually covered all Spanish possessions, insular and continental, in the New World. We may ask, nevertheless, why Columbus, in his letter to Luis de Santangel, immediately on his return from the first voyage, and in the first sentence of the letter, reported that he had "passed over to the Indies with the fleet which the most illustrious King and Queen, our Lords, gave me; where I found very many islands peopled with inhabitants beyond number." Why not "India"? Columbus possibly wanted to use the vaguest, most inclusive term he could find to suggest India without doing violence to the public imagination back home. The term "Indies" was the least specific term applicable to the newly discovered lands.

Ferdinand Columbus reported that his father called the lands he discovered "the Indies"

not because they had been seen or discovered by others, but because they were the eastern part of India, beyond the Ganges, to which no geographer had ever set bounds on the east, or made it border on any other country eastward, but only upon the ocean. And because these lands were the unknown eastern part of India and had no name of their own, he named them after the nearest adjoining land, calling them the West Indies. He had the more reason for doing this because he knew all men had heard of the great fame and wealth of India; and by using that name he hoped to arouse the interest of the Catholic Sovereigns (who were doubtful of his enterprise), telling them that he was going to discover the Indies by way of the West.

One can appreciate Columbus' problem of nomenclature for the lands between Asia and Europe. What distinguishes Asia from Europe? The line can be rather clearly drawn in the land bridge between the two, but how were Europeans to be expected to classify peoples in the seas between Asia and Europe in which they had never traveled? Had Columbus arrived at the Philippines instead of Española, would he have acted or thought or written differently? Would any European have known how to classify Philippine natives, Borneo natives, New Guinea tribesmen, Formosan aborigines, Polynesians? What empirical evidence makes all these peoples and their lands Asiatic or near-Asiatic? Europe was aware of myriad islands supposed to exist in the seas to the east and south of China and India, but no European of the time knew by direct acquaintance the locations of the lands or the character of the people, either in the offshore islands or on the mainland itself.

Marco Polo had reported not only about the incredibly civilized, powerful, populous, and wealthy kingdoms like China and Japan, but of islands such as "Necuveran" in which "they have no king or chief, but live like beasts. And I tell you they go all naked, both men and women, and do not use the slightest covering of any kind. They are Idolaters." To condemn Columbus for failing to recognize the difference between Polo's China and his own discoveries is to ignore Polo's reports of the "savage" islands in the Sea of India and to overlook his warning that he had described only the most noteworthy of these islands "for no man on earth could give you a true account of the whole of the Islands of India."

No true empirical evidence existed to "tell" the discoverers whether or not they had reached Asia. To assume that such "empirical evidence" existed in the reports of Polo is to stretch the meaning of the phrase to an unrecognizable point. Columbus was a sailor who knew what he had seen and where he had been, and his theory of reaching Asia by a short sail west, ridiculed by most, seemed to have been vindicated. It was logical for him to assume that he was better qualified to name the lands he had found than any armchair strategist.

In a sense, cannot one say that "America" — or rather the unknown, unnamed lands discovered by Columbus — was indeed a part of Asia, since it had been settled by men from the Asiatic land mass (the "Indians") and since it had been at one time joined physically at the present straits bearing the name of the eighteenth-century explorer, Vitus Bering, who, at that late date, proved that "Asia" and "America" missed, by a few miles, being one "continent"?

Columbus himself, on April 2, 1502, before starting on his final voyage, had copies of all his contracts, privileges, and commissions made and certified by the royal notary, and deposited in the Bank of St. George at Genoa. He signed his letter to the lords of the bank with the title "The Great Admiral of the Ocean Sea, and Viceroy and Governor of the Islands and Mainland of Asia and the Indies belonging to the King and Queen, my sovereigns, and their Captain-General of the Sea, and a member of their Council."

In this instance his title, repeated by his son Diego in his will of 1509, is as full as he dared to claim it, and it demonstrates Columbus' conception of the theoretical location of Asia combined with his knowledge of Spain's actual power over the lands he discovered. It is not proof of his assumption or intention, before the voyage, to take over the government of the "Asia" known to fifteenth-century Europe.

The medieval world tended to conceive of a central land mass, an *orbis terrarum*, inhabited by humans and located in the Northern Hemisphere. The problem of whether an antipodal land mass existed in the Southern Hemisphere had been debated fruitlessly from classical times. The concept of an antipodal land mass, an "orbis alter," tended to be denied by Christian writers since it was hard to conceive that the gospel had been preached in any such lands. Nevertheless some writers conceded the existence of the antipodes, while denying the presence of inhabitants there. Among these writers was St. Isidore of Seville who conceived of the antipodal regions, uninhabited in his view, as a fourth "part" of the world, along with Europe, Asia, and Africa.

The term "world" appears in many senses in the writings of classical and medieval scholars, theologians, and cartographers. There could be many "worlds" or orbs within the Ocean Sea on the face of the earth. Indeed, Seneca's famous prediction that there would come an age when the chains of the ocean would be broken, "novos orbes" would be discovered, and

Thule would no longer be ultimate, illustrates the frequent, often poetic or colloquial use of the term "world," as one part of the globe, not the entire globe itself.

Peter Martyr's frequently reported phrase "Colonus ille Novi Orbis repertor," used for the first time in his letter to Cardinal Ascanio Sforza from Barcelona, November 1, 1493, does not imply the conception of a "new world" in the sense of an American continent, though this claim is often made. The phrase is perfectly consistent with either an Asiatic or non-Asiatic location and also with a land area of less than "continental" size.

Alexander von Humboldt long ago demonstrated that the phrase "new world" was often applied to unknown parts of a known region even when both were parts of the same land mass.

The popular meaning of the phrase "new world" is suggested by Bartolomé de las Casas' report of Columbus' reception on his return from his first voyage. Though written after the event it may well suggest the contemporary use of the term. Las Casas reported that the sovereigns, learning of Columbus' arrival, "ordered that a solemn and very beautiful reception should be given him, for which all the people came out and the whole city, filling the streets and marvelling on seeing in that venerable person the one who was said to have discovered another world [*otro mundo*]. . . ."

Columbus referred to the areas he had discovered as "another world" (*otro mundo*) both in the course of his third voyage in 1498 and in his letter to the nurse of Prince Don Juan of Castile in 1500, when he was returning from the Indies as a prisoner. In the latter letter, after quoting from St. John and from Isaiah concerning a "new heaven and a new earth," Columbus also pictured himself as the messenger chosen by God to undertake "a new voyage to the new heaven and world [*viaje nuevo al nuevo cielo e mundo*], which up till then had remained hidden." Both Columbus and

Vespucci referred to the newly discovered lands both as a part of Asia and as a "new world." How futile, then, to claim, as O'Gorman so insistently does, that Vespucci had "empirical evidence" that the southern mainland was not merely an Asiatic peninsula while Columbus, with his a priori ideas, believed that it was. The empirical evidence of discovery of a coastline is the same whether one calls it Asia or something else. Neither Columbus nor Vespucci nor other Europeans knew, by direct knowledge, of Asia or any lands that might lie on the sea between it and Western Europe. Both saw the lands discovered as a new world. Does one need to emphasize the obvious in pointing out that Columbus was more insistent in calling the lands he encountered parts of Asia?

One does not need a universe in which to place a "new world." There is neither need nor logic in thinking such an expression equivalent to a new "continent," assuming we know what that word means. Perhaps historians are too little schooled in literature to appreciate the extensive use of metaphor and hyperbole. A doer, a seaman like Columbus, is less apt to misunderstand the meaning of such a term — as used in speech and writing — than a too literal book-bound scholar.

Bartolomé de las Casas, despite the abuse to which he is subjected by latter-day historians, takes what to me is the most satisfactory and scientific explanation of what we mean by Columbus' discovery. He cites myths and rumors of unknown or forgotten lands to the west, as well as the belief that Asia, or lands off Asia, was the goal, and after discussing them concludes that the question of exactly what land Columbus thought he had found makes no difference to the history of the discoveries which he is writing. For this attitude he is castigated by O'Gorman for "a thoroughly jumbled and indigestible hodgepodge" of comment on Columbus' motives, and for a thesis which causes "the many inconsistencies in his work." It is odd that the present-day generation of presumably hardheaded historians and writers of Latin America, such as O'Gorman, Arciniegas, and Levillier should in fact be true, if misguided, metaphysicians while Las Casas, the man they denounce as a poor, misguided, medieval friar, is the real pragmatist and the true historian whose sophistication of method and knowledge of the events cannot fail to command our respect.

What O'Gorman fails to do is to carry his theory to its logical conclusion. Certainly Columbus did not discover "America" in a strictly logical sense. But if America is not what Columbus found, neither does it make sense to call America the lands in which our forefathers were born, in which we were born, or in which our children will be born. In fact, "America" changes in population, in industry, in agriculture, and in every conceivable human way every instant of every minute of every day. America is never the same; it is ever changing. The America Vespucci knew is not the America we know, either in human or geographical terms. What use is the term then? And are we to denounce with equal vigor the practice of calling the native inhabitants of the Americas "Indians"? Do we make allowances for those who use the term because "we all know what they mean"? If so, when do we apply the concession: 1493? 1500? 1515? 1542? And to whom? How do we know what the persons using the phrase meant by "Indians"? Obviously, one must use conventional signs to signify meaning. This is what O'Gorman and all the historians he

criticizes do, though some do so with a greater degree of historical accuracy than others.

May we not conclude that an examination of the basic meaning of the words used to describe the early discoveries is in order when we get such extremes of interpretation as Vignaud on the one side, claiming Columbus' intention all along to find new lands rather than Asia, and O'Gorman's *idée fixe* that the world Columbus found was not America because he could not conceive it, and not Asia because he did not find it, but rather a world in limbo, existent in thought, but not in fact. Both Vignaud and O'Gorman rival each other in the persistence with which they have presented their theses in book after book. Yet their excessive zeal and their extreme divergence should be a double warning to us to re-examine the original texts and attempt to rewrite the history of the discoveries with an agreed upon vocabulary, one reflecting the reality of the fifteenth century without the admixture of the philosophy of later centuries.

My plea, then, is that scholars in many fields, cartographic, historical, linguistic, belletristic, search out more carefully and thoroughly the terms of the Age of Discovery and provide us with a more complete statistical sample upon which to base our assumptions. Until we know precisely what Columbus and his fellow explorers were talking about we will hardly be able to translate their intentions and actions into historical truth.

The English Discovery of America

DAVID B. QUINN

Thanks to a long list of distinguished books and articles on many aspects of English expansion in the late Middle Ages and Renaissance, including *The Voyages and Colonizing Enterprises of Sir Humphrey Gilbert*, 2 vols. (1940); *Raleigh and the British Empire* (1947); and *The Roanoke Voyages, 1584–90*, 2 vols. (1955), David Quinn has become one of the best known and most respected experts in the field. Born in 1909, he was educated primarily in England and Northern Ireland, receiving his Ph.D. from the University of London in 1934, and a D.Lit. from Queen's University, Belfast. He has occupied several positions of academic and literary importance, and is currently Andrew Geddes and John Rankin Professor of Modern History at the University of Liverpool.

In 1956 Dr. Louis André Vigneras published a letter he had found in the archives at Simancas which has greatly affected and will continue to affect consideration of the circumstances of the discovery of America. In Spanish, and undated, the letter was addressed by John Day, an Englishman, to a Spanish official, the "Almirante Mayor," who is to be identified either as Fadrique Enriquez, Grand Admiral of Castile, or as Christopher Columbus, Admiral of the Ocean Sea, often referred to also as the "Almirante Mayor." Dr. Vigneras prefers the Columbus identification and it seems the much more probable one. The letter is the work of a man of some learning, familiar with the geographical knowledge of the time, who has been carrying on a correspondence with the Grand Admiral, exchanging books with him, and sending him information on English voyages on at least one earlier occasion. Where its information can be checked against other evidence it is correct, which suggests that its unsupported statements are serious and probably authoritative ones. The letter is mainly concerned with reporting a successful voyage from Bristol by an unnamed ex-

plorer which has found across the ocean a land which Day identifies with "the Island of the Seven Cities." Both by its general character and by specific details — the grant, for example (on 13 December 1497) of a pension of twenty pounds by the king to the explorer on his return — this voyage can be clearly and unambiguously identified as that made by John Cabot in 1497 during which he coasted a substantial part of the Newfoundland and mainland shores across the Atlantic. The letter, moreover, states that the explorer had earlier made an unsuccessful voyage from Bristol, thus adding a piece of hitherto unknown information on John Cabot, while it also gives some details of the preparation for a further voyage which Cabot was making to follow up his discovery. From this last information it is possible to tie down the composition of the letter to the latter part of December 1497 or the opening month or so of 1498. The general considerations are discussed by Dr. Vigneras. For the Cabot voyages the letter is an important source, the most important, indeed, to be published in the present century, while the details it gives of the 1497 discoveries will continue to provide ma-

From David B. Quinn, "The Argument for the English Discovery of America between 1480 and 1949," *The Geographical Journal*, CXXVII (1961), pp. 277–82. Reprinted by permission of Professor Quinn.

terial for interpretation and controversy. One passage in it goes beyond the Cabot voyages themselves and raises the question of the priority of the discovery of America in a novel form. Its interest is such that it is worth segregating it from the Cabot material and considering what its implications may be if it is taken literally as a statement of fact.

The text reads, in translation: "It is considered certain that the cape of the said land [that found by Cabot in the 1497 voyage] was found and discovered in other times by the men of Bristol who found 'Brasil' as your Lordship knows. It was called the Ysle of Brasil and it is assumed and believed to be the mainland that the Bristol men found." (The Spanish being: "Se presume cierto averse fallado e descubierto en otros tiempos el cabo de la dicha tierra por los de Bristol que fallaron el Brasil como dello tiene noticia Vra Sª la qual se dezia la Ysle de Brasil e presumese e creese ser tierra firme la que fallaron los de Bristol.") The Spanish of the letter shows few signs of being written by a foreigner, but Dr. Vigneras has found that John Day, its author, as an English merchant, appears also in a Spanish document of 1500. The literal meaning is clear enough. The land, or part of the land, which Cabot found in 1497 is equated with "Brasil" or the "Isle of Brasil," which the Bristol men had found already some time before. Cabot's discovery, although the possibility of a rediscovery of land found and lost again is not ruled out, had not, Day is asserting, any claim to absolute priority. When, then, could this first discovery have taken place? Or between what limits can we place it? The major ambiguity lies in the words, "en otros tiempos," with which Dr. Vigneras has already wrestled. The expression is a vague one, "in times past," rather than "in past times," having only the implication that the "times" were not very recently passed, but even that not very clearly. Certain dates, 1480, 1481, 1490 give us a framework of known facts in which to insert a

series of questions and an argument on the implications of the statement.

1. Could the discovery have taken place before 1480? Clearly it could have done so, but no evidence whatever of specific English voyages of discovery into the Atlantic before that date has yet come to light. That being so, nothing useful can be said except that the first positive evidence we have, that for 1480, which follows, is slightly weighted against a discovery before that date, and that for 1481 more heavily.

2. On 15 July 1480 a ship, partly owned by John Jay the younger and with "Thloyde" (identified as John Lloyd with some probability, though it could be Thomas Lloyd) as master, left Bristol for the Island of Brasil, west of Ireland, and returned by September 18 following, having through bad weather failed to find the island. The Latin of William Worcester on its objective reads: "usque ad insulam de Brasylle in occidentali parte Hibernie." Since the Island of Brasil appeared on many maps, in many different locations, from 1325 onwards, without apparently having been discovered in practice, this would appear on our present information to have been an unsuccessful voyage of discovery to an island known only in theory. Nevertheless, the alternative, that it was an unsuccessful voyage to an island or land already known and discovered before 1480, cannot be entirely ruled out. At least, however, the discovery did not take place in 1480 as the result of this expedition.

3. On, or shortly after, 6 July 1481 two ships, the *George* and the *Trinity* of Bristol, partly owned and victualled by Thomas Croft, one of the collectors of custom for Bristol, left the port "to serch & fynde a certain Isle called the Isle of Brasile." The terms of their objective would, more strongly than the document of 1480, indicate that the Isle of Brasil had not been located and that this was another voyage of discovery. Moreover, on 18 June 1480, probably too late to be connected with the 1480 voyage, a licence was given

to Croft and three Bristol merchants, William Spenser, Robert Straunge and William de la Fount, to trade for three years to any parts, with any goods except staple goods, despite any statute to the contrary, with two or three ships, each of sixty tons or less. Since Croft was precluded by his office from engaging in trade and was questioned on 24 September 1481 about shipping forty bushels of salt in the *George* and *Trinity* on 6 July 1481, it would appear that this licence was for exploration, not commerce, while Croft's excuse that the two ships which he had helped to victual were intended not for commerce but for the search for the Isle of Brasil, was accepted. The 1481 voyage, of the failure of which there is no record, and of the return of which the proceedings against Croft are probably circumstantial evidence, is one which could have resulted in the English discovery of America. A discovery by this expedition would fit, without straining, the requirements of John Day's letter. Moreover, it is the earliest known voyage which could have so succeeded. 1481 is therefore the earlier limit on our present information for a successful discovery and could be the year of the discovery itself.

4. If the discovery did not take place in 1481, Croft and his partners, provided the licence of 1480 was for the purpose which has been presumed, had still authority to set out ships in 1482 and in 1483 up to June 17. Evidence is still entirely lacking that any such further voyages were made or, if made, that they had any results, but it is within the years of the currency of the licence that the English discovery of America is least unlikely to lie.

5. The years between 1483 and 1490 are as blank of even the suggestion of evidence for a voyage as those before 1480, but they are still within the period of discovery appropriate to the Day letter.

6. One of the Spanish representatives in England provides a well-known piece of evidence about English western voyages which reaches back, perhaps, to 1490. Pedro de Ayala wrote from London to Ferdinand and Isabella on 25 July 1498 to report on Cabot's discoveries in 1497 and on the progress, so far, of his 1498 expedition. He added: "Los de Bristol ha siete años que cada año an armado dos, tres, quatro caravelas para ir a buscar la isla del Brasil, i la Siete Ciudades con la fantasia deste Ginoves," which has, since 1862, been invariably translated: "For the last seven years the people of Bristol have equipped two, three, four caravels to go in search of the island of Brazil and the Seven Cities according to the fancy of this Genoese." It is not certain which years are meant. Is Ayala writing of seven years before Cabot's voyage of 1497 or of seven years before his letter? The range is either 1490 to 1496 or 1491 to 1497, and choice between the alternatives is not easy to make; both must be regarded as possible. How far Ayala was speaking precisely and authoritatively it is also impossible to say, but it is reasonable to take his statement at its face value that a series of Bristol voyages began in 1490 or 1491 and was continued in, perhaps, each of the six years following.

To determine how much or how little John Cabot had to do with these voyages is a delicate matter. "According to the fancy of this Genoese" has been taken, almost invariably, to mean that John Cabot, Genoese by origin though Venetian by adoption, inspired this series of Bristol voyages and proposed their objectives to those who took part in them. This does not necessarily follow. The phrase as it stands can mean simply that in Cabot's "fancy" the objectives of the Bristol voyages were the Isle of Brasil and the Seven Cities. He would stand outside the voyages entirely and his comment would be that of an observer only, made to Ayala's informant near to the time of writing in 1498. An alternative translation of the passage could read: "The Bristol men for seven years have fitted out yearly two, three, or four small ships to go in search, as this Genoese fancies, of the Isle of Brasil or the Seven Cities." Which interpretation is correct must remain a matter for argument. Each appears to be legitimate.

The alternative interpretation fits usefully into a pattern formed by the newer documents. It is in line with the evidence already used on the 1480 and 1481 voyages. The English are continuing in the nineties their westward voyages from Bristol, only now they are using as many as three or four little ships instead of one or two; they are said to be looking for the Seven Cities in addition to their old objective, the Isle of Brasil. Moreover, the evidence found by Professor M. Ballesteros Gabrois in the Aragonese archives, if it is to be accepted, puts John Cabot in Valencia between the middle of 1490 and the end of February 1493 at least, and so rules him out from influencing some of the earlier voyages of the series. This involves identifying the Juan Caboto Montecalunya, a Venetian engaged on harbour works at Valencia, with the "English" John Cabot. While this is not certain it is highly probable. The discoveries of R. Gallo (1948) on the "English" John Cabot's activities in Venice between 1476 and 1485 make it unlikely that there was a second John Cabot with Venetian nationality, though the cognomen "Montecalunya" remains mysterious. The consequence of accepting this identification would be that the voyages of 1490 (if there was one), 1491, 1492 and 1493 (probably), of the series were purely English expeditions, and so they could be considered as coming within the range of the independent English discovery described by John Day. Dates as late as 1490 and 1491 could be covered by his "en otros tiempos"; later dates, 1492, six years, and 1493, five years, before the Day letter, seem too near, or at least to be at the outer limit of credibility: 1494, if worth considering, would be rather absurd. We are entitled to say, remembering that we have selected one meaning of two from the Ayala letter and have accepted the Valencia material, that 1490 and 1491 come within the probable range of the independent English discovery of America, and

1492 and 1493 within the possible limits.

7. Robert Thorne the younger, in 1527, claimed that his father, Robert Thorne the elder, and Hugh Eliot, merchants of Bristol, were "discoverers of the New Found Landes." The claim appears to have been made in good faith and, accepting Day's statement of a pre-Cabotan English discovery, it seems not unlikely to be true, or at least to indicate that these men had something to do with a voyage to the Isle of Brasil before Cabot came on the scene. No date is associated with the claim, but John Dee in 1580 adopted it and associated it with the date 1494, doing so only tentatively, placing it "Circa An. 1494," and leaving no evidence to show whether or not he had specific reasons for the choice of date. "1494" therefore has no special authority: a Thorne-Eliot voyage before 1494 which had a successful outcome is as possible as one in that year if not more so. 1494 can, however, be dragged in as the furthest forward limit of the discovery recorded by John Day and, as already indicated, it is already so late that it can legitimately be thought of as beyond the limit.

8. John Cabot, if he still had unfinished business at Valencia at the end of February 1493, is unlikely to have come to England in time to take part in westward voyages from Bristol before the end of the sailing season (September) in that year. 1494 is therefore the first year in which he, if the Valencia evidence be accepted, is likely to have been available to make a voyage from Bristol. John Day records that he did make one unsuccessful voyage before 1497. On the arguments advanced so far this would leave 1494, 1495 and 1496 open to him for it. It is difficult to say with any confidence that one year is much more probable than another. The first is still a possible Thorne-Eliot year and is therefore a shade less likely for a Cabot voyage. Dr. Vigneras argues that Cabot would not have made a voyage until he had got a royal licence to do so and so could not have made his first, unsuccessful voyage until 1496. This is reasonable but it does not exclude

alternative suppositions. If Cabot intruded himself at Bristol he may have found himself handicapped by secrecy and obstruction so that his first venture had little chance of success and he may therefore have sought a royal licence so that he could overcome it. This is pure speculation, but it is made to show that Cabot could have made his first voyage in, for example, 1495. If 1496 is regarded as more likely, however, following on Cabot's petition to Henry VII and the issue of a patent on March 5 granting him powers to occupy and govern lands found, and to trade with them through the port of Bristol, a further point remains. In that case Bristol voyages made in 1495 as well as in 1494, in Ayala's series, would have been purely English voyages. The limiting date of an English discovery could therefore be pushed up to the very eve of the Cabot grant but, if it is, John Day's "in other times" must be called in question because if 1494 is an absurd date to associate with it, 1495 is impossible. A run of annual Bristol voyages, beginning about 1490 and continuing to include 1495, though not including a discovery in the later years, seems credible. The series would then be continued or paralleled by an unsuccessful Cabot voyage in 1496.

9. In summary, then, since, according to John Day, the English discovered America before 1497 they must have done so either before 1480 or between 1481 and, at the furthest limit forward, 1494. 1481 or a date near it would best fit the phraseology of the Day letter on the information now available. A date of 1490 or 1491 is still possible though less likely, but it seems desirable to bring in at least one of the years covered by Ayala's evidence. A date between 1492 and 1494 appears progressively less acceptable and 1495 unacceptable (though of course the drawing of a line in this case must be at least partly subjective). Allowing ourselves room for speculation on years both before and after, we can say that an argument on the present basis indicates that the English discovery could reasonably have taken place between 1481 and 1491, with the initial date, 1481, and the concluding one, 1491 (if it is the first of Ayala's series), as slightly less unlikely than the others, though with the chances otherwise in favor of a year in the early part of the series rather than the later. Further than this it would seem undesirable to go until something fresh can be adduced. The sequence of information is so fragile and incomplete that any single scrap of new evidence can upset it. It does not provide a basis for any dogmatic statement other than that made by John Day himself. Nevertheless, with all its limitations, it does provide a rational case for placing the English discovery of America in the decade before Columbus sailed in 1492, and possibly as early as 1481.

III. THE SPANISH CONQUEST

The Destruction of the Indies

BARTOLOMÉ DE LAS CASAS

Bishop Las Casas had a long and turbulent life (1474–1566) as "Apostle of the Indies." Born in Seville where his father was a successful merchant, he accompanied the new governor, Nicolás de Ovando, to the New World in 1502 and there began his life-long involvement with the Indians. He was ordained a priest in 1512 and three years later renounced his *encomienda* and returned to Spain. In 1523 he became a Dominican, and for the next seventeen years wandered about South and Central America as a missionary. In 1540 he returned to Spain where he wrote his *Brevissima relación*. He was sent to America as Bishop of Chiapa in 1544 but remained there only three years. The last nineteen years of his life were spent in and out of court, writing and rewriting, debating and denouncing. His most valuable books are: *Historia de las Indias; Apologética historia de las Indias;* and *Del único modo de atraer a todos los pueblos a la verdadera religión.*

I N 1492 the Indies were discovered. A year later the Spanish Christians began to settle them, so for forty-nine years now there have been a great many Spaniards living there. The first land invaded for the purpose of settlement was the large and happy island of Hispaniola, which is six hundred leagues in circumference. There are other very large and innumerable islands surrounding it, all of which — and this we have seen ourselves — were as fully populated with their native Indian people as any country in the world. Ten thousand leagues of the mainland coast, which is over two hundred and fifty leagues from this island at its closest point, have been discovered and every day they discover more. All of the lands discovered up until the year forty-one are as crowded as a beehive, almost as though God had put in them the entire mass of humanity, or at least the major part of it.

This infinite number of people have all been created by God as the most simple, obedient, faithful, humble, patient, peaceful, and relaxed people in the world; without malice or duplicity, strife, upheavals, quarrels, hatred, nor desires for vengeance. They are similarly the most delicate people, slight and weak in constitution and less able than others to stand up under work without easily dying from some sickness or another. Even the sons of our princes and lords, who are brought up in royal and pampered lives, are no more delicate than they, even though many of them are of peasant lineage. They are also extremely poor people who possess, or even desire, very few temporal goods. For this reason they are neither arrogant, ambitious, nor covetous.

Their food is such that not even that of the Holy Fathers in the desert seems to have been more scanty, less appetizing, or

From Bartolomé de las Casas, *Breve relación de la destrucción de las Indias occidentales* (London: Schulze y Dean, 1812, reprinted from the original Seville 1552 edition), pp. 13–18, 125–129. [Editor's translation].

poorer. Their usual clothes are skins, covering their shame, and at most they drape themselves with a cotton blanket [manta] about one and a half or two yards square. Their beds are the top of a mat, but mostly they sleep in sort of hanging nets which, in the language of Hispaniola, they call hammocks.

They also have clean, detached, and lively minds, very capable and amenable to all good doctrine. They are ready to receive our holy Catholic faith and to be endowed with its virtuous customs, for they have fewer difficulties with such matters than anyone God has created in the world. They are so eager to know these things, once they begin to learn about matters of the faith and participate in the sacraments of the Church and the divine service, that, to tell the truth, it is necessary for the clergy to be specially endowed by God with the gifts of patience in order to put up with them. And finally, for several years I have heard many Spanish laymen frequently say — not being able to deny the kindness which they see in them — that these people would certainly be the most fortunate on earth if only they knew God.

As soon as these gentle sheep, gifted with such qualities by their Creator, were known, the Spaniards entered in among them like vicious wolves, tigers, and lions that had been starving for many days. And for forty years, from that time until the present (and still they continue), they have done nothing but tear apart, kill, distress, afflict, torment, and destroy them with strange, new, and diverse manner of cruelties never before heard of nor read about, some of which will be described below. The extent of this cruelty has been such that whereas there were once over three million souls in the island of Hispaniola, that we saw, now there are no more than two hundred natives left.

The island of Cuba, which is almost as long as the distance from Valladolid to Rome, is now almost completely depopulated. The islands of San Juan and of Jamaica, both very large, happy, and beautiful, are desolate. The Lucaios Islands, next to Hispaniola and to Cuba on the north, are more than sixty in number, counting those known as the Giants along with others both large and small; and even the poorest of these is more fertile and beautiful than the King's garden in Seville, and is the healthiest country in the world. In these islands there were more than five hundred thousand people; today there is not a single creature. All were killed being transported to Hispaniola, after it was seen that the native population there was disappearing.

Three years later a ship went in search of the people who had been left behind after the rounding up, because some good Christian was moved by compassion for all who might be converted and won to Christ. Only eleven persons were found; these I saw. More than thirty other islands around San Juan were depopulated and lost for the same reason. In all, these islands total more than two thousand leagues of land and are now completely depopulated and deserted.

We are sure that on the mainland our Spaniards, through their cruelties and infamous works, have depopulated and desolated more than ten kingdoms larger than all of Spain, including Aragon and Portugal, all filled with rational men, and have left a desert of more land than twice the distance from Seville to Jerusalem, which is over two thousand leagues. We give this as an accurate and truthful count that in those forty years, through the above mentioned tyrannies and infernal works of the Christians, more than twelve million souls — men, women, and children — have been unjustly and tyrannically killed. And I think I am not being deceived in believing that it is really over fifteen million.

The so-called Christians who have gone there have used two general and principal methods in extirpating these miserable nations and erasing them from the face of the earth. One is by unjust, cruel, bloody, and tyrannical wars. The other (after all those who might aspire to, desire, or think about liberty have been killed, and also those who would escape from the torments they suffer, such as all the native Lords and adult males — since usually none are left alive in the wars except the very young men and the women) is by oppressing them with the hardest, most horrible, and obdurate servitude that either men or beasts could be put into. All of the numerous and diverse other ways (which are infinite) of exterminating these people are reduced, resolved, or subjected, according to kind, to these two methods of infernal tyranny.

The reason for the Christians having killed and destroyed so great a number of souls is only because they have had gold, the desire to become rich in a few days, and to rise to high status beyond their class, as their ultimate goal; that is, for their insatiable greed and ambition, unmatched anywhere in the world. They have had no more respect for these lands so tranquil and rich, and their people so humble, patient, and easy to subdue, nor given them any more consideration (and I speak the truth for I have witnessed this all the time) I shall not say, than to the beasts, because would to God they had considered and treated them as beasts instead of as dung in the market-place.

Thus have they cared for their lives and their souls, and as a result, all these many millions have died without faith and without the sacraments. And it is a notorious and well-advertized truth, known and admitted by all whether they are tyrants or murderers, that the Indians throughout the entire Indies have never done any harm to the Christians. In fact they even took them as coming from heaven, until they and their neighbors had suffered so many evils, robberies, killings, violences, and vexations at their hands. . . .

Another thing ought to be added, that is, from the very beginning to the present time, the Spaniards have taken no more care to have the faith of Jesus Christ preached to these people than if they were

dogs or some other animals. Heretofore they have prevented the churchmen from doing their work by all sorts of afflictions and persecutions, causing them to be unable to preach to the Indians because they feared it would impede their aquisition of gold and riches, which they had greedily promised themselves.

And today in all the Indies there is no more knowledge of God among the people — whether He is wooden, whether He is in heaven or in the earth — than there was a hundred years ago, except in New Spain [Mexico], which is only a tiny corner of the Indies, where the churchmen have labored. And in this way all have perished, and are still perishing, without faith and without sacraments.

I, Fray Bartolomé de las Casas, or Casaus, friar of Santo Domingo — who, by the mercy of God go about this Court of Spain trying to cast this hell out of the Indies, to prevent those innumerable souls redeemed by the blood of Jesus Christ from hopelessly perishing forever without knowing their Creator and saving themselves (and moved also by the compassion I have for my native land, which is Castile, so that God may not destroy it for such great sins against its faith and honor, and against its neighbors) — was induced [to write this book] by several notable persons, residing at this Court, who are zealous in honoring God and compassionate for the afflictions and calamities of others. Although I had intended to do it for a long time, my continuous occupations had prevented me from carrying it out.

I completed it in Valencia on December 8, 1542 at a time when all of the violences, oppressions, carnage, depopulation, tyrannies, murders, robberies and destructions, the ravages, afflictions and calamities mentioned above were at their peak wherever there were Christians in the Indies; although in some parts they were more fierce and abominable than in others. Mexico and its immediate surroundings are a little less bad, at least there such things are not done publicly, because in Mexico, unlike in other parts, there is some justice, although very little for there too they kill with infernal taxes.

I have great hope, since the Emperor and King of Spain our Lord Charles, Fifth of this name, is becoming acquainted with the evils and treachery that have been and are still committed in those lands against the will of God and against his own (because until now the truth has been cunningly kept from him), that he will have to root out all of the evils and liberate that New World which God has given him, as he is a true lover and venerator of justice. May God Almighty prosper his glorious and happy life and imperial state for the reparation of all his universal Church and the ultimate salvation of his Royal soul. Amen.

Since the above was written, certain laws and ordinances were published by His Majesty in the city of Barcelona during the month of November 1542 [the New Laws] and in the city of Madrid in the following year, whereby it was ordered that henceforth it would be agreed that such evils and sins that are committed against both God and neighbors, to the total destruction and loss of that part of the world, should cease.

His Majesty issued these laws after many gatherings, disputations, and consultations in the city of Valladolid with people of high authority, education, and morals, and eventually with the agreement of all the others who gave their opinion by written vote, and who found themselves closer to the precepts of the law of Jesus Christ. These men are also free from the corruption and pollution of the treasures stolen from the Indies, which soiled the hands, and also the souls, of many leaders. From this stemmed their blindness so that they destroyed them [the Indians] without the least hesitation.

Upon publication of these laws, the authors of the tyrannies, who were then at Court, made many copies of them — since all were disturbed because it appeared now that the doors to participate in robberies and tyranny were being closed — and sent them to diverse parts of the Indies.

Those who had been responsible for the robberies in the Indies, and of completing the destruction with their tyrannies, had never observed the least bit of order but rather followed all of the disorder that could be established by Lucifer. When they saw the copies, before the arrival of the judges who were to enforce them, and knowing what they would have to do (according to what was said and believed by those from here who, up until then, had sustained them in their sins and violences), they became so disturbed that when the good judges came to carry out the laws they elected to forfeit their honor and obedience to the King, just as they had lost their love and fear of God.

Therefore, they decided to take the name of traitors, since they were cruel and licentious tyrants, especially in the kingdoms of Peru where today, in the year 1546, are committed such horrible, frightful, and abominable works as have never been done either in the Indies or in the world. These things are done not only to the Indians, all of whom or almost all have now been killed and their lands depopulated, but among themselves to one another. This is the righteous justice of God, since they are without the King's justice, which brings punishment from Heaven by permitting them to be their own executioners.

Encouraged by that uprising, those in all the other parts of that world [the New World] who have not wanted to obey the laws, and under pretext of supplicating against them, are as rebellious as the others. For they resent giving up the estates and properties they have usurped and object to releasing the Indians they have held in perpetual captivity.

Where they have ceased to kill quickly

with swords they now kill slowly with personal service and other unjust and intolerable vexations. And until now the King has not been powerful enough to hamper it because everyone from the least to the most important goes about robbing, some more and some less, some publicly and openly, others secretly and dissemblingly. And under the pretext of serving the King they dishonor God, and rob and destroy the King.

Letter to the Emperor Charles V

TORIBIO DE MOTOLINÍA

Toribio Paredes de Benavente, known always by the Indian cognomen of Motolinía ["poor man"], joined the Franciscans at the age of seventeen. He was one of the twelve missionaries from that order sent to Mexico in 1524, at the request of Cortés. Laboring in several parts of New Spain, where he also applied himself to the mastery of Indian languages, he soon became one of the best-loved friars in the New World. Motolinía was also something of a historian; not as systematic nor as literary as Las Casas, but his *Historia de los Indios de Nueva España* is nevertheless a valuable contribution to the historiography of the conquest, especially in its depiction of Indian life, customs, and religion. His quarrel with Las Casas had many roots, both personal and institutional, and after the promulgation of the New Laws in 1542 he became increasingly hostile to the controversial Dominican. His famous letter of 1555 to the Emperor Charles V is an example of the fire aroused by the controversy over Spanish Indian policy.

S ACRED CAESAREAN CATHOLIC MAJESTY — Grace and mercy and peace from God our Father and the Lord Jesus Christ.

Three things in particular move me to write this letter to Your Majesty, and I believe it will be the means of removing some of the doubts which Las Casas, former bishop of Chiapa, has caused Your Majesty and your councils, especially with the things he has just recently written and published.

The first will be to acquaint Your Majesty with the conditions of this dominion of New Spain when the Spaniards entered it — just a few years after the Mexicans arrived — and how the Mexicans themselves had won or usurped it by war. The first native inhabitants of New Spain were called Chichimecs and Otomies. They lived like savages in caves and huts instead of houses. They neither plowed nor cultivated the land but ate the herbs and roots and fruits that they could find on the land. The wild game they caught with their bows and arrows were dried in the sun and then eaten. They neither worshipped idols nor made sacrifices, but the sun was their god, and they also prayed to other creatures. After these first settlers came the Culhuas, who journeyed from a distant land. They brought corn, other seeds, and domestic fowls, built homes, and cultivated the land. Eventually their population increased and, having proved themselves by

From "Carta de Fray Toribio de Motolinía," in *Colección de documentos para la historia de México*. Ed. by Joaquin García Icazbalceta (Mexico: J. M. Andrade, 1858), vol. I, pp. 253–61, 267. [Editor's translation.]

their superior ability and greater capacity to be more advanced than the former inhabitants, they gradually became masters of this land of Anahuac, which is its proper name.

After many years, Indians known as Mexicans settled the land. This name was taken from, or given to them by, an idol or principal god brought with them, whose name was Mexitle, known also as Texcatlipuca. This was the idol or demon most generally worshipped in these parts and to whom a great many men were sacrificed. These Mexicans established themselves in New Spain by war, but the principal overlords of this land were still the Culhuas, located in a town called Culhuacan, which is two leagues from Mexico. Later, also by war, dominion was exercised by a warlord and his people known as Ascapulco (Azcapatzalco), located one league from Mexico. This I have written in length to Count Benavente, explaining the rites and old customs of this land.

Let it be known to Your Majesty that at the time the Marquis del Valle [Hernando Cortés] entered this land, God our Father was very displeased that men suffered such horrible deaths, and that the demon, our adversary, was well-served by the great idolatries and cruel homicides that were continually practiced. The predecessor of Moteczuma, master of Mexico, called Abizozi (Ahuizotl), offered in sacrifice, in one temple ritual lasting three or four days, eight thousand four hundred men. These were lined up along four streets in four lines and then marched to the altar of sacrifice. When the Christians arrived in this New Spain they found in all the towns and provinces many dead men, more than ever before, murdered and sacrificed before the idols. Every day and every hour throughout the land they offered human blood to the demons, not to mention the many other sacrifices and services that were always made to the demons in public, not only in the temples (which almost covered the land) but also on the roads, in all of the houses, and by all of the people who entered into the services of the demons and idols.

Therefore, we must impede and remove these and other abominations, sins, and offenses that were publicly committed against God and our neighbors, and plant our holy Catholic faith and raise the cross of Jesus Christ everywhere, and the confession of His holy name. God has now laid the groundwork for the conversion of these people, where so many souls have been and are being saved every day, and has built so many churches and monasteries (the Franciscans alone have more than fifty inhabited by friars, not counting those of Guatemala and Yucatan) that this will be a land where peace and justice will abound. If Your Majesty could see how Easter and other paschal festivities are celebrated in New Spain, and how devoutly the activities of Holy Week, Sundays, and other celebrations are carried out, you would offer a thousand praises and thanks to God. Las Casas is wrong in saying what he says, writes, and publishes. Hereafter he will have to show by his zeal and works that he has helped the Indians and not hindered them.

I humbly beseech Your Majesty, by the grace of God, that (now that the Lord has discovered the land of Florida nearby, that from the river Panuco, which is part of Mexico, to the big river of Florida, where Captain De Soto travelled for more than five years, there is less than eighty leagues — which in our times and especially in this land is like eight leagues — and beyond the river of Florida there are also many towns, so that even the actual distance is less) Your Majesty, in the love of God, will have pity on those souls [in Florida] and compassion and pain for the offenses that are practiced there against God. Stop the sacrifices and idolatry that are made to the demons, and send a man of God and captain of the holy Church as soon as possible and by the best means in order that these faithless Indians may have the holy Gospel preached to them. And not in the manner Las Casas arranged, which gained nothing and added to Your Majesty's expense by providing and supplying a ship costing two or three thousand pesos, in which some Dominicans were sent to preach to the Indians of Florida with the instructions that he gave them. They docked at the port and before they had an opportunity to move inland they were attacked and half of them killed. The rest made it back to the ship where they had to relate the incident and how they escaped.

For this proposal Your Majesty will not have to spend much nor send much from Spain, only order it, and I trust in our Lord that within a short time great spiritual and temporal progress will follow. Here in New Spain there is more help than is needed, because there are many friars with experience who, if sent, would go obediently and would undertake any risk in order to save those souls. Likewise, there are many Spaniards, with cattle and horses, and all those who escaped from De Soto's expedition (which is more than a few) who wish to return to Florida, for the richness of the land. This expedition would be very good for this land because it would be an opportunity for the many lazy ones, whose inactivity causes them to think and do evil. This is the second thing that I, poor servant, beg of you on behalf of God.

The third thing is to beg Your Majesty, for the love of God, to command the lawyers, both of your councils and of the universities, to find out whether or not the conquistadores and *encomenderos* and merchants of this New Spain may receive the sacrament of penance and the other sacraments without their having to present a written public document under oath. Because Las Casas affirms that without this and other measures they cannot be absolved; and he imposes so many conditions on the confessors that there is nothing left but to send them all to hell. For this reason, it is necessary that this matter be taken up with the Pope, because it would help some of us — who have baptized more than 300,000 souls, and married and buried as many more, and confessed a great multitude besides — to know, since we have confessed ten or twelve of these conquistadores, whether they and we are both going to hell.

Las Casas says that everything the Spaniards have here is ill-gotten, even when they have earned it. There are many laborers and tradesmen and others here who gain their livelihood through work and sweat. And so that what is said and printed may be better understood, Your Majesty may recall that five or six years ago I was ordered by Your Majesty and your Council of the Indies to collect certain confessionals, hand-written by the friars, that Las Casas had left here in the Indies. I found all the copies I could among the Franciscans and gave them to Don Antonio de Mendoza, your viceroy, and he burned them, because they contained false and scandalous statements. Now, in the last ships that have arrived in New Spain some of these same confessionals have come printed and have caused no little uproar and scandal in this country, because many times in them he calls the conquistadores and *encomenderos* and merchants tyrants, robbers, violators, rapers, and predatory beasts. He says that they have always tyrannized and today are still tyrannizing the Indians, and also that all the tributes of the Indians are and have been taken unjustly and tyrannically. If such were the case Your Majesty's conscience would be in a fine shape, for Your Majesty has half or more of all the principal provinces and towns of New Spain, and the *encomenderos* and conquistadores have no more than Your Majesty gives them.

The Indians should be moderately taxed and should be well-treated and cared for, just as, by the grace of God, almost all of them are today, and they should be taught doctrine and given justice. This also is done, but nevertheless, Las Casas says all the above and more in such a way that his principal insults are directed against Your Majesty. He condemns the lawyers of your council, frequently calling them thieves and tyrants. He also insults and condemns all those who are or have ever been in New Spain, ecclesiastics as well as laymen, and Your Majesty's prelates and Audiencias. Certainly the Marques del Valle, Bishop Don Sebastián Ramírez, Don Antonio de Mendoza, and Don Luis de Velasco (who is governing now with the *oidores*), have ruled and governed and are governing very well, both the Spanish community and the Indians. Truly, for the few canons that Las Casas has studied, he presumes a great deal, and his disorder seems very great and his humility small. He thinks that everyone else is wrong and he alone is right, for he has literally said: All the conquistadores have been robbers and rapers, and more adept at evil and cruelty than men have ever been, as is manifest to all the world. This refers to all the conquistadores, he says, without any exception whatever. Now Your Majesty knows the instructions and commands carried by those who go on new conquests, and that they try hard to keep them, and that they are of as good a life and conscience as Las Casas, and with more commendable zeal.

I am surprised that Your Majesty and your councils have been able to suffer so long such a tiresome, turbulent, unreasonable, boisterous troublemaker, who in religious habit is just as unruly, ill-mannered, insulting, harmful, and restless. I knew Las Casas for fifteen years before he came to this country. Once he started out for the land of Peru but, unable to reach his destination, he stopped in Nicaragua, staying there for only a short time. From there he came to Guatemala and remained even less time; afterward he was in the province of Oaxaca, but did not stay long there either. After landing in Mexico he went to the monastery of Santo Domingo, but soon got enough of that and again turned to wandering about with his trouble-making and disturbances, always writing accusations and rumors, looking for the evils and cruelties that the Spaniards had committed throughout this land in order to distort and

exaggerate the evils and sins that have been committed. And in all this he seemed to cherish the role of our adversary, although he considered himself to be more zealous and just than other Christians, and even more than the missionaries. All the time he scarcely concerned himself with religion!

Once he was talking with some friars and told them that what they were doing was too little, that they had not suffered nor shed their blood. However, the least of them was a much better servant of God than was Las Casas, and served Him better and watched over more souls and had more religion and virtue than he, in spite of all of his perfection. His dealings have all been with a few malcontents to get them to tell him things he could write in support of his passionate feeling against the Spaniards, and to show them that he greatly loves the Indians and that he alone wishes to defend and favor them more than anyone. In this he busied himself a short while here, except when he was using them as carriers and abusing them himself.

Las Casas landed at the city of Tlaxcala as a simple friar with twenty-seven or thirty-seven Indian carriers, called *tamemes*. At that time certain bishops and prelates were examining a bull of Pope Paul's concerning marriage and baptism, and he silenced us and forbade us to baptize adult Indians. But an Indian who had asked for baptism many times and was very well prepared, catechized, and taught, travelled three or four days' journey to us to be baptized. So I, along with many friars, begged Las Casas to baptize that Indian who had come so great a distance and, after we had beseeched him many times, he consented but demanded many preparatory conditions for the baptism, as if he alone knew more than the rest, when really the Indian was well-prepared. So, since he said he would baptize him, he put on his surplice and stole, and three or four of us friars went with him to the door of the church where the Indian was kneeling.

Then I don't know what nonsense struck him, but he refused to baptize the Indian, and left us and went away. I then said to Las Casas: "How is it, Father, that all the zeal and love which you say you have for the Indians results only in using them as carriers and in running around writing about the Spaniards and annoying the Indians? Why, Your Grace alone uses more Indian carriers than twenty friars; and, since you will not baptize or teach a single Indian, it would be well if you paid some of those overworked carriers of yours!" At that time, as I have said, he had some twenty-seven or thirty-seven carriers with him — I do not recall the exact number — and mostly they were carrying accusations against the Spaniards and other such nonsense. When he went to Spain and returned as a bishop, he brought one hundred and twenty Indian carriers, without paying them anything. Now he is trying to get Your Majesty and the Council of the Indias to forbid any Spaniard to use Indian carriers, even if he pays them well (as now they are paid everywhere), and the only ones now used are three or four to carry bedding and food, for they are no longer to be found on the roads.

Afterward he always went about anxiously engaged in the business of important people, and especially the business of getting himself made Bishop of Chiapa. Since he did not negotiate what he had promised, Father Friar Domingo de Betanzos, who was well acquainted with the matter, wrote him a long and public letter in which he described his life, the disturbances and troublemaking, the harm, and the damage which he had done with his reports and indiscreet zeal wherever he went — especially in Peru where he had been the cause of many scandals and even deaths. Even where he is now he never ceases doing the same, pretending that he is doing it out of his zeal for the Indians. But, based upon a letter that someone has written him from here — and not always true — and one item in particular, which he has shown Your Majesty and the Council, he has tried to obtain a general decree and thus upset and destroy the government and the state here. This is what his zeal is all about.

When he became a bishop and arrived at Chiapa, which is the head of his bishopric, the people of that city received him — because Your Majesty had sent him — with great love and humility. They established him in his church with the pallium, and loaned him money to pay the debts he had incurred in Spain. A few days later he excommunicated them, imposed fifteen or sixteen new laws and conditions for the confession, and then left them and moved on. Betanzos wrote to him about this saying that he was making goats out of his sheep and had put the cart before the horse. Then he went to a kingdom called Vera Paz, which he says is such a great place with an infinite number of people. This country is close to Guatemala and I have travelled there visiting and teaching — very close in fact because I was within two days journey of it — and it is not one-tenth as large as is claimed there. One monastery here in Mexico teaches and visits ten times as many people as there are in the whole kingdom of Vera Paz. The Bishop of Guatemala is a good witness of this, and I have seen the people [of Vera Paz] and they are of less significance than any others.

Later, Las Casas became restless and came to Mexico, where he requested permission from the viceroy to return to Spain. Even though his request was denied he nevertheless went without it, leaving behind without hope those entrusted to his care, both Indians and Spaniards. Regardless of the fact that he had legitimate reasons to go to Spain, he should have returned soon and worked among his sheep for at least two or three years instead of abandoning them, even though the Spaniards considered them incorrigible, for he presumed to be the holiest and wisest of all the bishops.

Two clergymen visited Chiapa four years after Las Casas' departure and they saw Spaniards who, at the brink of death, were denied confession and were not absolved from their sins because of the rules laid down by Las Casas. There was no one to baptize the Indian children who sought baptism except for the two friars, who baptized many. Las Casas remarks in his confessional that the owners of *encomiendas* are obliged to teach the Indians who are under their jurisdiction — and this is right. It was later said that the *encomenderos* did not carry out their responsibility, but this is not true, for many Spaniards accepted this responsibility and taught the Indians according to their ability. Many other *encomenderos* have procured the services of friars and taken them to the towns where they have taught and administered the holy sacraments to the Indians. Time was when the Spaniards did not wish to see clergymen or friars in their towns. But for some time now many Spaniards have been getting friars, and their Indians have built monasteries to accommodate them. At the same time the *encomenderos* provide them with food, clothing, and vestments. It is no wonder that Las Casas does not know this, for he made no effort to learn anything but the evil, and not the good.

Las Casas was restless in New Spain and did not learn the language of the Indians, nor did he humble himself and try to teach them. He spent his time writing about the sins committed everywhere by the Spaniards. This is what he loves most, but it is certainly not the occupation that will get him to heaven. Furthermore, what he has written is untrue and unsubstantiated. If we look and take note of the atrocious sins and crimes committed alone in the city of Seville, and see the number of people who were brought to justice during the last thirty years, we will find more and uglier crimes and wickedness than those committed in all of New Spain since the conquest thirty-three years ago. If there is to be compassion for this land, it should be for the city of Chiapa and its inhabitants, because after Las Casas became bishop it deteriorated into ruins, both temporally and spiritually, for he infected everything. I pray to God that it will not be said of him that he left the souls in the hands of wolves and ran away: *quia mercenarius est et non pastor, et non pertinet ad eum de ovibus.*

Whenever a bishop renounces his bishopric to leave a church which he had received as his spouse, great and solemn is his obligation and greater should be his attachment to it than to any other profession of lower status. In order to leave and abandon it there must be a great cause, and wherever such a cause is absent the renunciation is apostasy. To apostatize from the high and perfect state of a bishop is worse than anything. If this were to happen because of grave sickness or in order to intern oneself in a strict monastery whereby the individual would never again see man or engage in mundane affairs, even then we do not know whether God would forgive such a bishop. But, to become an attorney of law, and to try to have himself made attorney at Court, as Las Casas now does, in order to make it appear that the Indians are demanding him as their protector! When the letter in which this was ordered was read in a congregation of Franciscans, they all burst out laughing and could not respond to such madness. He will not show the letters from the chapter or congregation of Franciscans there, but he still tries to induce people here to send him money and commissions.

Who will be pleased by these things? I believe Your Majesty will abhor them, because it is clearly a temptation of our adversary to cause unrest for you and for others. Your Majesty should have him locked up in a monastery so that he will not make more trouble. Otherwise I am afraid he will go to Rome and be the cause of disturbance at the Roman court. . . .

I say all this in the hope of serving Your Majesty and letting you know what I think of this country and what I have seen in the thirty years since we came here by command of Your Majesty. . . . Receive this letter, Your Majesty, in the spirit in which I write it, and let it not have more weight than is reasonable, just, and right.

I remain the least of your chaplains, praying God that His Grace will always dwell in the blessed soul of Your Majesty so that you will always do His holy will. Amen.

Las Casas and the Black Legend

RAMÓN MENÉNDEZ PIDAL

Spain's ranking historian and modern humanist was born in La Coruña in March 1869. From 1899 to 1939 he was professor of Romance philology at the University of Madrid, and during the last decade of that period was also president of the Real Academia Española. He served for an extended period as head of the Centro de Estudios Históricos, and was founding editor of *Revista de Filología Española*. Above all, he is known as a penetrating and persuasive writer on Spain and Spanish history, emphasizing always the native roots of Spanish culture and the conservatism and continuity of Spanish history. His distinguished works range over many subjects, the most influential being *Orígenes del Español* (1926); *La España del Cid*, 2 vols. (1929); *Los Españoles en la historia y en la literatura* (1951); and *Romancero hispánico*, 2 vols. (1953). The following article is a brief résumé of his most recent contribution, *El Padre Las Casas: su doble personalidad* (1963).

EVERY CONQUERING NATION provokes complaint and dislikes from the conquered, who protest against habitual administrative immoralities and against cruelties in the use of force. Let us remember the anti-French black legend conceived in Spain during the shooting and plundering of 1808, when Don Manuel José Quintana denounced "the ferocious vandals of the Seine."

The anti-Spanish black legend was born during the domineering expansion of Spain, beginning with the conquest of the kings of Aragon in Sicily and Sardinia, as Sverker Arnoldsson demonstrates in his authoritative book published at Göteborg in 1960. This primarily anti-Catalonian legend existed in Italy from early times.

Twenty-five years after the Sicilian Vespers (1282), the legend was well propagated when one of its topics was solemnly enunciated by Dante in his "Divine Comedy" with the verse "l'avara povertà di Catalogna." During the entire fifteenth century the Catalans were showered with accusations about their being misers, dishonest in their dealings, members of an impure race, and "circumcised pigs." The Catalan domination was described by Pontano as "insolent in the extreme."

Next came the supremacy of Castille, and the Italian legend was superseded by a German anti-Spanish legend, resulting from the Schmalkaldic war, 1546–1552, also called the "War of the Spaniards" ("der Spanierkrieg") because of the pre-

Ramón Menéndez Pidal, "El padre Las Casas y la leyenda negra," *Cuadernos Hispanoamericanos*, No. 157 (January, 1963), pp. 5–14. Reprinted by permission of the Instituto de Cultura Hispanica [Editor's translation].

dominance of Spaniards in the army of Charles V. Among the many songs in which the Germans expressed their feelings about that passionate war, very few praised the Spaniards. The majority censured them as being haughty, dishonest, corrupt fornicators, disloyal, and treacherous; "we shall not be governed by wicked Italians nor vile Spaniards who come with the Emperor in the name of the Pope."

Nothing remained, either of the particular anti-Catalonian phase of the legend or of the general anti-Spanish, except a few condemning judgments formulated by some writer of satirical songs that soon evaporated into thin air. These opinions and songs, having long passed the period when they were written, are remembered only by a few erudite historians. But the Spain of Philip II presented a better target than did the kingdom of Aragon or the empire of Charles V, and produced many scandalous books on the theme of cruelty. The Inquisition provided the first serviceable theme for attack. It was denounced to the world by a fugitive of that tribunal, pseudonymously known as Reginaldus Gonsalius Montanus, in his book *Sanctae Inquisitionis Hispanicae artes aliquot detectae* (Heidelberg, 1567), and years later denounced again by another fugitive, the famous Antonio Pérez.

During this time another theme of major political interest was exploited. Girólamo Benzoni, of Milán, had published his *Historia del Mondo Nuovo* (Venice, 1565), inspired by the history of Gómara, but emphasizing the aspects of cruelty which the Spanish chronicler had denounced. Thirteen years later Benzoni's book began to spread, and in 1578 it was translated into Latin, in 1579 into French and Dutch, and later into other languages. However, Benzoni was not the first to scandalize Europe with the cruelty of the Spaniards in America, for in 1571 an anonymous writer in the Andean valley of Yucay informed the viceroy of Perú that the book *Destruición de las Indias* and others printed by the friar Bartolomé de las Casas in 1552 were in

the hands of all the enemies of the Catholic Church, both English and French, and that they were attacking Spanish ships on the sea and entering by way of rivers in America to assault the roads and territory inland. A little later, in the year 1578, precisely when Benzoni's book was being translated into Latin, the book *Destruición* was also being translated into Latin and Dutch, with many segments of other works by Las Casas; and in 1579 the whole of Las Casas' works was translated into French.

In January 1579 the Seven United Provinces adopted protestantism by the Union of Utrecht, thereby maintaining war with Spain. From then on, and much later, during the anti-Catholic Thirty Years' War (1618–1648), reprints of the *Destruición* and other texts by Las Casas became innumerable. We know of twenty-one editions in Dutch, eight in Italian, six in French, four in German and two in English. All the enemies of Spanish Catholicism carried on their shoulders the "Reverend Bishop Don Friar Bartolomé de las Casas," who dedicated every line of his work to describing the bloody brutality of the Spaniards; terrifying to the point of being even grotesque, impossible, and absurd — but sufficient to blacken and to definitively consolidate the black legend. During the eighteenth century the printing of new editions diminished, but the legend took another decisive step, establishing itself in Hispanic America historiography when, at the beginning of the nineteenth century, the printing of new editions was resumed in the original Spanish language in order to kindle the war of the American liberators against Spain. A new edition of the Spanish text was printed in London (1812), in Bogotá (1813), and many times after that until 1898 when it was reprinted in English in order to interest the North Americans in the independence of Cuba. But even then Las Casas' incendiary mission had not burned out, for in 1936, in order to justify the genocide practiced in Europe by the Nazis in their anti-Christian annihilation of other races, the *Destruición* was translated into German once more, placing, *under the sign of the cross*, the mass extermination of the American Indians — witnessed by no less than a Catholic prelate, the Bishop of Chiapa. The Nazis, under the sign of the twisted cross, would destroy the inferior races.

The uniqueness of the black legend of Spain lies in fact that it was more violent and more lasting than those legends written about other countries. Books written against the Spanish Inquisition, or Benzoni's book written against the colonization of the New World, would have been read only by scholars and the Spanish legend would have vanished and faded away like those of other countries if it had not been for the slanted book of Las Casas. That book had two qualities making it superior to the others. In the first place, its brief length and its extraordinary depth, dedicating all its lines, word for word, to the description of colossal cruelties, made it interesting reading and contributed to its rapid circulation. Secondly, because it was written by a Spanish bishop, the writings were accepted as authoritative and used as an effective weapon by the enemies of Spain against Catholicism and the Spanish crown. By this, Las Casas was responsible for the intensification, solidification and propagation of the black legend against Spain. For four centuries, the *Destruición* has been widely accredited, accompanied at the same time by the slow demoralization and collapse of the Spanish empire. This extraordinary discrediting is unparalleled in the history of any other nation.

Because of the exceptional political value of the *Destruición,* Spain is known in the history of European colonization as the only destroyer of the American Indians, when in fact it was the sole colonizer to worry about preserving them as a unit, the only colonizer in the sixteenth century to undertake measures to repress the prevalent racial discrimination toward nations of inferior culture. Spain came to assert scrupulously equality before the law, even to the point of legislating, in order to protect the weak, that an offense committed against an Indian was punishable with greater severity than an offense against a Spaniard.

But at any rate, the exceptional anti-Spanish black legend is a fact that took four centuries to complete and is therefore difficult to reduce to historical truth, although many have worked to expel the testimony and spirit of Las Casas from Hispanic American historiography. This critical re-examination began with an emigrant Catalan Jesuit, the abbot Don Juan Nuix (*Reflessioni imparziali,* Venice, 1780), who considered the anti-Las Casian corrections of the Scot, W. Robertson, insufficient. Since then many others have continued along the same lines, for example, Ch. F. Lummis (*The Spanish Pioneers,* New York, 1894), J. Juderías (*La leyenda negra,* 1914), Constantino Bayle, S.J. (*España en Indias,* Vitoria, 1924), the Argentine R. D. Carbia (*Historia de la Leyenda Negra,* Madrid, 1944), and many more. I believe that fighting the legend head-on and in its entirety runs the risk of a reaction, resulting in the fabrication of a "golden legend," just as false in its apologetic sense as the black legend is in its vituperation. It is better to lay aside the ugly writings and to clarify descriptively the happenings of the conquest and the Hispanic American administration, looking objectively at its accomplishments and defects, endeavoring to forget that the black legend exists.

Personally, I have wanted to study the biography of Las Casas, the great architect of that legend, a biography that has always been written with a spirit of passion and praise. I have wondered about Las Casas' exaggerations, known to all but explained by none, and desired to examine the specific elements of that exaggeration. In order to accomplish this, it was necessary for me to study the personality of Las Casas from new documents, and I found this biography to be very different from the usual biographies filled with extraordinary Las Casian triumphs over wicked persecutors. There were no such things.

From 1502 to 1514 Friar Bartolomé de Las Casas came to the islands of Santo Domingo and Cuba as a soldier, later as a priest, in charge of an *encomienda* of Indians. The encomienda was an institution by which a Spaniard would benefit from the many jobs carried out by Indians, in exchange for teaching them Christian doctrine and making them live in villages, thus changing their savage existence to a sedentary life of remunerative labor. In 1511 the Dominican missionaries preached against and condemned the many abuses committed by Spanish *encomenderos* against the Indians, but the clergyman Las Casas at that time defended the legitimacy of such an institution.

In 1514 a sudden change came over Las Casas when he felt that he was called by God to preach against the *encomienda* as an unjust institution. According to this new calling, the *encomienda* was unacceptable because the only legitimate inhabitants of the New World were the Indians, and the only purpose for the Spaniards' coming was as missionaries to convert the Indians to the Christian faith, without the help of the military. In order to carry out his peaceful colonization without arms, Las Casas obtained from Charles V the territory of Cumaná (Venezuela), where he took his friars and colonists in 1521. But, at the first moment of carelessness the Spaniards were killed by the Indians and the experiment was over. The biographies written about Las Casas want to absolve him from all blame, but even the most enthusiastic recognize that he neglected all the necessary preparations for such an enterprise.

Being much afflicted by this disaster, the clergyman Las Casas became a Dominican Friar in 1523. He spent sixteen years of monastic retreat on the island of Santo Domingo and a little time in Guatemala and Nicaragua, although always yearning to return to Spain to plead his case before the Court and the Council of the Indies against the *encomienda*. This institution had already been reformed and purified by then, both in theory and in practice, since the Dominicans of Santo Domingo had been reproving it since 1511, but Las Casas continued to condemn the institution for the rest of his life, even against the wishes of other theologians and missionaries. Similar to his condemnation of the *encomienda*, Las Casas preached against all types of Indian slavery. It must be said here that although the enslavement of prisoners in just wars was accepted by jurists and theologians, and even by Las Casas himself, he maintained that all wars against Indians were unjust. In this belief he again disagreed with all the other theologians, whose principal leader was Friar Francisco de Vitoria (the founder of modern international law), for they all recognized various cases of just wars in the Indies and, therefore, many cases of possible slavery.

In spite of Las Casas' repeated petitions for a hearing before the Council, that body did not summon him, and his Dominican superiors detained him for those sixteen years without authorization to make the trip. Undoubtedly the disaster at Cumaná had discredited him completely.

But eventually, without any authorization, Las Casas reached Spain in 1540, and in 1542 managed to obtain an audience with the Council in Valladolid while Charles V was in residence there. Charles V at this time was plagued with doubts about the legitimacy and morality of his domain in America, because of the opinions of many clergymen who accused the Spaniards of abuses and cruelties in the Indies. Friar Bartolomé surpassed them all in his passionate and eloquent delivery, claiming that the recent conquest of Peru ought to be abandoned because the Incas were the only legitimate owners of the land. Charles V was inclined to give up his claims of Peru, but the great theologian

Francisco de Vitoria persuaded him that
an exclusively Indian domination of the
New World was indefensible, and that if
the Spaniards were to withdraw from Peru
Christianity would disappear there also.

Las Casas became insistent before the
Council and brandishing his opus, the *Destruición de las Indias,* like a terrible
weapon, he accused all the discoverers of
the New World, one by one, of horrible
crimes, violent acts and robbery, and of
being the instigators of the death of twenty
million Indians. Such accusations were
made for the purpose of prohibiting explorations by soldiers. Again his cries fell on
deaf ears, for his exaggeration of the atrocities was evident and the fact remained
that Charles V continued to grant rights
of discovery to the military. These rights
were granted with moderation for a number of years, imposing on the captains the
obligation to act in accordance with the
wishes of the missionaries, who were
charged to authorize only defensive wars.

The great jurists and theologians, like
Vitoria and many governors with a true
sense of justice, enacted and put into practice some very moderate laws, approved by
Charles V and sanctioned in Barcelona on
the 20th of November 1542. These so-
called *New Laws* restricted the *encomiendas* and the practice of Indian slavery.
However, even these moderate laws pro-
voked bitter criticism from Las Casas because they contradicted his juridical opinions.

In spite of his opposition to these laws,
in spite of his condemnation of the discoveries and the Spanish population of the
Indies, and in spite of his opposition to
existing laws approved by the jurists, theologians and missionaries, Las Casas exercised great influence on both the Council
and the magistrates, during the years 1542–
1547. In 1543 Charles V appointed him
bishop of Chiapa (Guatemala) so he could
practice his theories in that diocese. Once
he became bishop, Las Casas, in order to
implant his juridical ideas into his diocese,
wrote a *Confessional* with Draconian standards, according to which a confessor should
not allow any Spaniard in the Indies to
confess unless he submitted first to certain
previous guarantees. Thus if the Spaniard
had any Indian slaves, they should be set
free immediately, and if he was an *encomendero,* he must put his entire estate,
formally notarized, into the hands of the
confessor who would in turn restore to the
Indians all the tributes that had been taken
from them. Only after these requirements
were met could the confession begin,
whether the penitent was in good health
or whether he was on the brink of death.
This, of course, was contrary to existing
laws which upheld the practice of slavery
and the *encomienda,* and upon application
in the diocese of Chiapa this Confessional
caused excommunications and continued
disturbances among the members of the
diocese and also in the Audiencia of Guatemala. So bad was the situation that the
new bishop only remained in his diocese
a few months in the years 1545–1546, and
even this short stay in office became possible only after he himself had suspended
application of his absurd confessional.
Finally, his juridical doctrines were unani-
mously rejected in a conference of prelates held in Mexico in 1546. Let us say
by way of summary that during the few
months of episcopal leadership Las Casas
did nothing more than excite disturbance,
issue excommunications right and left to
the members of his diocese, to the viceroy,
to the presidents and to the jurors of the
Audiencia, and propose juridical theories
that were rejected by all the bishops of the
viceroyalty. With a feeling of dejection
and without any power, Las Casas abandoned his diocese forever, thus ending this
four-year period in which he had his greatest influence in American affairs.

From the age of seventy-three until his
death at ninety-two, having left America
for the last time and returned to Spain,
Las Casas lived the last twenty-one years
of his life in progressive mental depression.
This was the second period of great discredit for Las Casas, just as the one fol-

lowing the disaster of Cumaná, and now, although less extreme, he was submerged into deepening obscurity.

Nevertheless, at the beginning of this long period of discredit, Charles V, very scrupulous in moral matters, was still bothered by doubts of conscience and therefore arranged for Las Casas to discuss publicly his peculiar theories with the royal chronicler Juan Ginés de Sepúlveda, a partisan of the conquests. The disputation took place in Valladolid, in the years 1550 and 1551, before the Council of the Indies and many jurists and theologians. Biographies depict these disputes as another triumph for Las Casas. But the results of the extensive discussion were ambiguous, although in many ways favorable for Sepúlveda, and definitely condemning for Las Casas. The verdict of the four theologians, which was the main one, was divided: The Franciscan voted in favor of Sepúlveda, and the three eminent Dominicans, Friar Domingo de Soto, Melchor Cano and Bartolomé Carranza, did not vote in favor of Las Casas, even though he was a member of their order. Consequently, the Council and Charles V decided that the expeditions of discovery and pacification were to continue, although they were to be regulated more closely.

Las Casas, having retired to the convent of San Gregorio in Valladolid, suffered continued disappointments. At times he was forced to recognize that the Dominicans, Franciscans, and Brothers of Mercy worked piously in allowing some Indian slavery, in accordance with the laws, and he also discovered that his most intimate brothers in the faith repudiated the *Confessional* in the very diocese of Chiapa, and that they had discarded it everywhere. Later, during the succeeding years of his life as Las Casas found his closest missionary friends writing him in defense of the *encomienda* and contradicting his doctrines, he saw that he had been abandoned by all. Thus, in obscurity, Friar Bartolomé died in 1566. In conclusion, instead of a life of positive results, a life of efficient propaganda in favor of the Indians, a life of direct action against anti-slavery laws, we find a life wandering in a vacuum, barren.

What was the cause of this growing obscurity of Las Casas? The answer to the question is indicated in the account we have given. The doctrine of Las Casas was inapplicable in practice, not because it was in opposition to the laws of the kingdom, which should have been changed if they were unjust, but because it was an unsound doctrine out of touch with reality, coming from a confused mind. The action, the entire life of Las Casas, abounds in the inherent contradictions of vain fantasies, and in rigid application of his doctrine, forcing him to contradict himself on serious occasions. When he wanted to colonize Cumaná, without taking the necessary precautions, he had to turn to the Audiencia of Santo Domingo for armed men to aid him. In the short time he practiced his religious mission he had to appoint confessors who disregarded the norms of his confessional. While he was in the territory of Vera Paz carrying out his unarmed colonization, he started by using the Christianized Indian chiefs in place of the *encomenderos* and ended by asking the friars to make all-out war against the aggressive Indians.

We should bear in mind that we must distinguish two patterns of behavior in Las Casas. There is a normal Las Casas, an enthusiastic man who gives up a life of comfort and genuine ambitions in order to submit himself to asceticism in its strictest form. Consecrated to the defense of a noble cause, he devoted to it all of his moral and physical energy, unabated even in the last years of his long life. This advocate of the Indians, the most diligent of all those who carried that honorable title, worked with vigorous effort. He was the most energetic in making trips, reports, petitions, admonitions and disputes; he wrote more than anyone, and he proved himself to be one of the ablest and most zealous propagandists. So passionate was he that his contempo-

raries liken him to a "fire that burns everything" or to a "master of persuasion." He
was consulted by many as a person of
acknowledged experience and he was respected by all — even those who repudiated
his doctrines.

But alongside this normal Las Casas, of
exemplary life, there is an abnormal Las
Casas. From the very moment of his conversion in 1514, he showed signs of mental
abnormality, manifested in continuous unreasonable contradictions. In 1514 he undertook an ascetic life of stern renuncia-
tions, but contradicted the humble self-
sacrifice, which is essential to the ascetic,
by exhibiting greed, vanity, conceit and
praising himself for his sanctity and his
superior intelligence to all those who surrounded him. And keep in mind that this
arrogance, according to the warnings of the
Ascetics of the Desert, widely read in the
sixteenth century, was the insidious sin by
which the devil would overcome the virtuous man who had not committed any other
offense. In spite of his asceticism, Las Casas
was a Sevillian braggart who in his boast-
ing did everything possible to increase the
facetious fame "enjoyed" by his countrymen.

There is another notable contradiction.
Las Casas affirmed that all the money
brought from America was stolen and that
the Spaniards were obligated to return it
to the Indians. Nevertheless, during his
entire life he collected a pension ranging
from 300 to 500,000 maravedís, paid from
rent received from the Indies. We would
like to excuse his thinking that he justified
his pension because it was used for a good
purpose, even though he collected stolen
money to preach against stealing money;
but this cannot be justified with Las Casas,
since he condemned the whole charitable
groundwork laid by the Spaniards in America.

Another illogical contradiction, about
which Las Casas was as persistent as on
the previous one, was that of slavery. He
asserted that all the Indian slaves should
be set free, because the wars by which they
were enslaved were all, *without exception,*
unjust. But he considered *all* Negroes as
legal slaves, and he greatly lamented the
envy of millions of Negro slaves in America by affirming that the Portuguese, who
enslaved them, were waging just wars in
Africa, *all without exception.*

Let us give an example of another contradiction in his erudite character — the
defacing of scientific data. In his apology
of the Indies, Las Casas claimed that the
island of Hispaniola, or Santo Domingo, is
larger than England, and by this he proceeded to contradict the data given about
England by Diodorus, Caesar, Pliny and
San Isidore. According to Las Casas, all
these authors were mistaken; he knew this
because of "real experience" in the art of
navigation — quoting out of thin air, as
Las Casas frequently liked to do — he was
certain that the island of Hispaniola is
larger. And if we ask ourselves, why Las
Casas, in order to emphasize the fact that
Hispaniola is a very large island, engaged
in an absurd comparison with England, or
why he involved himself in a foolish discussion of numerical figures, we must recol-
lect a fortunate psychological intuition of
Cervantes. Recall that Don Quijote, while
in the Sierra Morena, wanted to commit
the one hundred insane acts that Orlando
performed when he learned of the in-
fidelity of the beautiful Angélica. When
Sancho replied that Dulcinea had not given
him any motive for such acts of insanity,
Don Quijote reminded him that therein
lies the finesse: "for what merit is there in
a knight-errant going mad for a good
cause? The real test is to lose one's mind
without a motive," in order thus to be of
better service to one's lady. Las Casas
could have been satisfied letting England
be larger than Hispaniola, but the real test
was to lose one's mind without a motive in
order to be of better service to the grandeur
of the Indies. Abundant cases such as this
tell us that Las Casas not only exaggerated
the praise to himself and the Indies, he
fatally and unnecessarily deformed the
facts that he wanted to depreciate and

despise, in order to favor the prejudices cultivated by himself.

Let us add, finally, the most serious contradiction. Las Casas was a virtuous friar, but in order to defend the Indians from the cruelties of the Spaniards, Las Casas employed a great part of his time in slandering the conquistadores with deceit and false charges, recognized even by those biographers who most admired the virtue of this zealous advocate of the Indians.

These monstrous defamations can hardly be understood in a man so seemingly virtuous, unless they result from a defective psychological constitution. Likewise, the many other doctrinal and intellectual contradictions are incomprehensible in such a scholarly man, given to study, meditation, and polemics, unless we see in him an abnormal mentality. The virtuous Las Casas is not at the same time the defamer; the studious Las Casas is not at the same time the malicious distorter of facts. Las Casas was a mental case, a paranoiac who, of necessity and involuntarily, falsified the true facts.

Being a layman in psychology and psychiatry, I use the term "paranoiac" in its common sense, I expose and deal with all the abnormal traits that the biographers fail to note in the life of this famous Dominican, and I submit them to the specialists that they may deal with them expertly. I hope that the future biographies of Las Casas will not be based, as they have been up until now, on the endless eulogies that biographers give him, and that the eminent Las Casas advocates will refrain from praising the scorn that Las Casas hurled on all those who disturbed the fantasies which he engendered. And I hope they do not go on believing that England is smaller than the island of Hispaniola. I hope that a severe criticism will be substituted for the usual incredible gullibility.

And thus I come to a close. I came to talk about Las Casas and the Black Legend, to say that we must not pay much attention to that legend, that lamentable mishap of Spain. Instead of exploding against the slander of Las Casas, the great inventor of Spain's discredit, let us try to explain it. And, in the final analysis, we must applaud the freedom that Charles V and Philip II gave to Las Casas to publish his accusations, even though these accusations came from a sick and disordered mind. But we must at the same time lament that adequate rectifications were not made then, and lament, above all, that in the time of Philip III pusillanimity was so great that the rectification which Captain Vargas Manchura intended to publish was prohibited. Let us resign to this apathetic indifference, typically Spanish of course. Let us forget the Black Legend or the Golden Legend, and concentrate instead on the impartial historical criticism of our work in America, in order to shed light on our conduct in the past and in the present.

Menéndez Pidal versus Las Casas

LEWIS HANKE

Lewis Hanke's career as a Latin American historian has been varied and colorful. He was born in 1905, received his A.B. and A.M. degrees at North-western University, and his Ph.D. from Harvard. Since 1935 he has traveled widely in Latin America and in Spain, taught at Harvard, the University of Texas, the University of Hawaii, and the American University of Beirut. He has been director of the Hispanic Foundation at the Library of Congress, is a member of the board of trustees of the Hispanic Society of America, and for many years directed the Institute of Latin American Studies at the University of Texas. Since 1961 he has been professor of Latin American history at Columbia University. In addition to writing many books on aspects of the Spanish conquest (see bibliography) and on Latin American history, he has edited *The Hispanic American Historical Review*, the *Handbook of Latin American Studies*, and is general editor of a new series, *Borzoi Books on Latin America*.

BESIDE THE GREAT CATHEDRAL in Mexico City visitors observe a large statue of a friar and an Indian, with these words below:

> Stranger if you love virtue,
> Pause and venerate this man.
> This is Friar Bartolomé de Las Casas,
> Father of the Indians.

Other monuments of respect for this sixteenth-century Dominican stand in most Spanish American countries. But the visitor will find no monument to Las Casas in Madrid, where the most venerable and highly respected Spanish scholar, Don Ramón Menéndez Pidal, published in 1963 a large book attacking the Dominican and recording his passionate conviction that Las Casas was unworthy of such devotion, being instead a megalomaniac, an egotist, whose true villainy no one has until now fully plumbed despite the hundreds of publications written about him. Don Ramón has assumed the task of writing the "true history" of Las Casas as a patriotic

duty and in so doing has produced, at the age of 93, probably the most remarkable, most complete, and most carefully-planned of all the many assaults on the Dominican made in the last 450 years; that is, since 1514 when Las Casas first determined to defend the original inhabitants of the New World from what he considered to be the un-Christian despoliation and destruction of the Indians by his fellow countrymen. . . .

In the centuries since Las Casas on his deathbed summed up his life's work, he has seldom been taken at his own valuation as a modest defender of the Indians who, though he had accomplished little, had always been right in his action on their behalf. Disputes began during his own lifetime, and the Franciscan Toribio de Motolinía probably represented a large body of opinion in the Indies when he complained to the Emperor Charles V in 1555: "Truly, for the few canons Las Casas has studied he presumes a great deal, and his disorder seems very great and his

From Lewis Hanke, "More Heat and Some Light on the Spanish Struggle for Justice in the Conquest of America," *The Hispanic American Historical Review*, XLIV (1964), pp. 309–16, 319–22, 324–5, 328–30, 333–4, 338–40. Reprinted by permission of the author and Duke University Press. [All translations of Menéndez Pidal in this selection are by the editor.]

humility small; he thinks everyone is wrong and he alone is right."

Time has not wrought its usual softening influence; on the contrary, until today his memory has been kept fresh by keen and active disputation. The Dominican scholar Venancio D. Carro, who has done so much to elucidate the theological background of the conquest, goes so far as to say that the struggle for justice in America not only did not originate with Las Casas but that the controversy "developed and would have continued its course even though Las Casas had never lived." Another eminent Spanish scholar, Américo Castro, attributes such influence to the Dominican that he declares that his "anarchical doctrines" were largely responsible for the Spanish American revolutions that began in 1810; one "need not search for foreign ideas and influences to explain the independence of the Hispanoamerican colonies." Another writer asks whether Las Casas was not a *converso*, and the Soviet historian D. E. Micjnevich looks upon him as merely a kind of *rara avis* (*mirlo blanco*) among the Spanish clergy in America. And always there are writers who contemplate the many problems present in Latin America today and conclude, as does Paul Johnson in the London *New Statesman*, that "The origins of the continental *malaise* can be traced back to the Spanish conquistadores. It is impossible to be too critical of this mindless bunch of ruffians." Nor is this opinion confined to non-Hispanic writers. The Venezuelan Francisco J. Herrera Luque argues in a recent volume that the pressing social problems of his country may be traced back to the actions of 16th century Spaniards and treats the "*criminalidad,*" the "*patografía,*" and the "*sintomatología psiquiátrica*" of the conquistadores, and has a special chapter on "*Pizarro el esquizoide.*" Now that Don Ramón is stigmatizing Las Casas as a paranoic, perhaps we are on the verge of a psychiatric interpretation of the conquest.

Significantly enough, no official or religious group has come forward to claim ownership of Las Casas and exploit him for its own purposes, except for such *indigenistas* as exalt Indian virtues at the expense of the Spaniard. His own Dominican Order has paid little attention to him. Nor has the Order ever published any of his treatises or a single major work about him. Spain itself has been bitterly divided on his true worth. While America has on the whole considered him a noble figure, one of the most forthright denunciations in recent years was made by an Argentine historian. But the most sustained and the most uncompromising attack has been the recent volume by Don Ramón Menéndez Pidal.

It is a difficult work to review; indeed, a proper treatment of all the many topics included in it might require another volume of similar size. It is likely that no other life of Las Casas will be so widely discussed in this generation. The battle lines are already forming, and 10 years hence there will doubtless be so many items in print that another supplementary volume will be needed to bring the standard bibliography up to date. Many of these writers will enthusiastically support Don Ramón and his conviction, frequently stated, that previous biographers of Las Casas have obscured him by burning too much incense to his memory. Similarly one can see those who support Don Ramón already beginning to produce a powerful and pungent cloud of smoke offered to him, the great detractor. Those who oppose him, and there must be many even in Spain though they do not all see fit to publish their conviction, are doubtless preparing their broadsides. For Don Ramón reiterates over and over again that Las Casas was a hopelessly biased writer who simply could not tell the truth in describing Spanish action in America or the nature of the Indians. Although in some few respects a normal person, he was a propagandist rather than a thinker who incorporated in his works some Christian ideas, though at times incorrectly. Essentially, however, Las Casas was abnormal, declares Don Ramón, who employs his rich Castilian vocabulary in attempting to convey to the reader an idea of Las Casas' defects. . . .

Few new documents are offered to substantiate all these charges; the volume is rather a massive and carefully organized collection of what the opponents of Las Casas have been saying these past 450 years. The result is a magnificent example of tendentious writing by a practiced hand. Before examining in detail some of the more important propositions of the book, it would be well to consider briefly the spirit in which Don Ramón has written his study:

It was a disagreeable task, reluctantly undertaken, but it was his duty to perform it. After 400 pages devoted almost wholly to blasting Las Casas, he concludes: "I have nothing more to say. I have fulfilled an unpleasant duty demanded by historical criticism." One feels that Don Ramón has acted with the supreme confidence of an Inquisitor who has performed dutifully in the torture chamber.

Underneath the meticulous prose, the many footnote citations, the extensive quotations from Las Casas, and the frequent protestations of the most rigid and scientific impartiality one can see boiling an intense and unquenchable passion. One wonders whether Don Ramón did not perhaps absorb this passion from Las Casas himself. One Spanish biographer of Las Casas, Manuel José Quintana, emphasized the "electric nature" of the great Dominican's spirit and stated that it was almost impossible for anyone to consider his opinions and activities, even centuries after his death, without becoming affected by the passions they aroused.

Don Ramón exhibits at times the same "pathological dogmatism" which he discovers so basic in Las Casas. He has never done any original research in the field, but uses extensively the contributions of Marcel Bataillon, Manuel Giménez Fernández, Juan Pérez de Tudela, and others, although on many individual points differing from them, even dissenting at times from Bataillon, who is by no means an un-critical admirer of Las Casas. Don Ramón blandly gives his own opinions on many complicated institutions and events without troubling to explain how he has arrived at his conclusions. Sometimes facts and interpretations inconvenient to Don Ramón's thesis are not mentioned, either by design or ignorance. Indeed, on some questions one might apply to him the description Motolinía gave of Las Casas: "He thinks everyone is wrong and he alone is right." Some readers, unaware of the extensive literature on the history of Spain in America and eager to dispose of such an irritating figure as Las Casas, may be led astray by Don Ramón's assumption of omniscience when he asserts his opinion as gospel truth on all these highly controversial and sometimes still unresolved problems. Others will penetrate the veil of Don Ramón's apparent objectivity to see clearly the unmistakable prejudices of this cleverly written diatribe.

In presenting his version of Las Casas, Don Ramón reminds one both of a Royal Canadian mounted policeman stalking a criminal in the wastelands of the north and of a prosecuting attorney rather than of a historian at work. The tendentious and unhistorical nature of Don Ramón's brief against Las Casas discloses itself in several ways:

1. HIS USE OF SOURCES

When a writer praises Las Casas, as Antonio de Remesal does on the Vera Paz attempt to preach the faith peacefully in Guatemala, Don Ramón denounces him. When the same writer disagrees with Las Casas, Remesal becomes a "mente sana." Even when there is no documentary proof of the charge that Casas abandoned his bishopric — and Bataillon doubts the veracity of Remesal on this point — Don Ramón accepts the story and even criticizes Fabié and Pérez de Tudela because they do not follow Remesal. His attitude is a simple one: "I see no reason to doubt, whenever he presents non-glorifying aspects."

Don Ramón inveighs against biographers of Las Casas who do not question Remesal's account of Vera Paz or do not analyze the way he reaches his many favorable comments on Las Casas. Yet he himself uncritically accepts the Franciscan Toribio de Motolinía, one of his stellar witnesses because of Motolinía's famous letter of 1555 to Charles V against the Dominican. He does not mention that Motolinía was possibly biased, due to his resentment that Las Casas worked actively and successfully against his appointment as bishop, which Manuel María Martínez, O.P., sets forth in an article not cited though easily available. The reader is told that Motolinía describes the number of Indians killed in the conquest and condemned Spanish actions "a veces con exageración lascasiana," but pro-Indian remarks by Motolinía do not disturb Don Ramón's confidence in him.

The well-known scandal of 1539 when Las Casas refused to baptize an insufficiently prepared Indian at Motolinía's request is described in considerable detail. Don Ramón does not disclose that Las Casas was upheld, in his insistence that Indians be instructed in the faith before baptism, by a commission of Salamanca theologians headed by Francisco de Vitoria, for whom Don Ramón shows great respect in other sections of the volume. . . .

Perhaps enough has been said to indicate that Don Ramón draws upon the great quantity of sources on the Spanish conquest captiously and in the spirit of a lawyer determined to win a case. Such a use of sources may be permissible or at least expected in the courtroom, but can one who aims at discovering historical truth employ such a questionable method?

2. HIS ATTITUDE TOWARD INDIANS

One wonders whether Don Ramón has ever seen an Indian, or been moved by the great drama of the confrontation in a New World of Spaniards with the many kinds of Indians ranging from almost Stone Age folk to highly cultured groups. Certainly

he has an exalted opinion of European culture, for he exclaims at one point that:

. . . all the nations of the world are more or less penetrated by certain standardized principles of civilization, whose roots and principal resources are in Europe, that genial colonizing Europe which since earliest times has spread its advanced culture and well-being to the four corners of the globe. Today the Hindus, Chinese, Arabs — all the empires which played a brilliant role in the past — have joined with the nations of Africa and Oceania in the universal referendum with which today they tacitly approve Western multisecular colonialism as the principal unifier of humanity. They give their vote of approval in the same suit and tie in which the principal leaders of all races prefer to dress; they want to abandon their national costume in order to dress in Western style, and in like manner they clothe their spirit with Western ideas of liberty which they did not engender.

Don Ramón betrays almost as much indifference to the Indians as he accuses Las Casas of showing. Las Casas, he asserts without citing his source, never worked with the Indians as a missionary, and showed a marked repugnance toward them; his motive was not love for Indians but hatred toward the Spaniards: "legista a palo seco, no ama a los indios." Don Ramón, looking back several hundred years through rose-tinted spectacles, sees few dead Indians, though his much respected authority Motolinía declared that so many had died in the mines that the birds and crows that came to feast on their dead bodies greatly obscured the sun. He sees, rather, a scene of contentment and cultural advance:

To the discredit of the Las Casian utopia, there flourished a *New Spain,* where the governors and the missionaries practiced and purified the *encomienda,* where the Indians emerged from a prehistoric age of stone, with [cannibalism] and human sacrifices, to enter into a civilized world, enriched already with the best plants and useful animals of the Old World and with institutions created by the old culture, beginning with the *encomienda* and progressing to the printing press and colleges of higher learning; a New Spain where the rulers, bishops and missionaries planted [elementary schools], colleges, workshops and hospitals for the Indians.

Where did Don Ramón obtain his knowledge of Indian culture? He ignores such principal sixteenth-century writers as Diego de Landa and José de Acosta, and does not refer to the greatest of them all, the Franciscan Bernardino de Sahagún, except to quote him on the superiority of the natives of Asia to the Indians. The two witnesses he calls to testify on the nature of the Indians were carefully selected to prove his point, for both witnesses sang the same tune. He quotes the Dominican Tomás Ortiz who held in 1519 that "never has God created a people so adept in vices and bestialities without a trace of kindness or lawfulness, and the Franciscan bishop Francisco Ruiz who reported that "although these people are malicious in contriving ruin and damage to the Christians, they are incapable of normal judgment to receive either faith or the other virtues of upbringing necessary for their conversion."

His bibliography is equally meager on modern studies of Indian cultures. He cites none of the numerous learned publications of the Carnegie Institution of Washington on the Mayas or the copious contributions of Mexican anthropologists, he ignores the *Handbook of South American Indians,* uses no articles from the *Journal de la Société des Américanistes* of Paris, the *American Anthropologist,* or the many volumes produced by the Congreso de Americanistas, although these volumes are full of descriptions and analyses of Indian cultures.

3. HIS INCONSISTENCIES, EXAGGERATIONS, AND DOGMATISMS

It may seem strange to apply these words to Don Ramón, for they are precisely the charges he makes against Las Casas.

The first inconsistency one notes is his attitude toward the writings of Las Casas. He naturally deplores above all the *Brevíssima relación de la destrucción de las Indias.* It is the "único fundamento de la fama mundial" of Las Casas which he describes and condemns at great length, for the horrifying material in this denunciation of Spanish cruelty to the Indians fascinates Spaniards, who have done a great deal to spread the *leyenda negra* through their fulsome refutations. One feels at times that Don Ramón believes that, except for this work by Las Casas, Spain and the world would have been convinced that on the whole the Conquest was a noble effort marked mainly by the glorious deeds of conquistadores or the kindly acts to Indians of encomenderos. He sees Cortés defended by Vitoria, praised by Motolinía, favorable to Friar Martín de Valencia's peaceful preaching projects, a "genial and courteous" gentleman even in his meeting with the rancorous Las Casas. He admits cruelties on some occasions and some oppressive encomenderos in the early days, but generally seems to agree with the first important apologia for the conquest written by Francisco López de Gómara, and referred to earlier. Nowhere does he consider the position of such a historian as the Mexican scholar Genaro García, and makes no reference to the latter's well-known study *Carácter de la conquista española en América y en México según los textos de los historiadores primitivos,* in which he states:

In order to give greater credibility to my studies, I not only refer continuously to the conquerors and most authorized historians, but I also transcribe their words literally; and in order that my work may not be objected to when trying to demonstrate what I have proven to be true, I will not quote our irreproachable Friar Bartolomé de Las Casas in my attempt to determine the character of the conquest.

Nor does he consider that the natural jealousy of other European nations would have in any case tempered their enthusiasm for the expansion of Europe by Spaniards.

Don Ramón at first praises other writings of Las Casas, such as the *Historia de las Indias* and the *Apologética historia,* but later attacks both works, so that his opinions fluctuate according to his mood of the moment.

Another inconsistency appears in his treatment of relations between the Dominican Domingo de Betanzos and Las Casas. He tells how Betanzos influenced Las Casas to enter the order, but later became his decided enemy. We do not learn that these two fiery figures were linked together for many years by their common devotion to the ideal of peaceful persuasion. Why did these two men fall out? One of the reasons probably was their divergent convictions on the nature of the Indians. These were the years when the subject was being fiercely debated, and when Pope Paul III issued in 1537 his bull "Sublimis Deus," proclaiming that "the Indians are truly men . . . capable of understanding the Catholic faith . . . are by no means to be deprived of their liberty or the possession of their property, even though they be outside the faith of Jesus Christ." Don Ramón pays slight attention to this bull, though it is central to Las Casas' doctrine in his treatise on *The Only Method of Attracting All People to True Faith*. Nor does Don Ramón emphasize that Betanzos' view on Indian affairs was so worrisome to some of his brother Dominicans that in 1549 they apparently prevailed upon him to renounce on his deathbed in Valladolid the anti-Indian memorial he had presented to the Council of the Indies long before.

Other inconsistencies, discrepancies, and doubtful judgments occur throughout *El Padre Las Casas. Su doble personalidad*, but they cannot all be considered here. . . .

Dogmatism is another characteristic of Las Casas shared by Don Ramón, since both men believed in the absolute validity of their convictions. Neither considers it necessary at times to do more than state them, and just as Las Casas sometimes delivered himself of broad generalizations without producing evidence, so does Don Ramón. He qualified Las Casas as "pathological" because he asserts that everything

the *encomenderos* did was wrong; Don Ramón is just as absolutist in his own way for, though the *encomienda* was a highly controversial institution, he maintains:

everyone can see that supervised living with the Spaniard is the only way the Indians would abandon inhuman and savage customs, like the sacrifice of men or children and cannibalism, and become accustomed to life in villages, to ordinary work, to marriage, etc. The *encomienda*, therefore, was beneficial; and for the Dominicans and Franciscans the *encomienda* appeared, in addition, toward 1530, as the only possible means of checking the rapid disappearance of the Indians who were threatened by their primitive existence and by terrifying epidemics.

Don Ramón endeavors to show that Las Casas was not taken seriously in his own time: "in general his contemporaries looked at him as an eccentric or an excusable maniac, whose extremism, however violent it may be, should not be taken too seriously." No evidence is adduced to document this generalization; considerable material could be cited to show that in fact Las Casas received much support for his ideas throughout his life and that his powerful political influence was recognized by many different kinds of sixteenth-century Spaniards. Friars wrote to him from many parts of the Indies to report atrocities and the needs of the Indians, oidor Cristóbal Lebrón appealed to Las Casas for help in his difficulties with the audiencia of Nueva Galicia, the ancient conquistador Bernal Díaz del Castillo even had the audacity to ask Las Casas for assistance in keeping his encomienda and offered a bribe, the conquistador-chronicler Pedro Cieza de León willed his manuscripts to him, the Council of the Indies used him on confidential missions when he was 90 years of age, and he was active as a witness on Indian affairs until a few weeks before his death. . . .

Enough has been said to illustrate how this veteran scholar, who indignantly denies that he is an antilascasista, exhibits in this extraordinary book some of the worst defects he attributes to Las Casas: inconsistency, exaggeration, and dogmatism. This curious book, which reveals Don Ramón's tendency to transform conjecture into certainty, does make one important contribution; it helps us to understand — as did the work of Don Ramón's spiritual ancestor Marcelino Menéndez Pelayo — those "two Spains that for so long coexisted or battled each other on the peninsula." Will future students reach the same conclusion on Don Ramón as the following on Menéndez Pelayo?

"Thus he has come to be a kind of symbol through which we can see the struggle and the tragedy of the history of Spain; he himself is a historical problem."

THE SIGNIFICANCE OF DON RAMÓN'S ATTACK ON LAS CASAS

How can Don Ramón's dedication to his objective of demolishing Las Casas be explained? Is it merely a strange aberration? I cannot believe this. The volume is rather an astonishing *tour de force* which required great energy and acumen in marshalling data. Some have interpreted his campaign as a political effort, but this seems unlikely, although it is true that his first publication against Las Casas appeared at the end of the Spanish Civil War in the Falangist periodical *Escorial*. The many lectures and articles against Las Casas, between his first lecture in Cuba in 1937 and the climax reached with this book of 1963, constitute a personal crusade, I believe, sustained by his own passionate and very Spanish convictions. . . .

However one describes the fatal fascination that draws Spaniards toward the conquest, one non-Spaniard at least believes that by attempting to diminish Las Casas they are thereby diminishing Spain itself. Let everyone freely admit that Las Casas not only exaggerated the statistics of Indian deaths, but that he also failed to give a well-balanced or full account of Spanish accomplishments overseas. But should Spaniards not be proud of the fact that the King and his councilors listened sympathetically to him no matter how horrible a tale he had to tell or how radical a solution he proposed for Indian problems? They allowed him to print and circulate his ideas widely while his opponents were not allowed to publish, and he received many marks of royal favor in his lifetime. But he could not stop the forcible conquest of the Indies, nor prevent the Indians from being exploited.

Don Ramón winces when he looks back at the life and reputation of Las Casas. How is it that some Spaniards from the sixteenth century onward have tolerated, even praised him, when such men as Motolinía opposed him? And when Captain Bernardo de Vargas Machuca composed such a convincing *Apologías y discursos de las conquistas occidentales*? Don Ramón laments the blindness and pusillanimity of some of his ancestors, and condemns their timidity and error. For the Captain's apologia was never allowed to be published, despite the fact that it was prefaced by laudatory sonnets by four Dominicans. The Captain had a different experience with theologians, for when he drowned an Indian child he was absolved in the confessional. His modern biographer comments: "Perhaps, perhaps Padre Las Casas would have condemned him to Hell."

Let us hope that the four-hundredth anniversary of the death of Las Casas — which falls in July, 1966 — will be the occasion for less heat and more light on the life and work of this great Spaniard. We may at least agree with Don Ramón Menéndez Pidal that the story of the Spanish conquest of America should be approached in the spirit of impartial historical criticism even if he himself has not led the way.

Now let us return to the great plaza in Mexico City where the monument to Las Casas as the apostle to the Indians stands so firmly. Will we ever see there a monument to Cortés, the conqueror of Mexico whose life and achievements are as integral a part of her history as those of Las Casas?

Cortés has long been a problem in Spain as well as in Spanish America, as Professor Marcel Bataillon reminds us in another of his acute studies, and it is not surprising that thus far Mexicans have emphatically refused to raise a monument to him just as Spaniards have never erected a statue to Las Casas in Madrid. Don Ramón at Oxford in conversation with Castro Leal expressed astonishment that Mexicans still cherished such feeling against Cortés and were not yet ready to forget the cruelties of the conquest. Why did they not remember instead the cultural contributions of Spain to Mexico, he asked with that curious naïveté that marks the attitude of some Spaniards toward Spanish-America.

The Mexicans' usual reply to this question is that their nation is not yet racially unified enough to permit any public recognition of the conquistador who symbolizes the action of the sixteenth-century imperialist invaders. Samuel Ramos, the Mexican philosopher, quotes Rubén Darío's cry that his soul was the object of contention "between the Cathedral and the pagan ruins," and then asks:

Isn't this, perhaps, a valid image of the drama of America? Today very serious problems persist because of the schism between the culture inspired in our cathedrals, and the other, which emanates from *our* ruins. When the two heritages met they could not be combined in the creation of a new synthesis.

But is it not possible that Mexico, despite her important Indian heritage, is still so profoundly Spanish that Mexicans also share the burden of Spanish American history and will no more tolerate compromise than the Spaniards? If we ever see a statue to Las Casas in Madrid and a monument to Cortés in Mexico we can be sure that a new day has dawned, that mature acceptance has at least been reached, on both sides of the Ocean Sea, of the strange but strong relationship which always existed between the soldier and the priest whom the Spanish sovereigns sent together to the New World to conquer and to Christianize that world. Men will then see the long struggle for justice as a vital part of Spanish American history. They will see how many kinds of fighters participated and will understand how strongly the struggle has influenced historical writing on the Spanish empire.

The day of serene historical judgment has not yet arrived. Thus the views of the conquest held by the Colombian Juan Friede and the Spaniard Ramón Menéndez Pidal underline the truth of Sverker Arnoldsson's statement: that the conquest has been so vigorously discussed for over four centuries because this great period of history created the still-smoking problems of today.

The conquest is the "living past" of both Spain and Spanish America. How long ago it all happened! And yet how persistently the historical consequences remain as part of our world, our time, our problems.

The *Mita* and Indian Enslavement

SALVADOR DE MADARIAGA

Salvador de Madariaga, born in La Coruña (1886), is a leading Spanish author and diplomat. Educated in Madrid and Paris, he moved to London in 1916 as a journalist, later (1928–31) holding the chair of Spanish literature at Oxford. His public career has been illustrious as director of the disarmament section of the League of Nations (1922–27); Spanish ambassador to the United States in 1931; permanent delegate to the League of Nations (1931–36); ambassador to France (1932–34); and minister of education and justice in the Lerroux government of 1934. For many years Madariaga has been an influential interpreter of Spanish culture. Among his significant books are *The Genius of Spain* (1923); *Englishmen, Frenchmen, Spaniards* (1928), a provocative study of national character; *Christopher Columbus* (1939); *Hernán Cortés* (1942); *Spain* (1943, rev. ed. 1958); *The Fall of the Spanish-American Empire* (1947); *Portrait of Europe* (1952); and *Latin America between the Eagle and the Bear* (1961).

As LANDS WERE ALLOTTED to captains and soldiers, and conquerors became settlers, some measure of forced labour was soon found necessary, and the settlers developed it as a matter of course. Nor were priests and even monks always averse to it. The trend of the Crown was to accept it, but only as a necessity to be reduced to its minimum, carefully regulated, and abolished as soon as possible. The Crown began by prohibiting the habit which had developed of using forced labour for private services such as "kitchen gardens, care of the buildings, the procuring of fire wood, hay and other similar services for though this may be inconvenient for the Spaniards, the freedom and preservation of the Indians matters more." And in this *Cédula*, addressed to Montesclaros (1601) he was requested to lead the community by giving up his own Indian forced labour. The settlers tried to resist the royal pressure, arguing that they could not find Spanish labour; but the Crown countered (1609) that, by better pay and treatment, they would easily find Indian free labour, "and they can also draw on blacks, *mestizos* and mulattoes, of which there is an abundant idle rabble in the provinces." Later in the century, these non-Indian castes were compelled by law "to come out to the market place and hire themselves."

But for a number of public and semi-public services, at any rate in Peru, forced labour was organized through the *mita*, an institution of Inca origin which Spanish law took over with some modifications. It amounted to recruiting Indians for compulsory labour for a certain period and for work defined on a criterion of public interests, strictly understood, though by no means in accordance with our modern standards. For instance, the building of private dwellings was looked upon as a work of public interest, as also, of course, mining and the tilling of land; but the cultivation of certain plants such as coca or even the vine and the olive tree, which were either obnoxious or considered superfluous, was not looked upon as of public interest and therefore *mitayos* were denied to planters who grew these crops. They were also refused for the cultivation of indigo on the ground that this was injurious to their health.

The *mita,* like the *encomienda,* was a compromise between the theoretical attitude of equality and freedom and the practical need of labour. The contradiction between the practice and the principle was keenly felt: "And it is obvious" — writes Solórzano Pereira — "that this is in flat contradiction to their liberty [of the Indians]; for liberty is nothing else than a faculty that a man has to do what he likes with himself and to live where and with whom he pleases. And this is incompatible with the practice of keeping the Indians by force in alien houses and farms." Comfort is sought in legal authorities and in the example of other contemporaries. The same author adds: "To-day, in Germany, noblemen take so many liberties with the persons of their peasants and plebeians, that there is no work however servile and hard to which they do not compel them, punishing them with rigour if they do not obey."

But if the principle suffered, the Indians suffered more still. The *mita* was meant to apply to a relatively low proportion of Indians; that which supplied the silver mines of Potosí, for instance, had been so calculated by Don Francisco de Toledo, that a given Indian would not have to serve on it more than twice in his lifetime. Even so, what did it actually mean? Here is a description by a personal witness, of the *mita* of the two thousand two hundred Indians who migrated every year to the mines of Potosí from the Province of Chuquito: "They all go usually with their wives and children, and having seen them twice I am in a position to say that they amount altogether to more than seven thousand souls. Every Indian of these takes with him eight to ten sheep and a few alpacas to eat; others who are wealthier, take with them thirty to forty sheep; on which they carry their meals of Indian corn and potato flour, their covers for sleeping, mats to guard against the cold, which

is sharp, for they always sleep in the open. All this cattle generally exceeds thirty thousand head, and nearly always amounts to about forty thousand. Now let us say that they are no more than thirty thousand, with the potato flour, the corn, quinoa flour and dried meat, and their new clothes; the whole is worth altogether more than three thousand *pesos* of eight *reales.* All this wealth in this manner takes the road to Potosí by stages and the distance of about one hundred leagues takes two months, since the cattle cannot travel quicker, nor their children of five and six years whom they take with them. Of all this mankind and common wealth which they take away from Chuquito, no more than two thousand souls ever return, and the remainder, about five thousand, in part, they die, and in part they remain in Potosí. There are others who go to the valleys nearby, and the reason is that when they want to return they have neither cattle nor food for the road."

Nor did the tragedy end there. For the Indians left at home dwindled, and therefore the liability to the *mita* increased, so that once in three years was considered luck. Here again, the Crown and its viceroys stood for the Indians; the local settlers and mineowners stood for their own interests. The actual lamentable facts are objectively put to the Viceroy Velasco by his adviser Alfonso Messía, in the document just quoted. The *mita* year meant for the miserable Indian stark ruin and the uprooting of his home, family and cattle. "And for this and the work, so excessive at that, of six months, four in the mines, working twelve hours a day, going down four hundred and twenty and at times seven hundred feet, down to where night is perpetual, for it is always necessary to work by candlelight, the air thick and ill smelling being enclosed in the entrails of the earth, the going up and down most dangerous, for they come up loaded with their small sack of metal tied up to their backs, taking quite four to five hours step by step, and if they make the slightest false step they may fall

seven hundred feet; and when they arrive
at the top out of breath, find as a shelter
a mineowner who scolds them because they
did not come quickly enough or because
they did not bring enough load, and for
the slightest reason makes them go down
again; and that for all that and four months
which their pilgrimages take, they should
receive just forty-eight *patacones,* who
would not feel compassion for them? . . ."

This picture is bad enough. But it refers
to one of the least badly governed provinces
in the Viceroyalty of Peru — that of Quito.
To the south, in what is to-day Peru
proper, another institution prevailed, not
permitted in the north, which, conceived
to favour the Indians and to induce them to
work and prosper, had also become, owing
to the cupidity of the Whites, an instrument of incredible oppression. The *reparti-
miento* was a system whereby petty governors were allowed to provide the natives of
their governorships with mules, European
goods and produce of the country, at
moderate prices. From a purely voluntary
distribution to be agreed by both sides on
equal terms, it had become a system of
compulsory purchase from the man in
authority, of the goods he had to sell and
at his prices. The natives of Peru who
fell into the hands of a heartless and avari-
cious *corregidor* were ground down to
moral and even physical death by this
disastrous system.

Nor could the tradesmen of Lima be
exempted from responsibility. Far from it.
In a relatively short time, the tensions and
pressures of this iniquitous machine had
found their level, and the trade community
had succeeded in appropriating the lion's
share of the spoils. An impecunious *corregidor,* fresh from Spain, came to Lima
to load his mules with goods to dump on
his Indians. He had to buy on credit. The
merchants dumped on him all their un-
saleable stock, and at exorbitant prices. The
results were enough to make one laugh if
they did not make one weep. The poor,
sparing, beardless, naked Indians were
"sold" mirrors and silk stockings, razors

("truly a mockery of that poor nation," indignantly remark Ulloa and Jorge Juan),
pens and ink and paper and playing cards,
as well as "combs, rings, buttons, books,
comedies, lace, ribbons and many more
things as useless as these. . . ."

Indians working in cloth factories, known
in Peru as *obrages,* fared still worse. They
worked from dawn till sunset, locked up,
save for a short time for a midday meal,
were paid just enough to keep body and
soul together, and when their task had not
been completed, were mercilessly flogged
and made to incur an unredeemable debt
which automatically made them practical
slaves of their employers. They often died
of starvation, "with their work in their
hands." "They provoke such compassion
when they are brought out from the works,
dead, that even the stoniest hearts are
moved. One can see in them only the
skeleton, which plainly tells the cause and
motive of their death." The owners "cannot imagine that a sick Indian deserves to
be sent to a hospital until he is so weak
that he dies before he arrives at the charitable institution, and happy are those who
keep enough strength to be able to die in
the hospital."

The two Spanish critics propose a number of remedies for this terrible state of
affairs, and they close their picture with
the following page:

The custom to condemn Indians to these
abominable places [the *obrages* or textile
works] has become so general that they are
sent to that civil death for many other motives; a short debt, even owed to a private
person, suffices for anybody, on his own authority, to lay on them such punishment. One
often meets on the roads Indians tied by
their hair to the tail of a horse on which a
mestizo drags them to the works; and perhaps
for the slight fault of having run away from
the domination of the very man who is drag-
ging them, out of fear of his cruelty. However
we may stress the tyranny with which the
encomenderos treated these Indians during
the first years of the Conquest, we can hardly
believe that it could have been as bad as that
which we have observed inflicted on them

by Spaniards and *mestizos;* and if in those days, the *encomenderos* used their Indians as slaves, the Indian had only one master, his *encomendero,* while now, they have as masters the *corregidor,* the owners of the textile works, the owners of estates, the owners of cattle, and, most scandalous of all, the ministers of worship; all of them, including the priests, treat the defenseless Indians more inhumanly than the worst that can be imagined against black slaves.

Such things need only to be stated. They carry their own condemnation and bear no defense. But as human facts they must be referred to their background, both psychological and historical, and given a sound interpretation in terms of the living experience in which they occur. In its essence, the heartless exploitation of the Indians "by Spaniards and *mestizos*" grows worse as the waning religion of the Spaniards is less and less able to control the dominant energy of the stronger nation. The matter can only be estimated in an adequate human context in relation to similar experiences of other nations when placed in comparable circumstances. The men of the period were hard even towards their own kith and kin everywhere. Bristol businessmen throve on kidnapped English labour which they mercilessly shipped to the West Indies. Settlers in South Carolina put a price on Indian prisoners caught alive and made handsome profits by selling them as slaves to the West Indies. "The Punishments for Crimes of Slaves" — writes Doctor Sloane describing Jamaica in 1708 — "are usually for Rebellions burning them, by nailing them down on the ground with crooked sticks on every Limb, and then applying the Fire by degrees from the Feet and Hands, burning them gradually up to the Head, whereby their pains are extravagant." And after much more to that effect, and worse, the good doctor calmly concludes: "These Punishments are sometimes merited by the Blacks, who are a very perverse Generation of people, and though they appear harsh, yet are scarce equal to some of their Crimes

and inferior to what Punishments other *European* nations inflict on their Slaves in the *East-Indies*." We perceive here the callousness, not only of the individual man, but of the "attitude. . . ."

The picture must now be completed in all its baffling complexity. It varies considerably from one part of the Indies to the other, and everything points to the view that Peru was the seat of the worst iniquity in this respect. Hardly a statement, however, can be generalized. Take roads for instance. "The bridges, roads and paths of all Peru" — write Ulloa and Jorge Juan — "had been constructed by the heathen Indians with great lavishness, and for the greater part allowed to decay owing to the neglect of the new inhabitants." So write two Spaniards of their own kith and kin. Let us now turn to an Englishman with a strong anti-Spanish bias. Thomas Gage (1648) says: "It was then a very evil way [the road through Los Angeles at the time of the Conquest] though now it be a reasonable wide open road, where Mules laden with wares from St. John de Ulhua, and the Sugar-farms daily pass." The status of the Indians varied considerably and was much worse in Peru than in New Spain. Peru itself was in those days a country as vast as varied, in which conditions were far from uniform or static; and we have the testimony of Ulloa and Jorge Juan themselves to prove that all was not as black as the cases they paint, moved by their indignation and compassion. Arguing against those who claim that *mita* to be indispensable to obtain labour, they point out the estates based on voluntary workers who, though by no means well paid, accept their poor salary and, with the help of their wives' labour, manage to live. We shall presently record numerous cases of rich and prosperous Indians, not merely individuals but classes and whole districts as well.

Due note taken, however, of all these reservations and qualifications, the fact remains that, particularly in Peru, a system of heartless exploitation of the Indian had taken root. Its chief lines must be clearly drawn. The parties to this drama were five: the Indians; the *mestizos* and mulattoes; the "Spaniards" (whether born in the Indies or in Spain) permanently settled in the Indies; the officials coming from Spain and returning thither after their term of office; the Crown. The Indians were the victims. The *mestizos* and mulattoes (as well as many caciques of poor Indian blood) were the instruments of exploitation. Permanently settled Spaniards (whether Creoles or born in Spain) were the chief cause of the evil, for without them the rest of the edifice built on the sweat and blood of the Indians would collapse. The officials were led by their own character or by the compelling force of the system to share in the spoils or to condone it or to ignore it. The Crown opposed it as much as it could and as the character of its officials enabled it to, though indirectly fostering it by selling offices.

Ulloa and Jorge Juan relate the case of a nobleman, Don José de Eslaba, appointed by Philip V as *corregidor* in Peru. This gentleman took in earnest his duties as Visitor of the *obrages* of Quito. Thereupon he was offered sackfuls of silver by the owners of the *obrages;* he spurned the money. Then, "persuaded that in all the offices of those lands men had to load their conscience if they acted after the corrupted ways of Peru, or risked their lives, if they tried to reform matters," he entered a Jesuit College and became a priest. They also report the case of Don Baltasar de Abarca, who, appointed visiting magistrate by the viceroy, "soon after leaving Quito to carry out his visit, found himself bound to flee from the province of Lima even before he had begun it, for as the owners of *obrages* realized that he meant to inspect them in earnest, they plotted his death with so much danger for him that he had no time to inform the viceroy." "This year" — writes the author of the *Annals of Potosí* (1657) — "came to Potosí the Lord Bishop Cruz de Santa Marta, of the Order of Preachers, who, having filled the viceroy and the *Audiencia* of Lima with scruples backed

by various reasons which he gave them, tried to abolish the *mita* of Indians for Potosí; and so that this could be done, the Indian Governors called on the Bishop with great quantities of gold and silver. The silver mineowners and other inhabitants gathered together in Potosí; there were terrible disputes and disorders [. . .] the Bishop, as he was in the midst of this arduous affair of the abolition of the *mita* for the silver mines, was found dead one morning, though he had gone to bed in perfect health."

These cases prove that the chief benefit and responsibility in this lamentable state of affairs accrued to the "Spaniards," i.e., the Creoles made or in the making — a conclusion which explains the action taken by the Viceroy, Duke de la Palata, in the case of a Creole, Don Ignacio de Aybar y Eslava, a citizen of Quito, who through his relations in Madrid secured the post of Protector of the Indians, and whom the Viceroy dispossessed of this post on the ground that his appointment was "but a step forward towards becoming a prosperous *obrage* owner and a bad protector."

What again was the attitude of the Crown? These episodes show that, insofar as it was in its power, the Crown fought strenuously to protect the Indians. This follows also from the abundant documents quoted by Solórzano Pereira as well as by practically every viceregal report. But there are more direct indications as well. Thus, in virtue of Law VI, Title VI, Book III, referring to military works, Philip II enacted that in the case of labour engaged by or for military engineers, for fortresses, ports and other defense constructions, the day's work should be limited to eight hours, Sunday free. In case of accident, the workers in the hospital (which, of course, was free of charge) were paid half their wages. The difference between the treatment under private employers and that under the Crown was such that the *mita* miner was paid four *reales* a day at most, the worker in an *obrage*, one *real*, a shepherd 18 *pesos* net, i.e., 80 *reales* a year; while the skilled carpenters and shipwrights at the Royal Arsenal of Callao (all *mestizos,* mulattoes or pure Indians) were paid three *pesos* (24 *reales*) a day. Yet another indication of the spirit of the Government is the way the complement of the ships of the Navy was recruited: the sailors were paid 18 *pesos* a month, but in those days when it was the custom in other navies to press-gang people for the service, in the Spanish Navy in the Indies "the men on board ship, from artillery-men to broom-boys, were all volunteers."

Without unduly straining the point, or closing one's eyes to the heavy responsibilities of the Crown itself in such matters as taxation of destitute natives, sale of offices and often poor choice of officials, it is possible to conclude that throughout the three centuries of Spanish rule in the Indies, the tendency to order, lawfulness, fair dealing to all, good government and protection of the natives came chiefly from the Crown; that the tendency to anarchy, to exploitation and ill-treatment of the natives, to selfish enjoyment of the immediate fruits of life without a too close consideration of the moral issues involved, came from the white men settled in the Indies, whether born there (Creoles, "Spaniards") or Spanish born ("Europeans"); and that the Spaniards who came and went as officials of Church or State were at times the loyal and courageous instruments of the straight tendencies of the Crown, but far more often either greedy time-servers and get-rich-quickers who eagerly shared in the spoils, or weak characters who were absorbed through fear, corruption or family ties by the system which it was their duty to repress. The fact must, however, be stressed again that the basis and foundation of this abominable system was undoubtedly the permanent white population of the Indies, whose lawless life flowed riotously and vigorously through the elaborate but weak and loose meshes of the Spanish laws.

The Spanish Struggle for Justice

LEWIS HANKE

THE PURPOSE of this work is to demonstrate that the Spanish conquest of America was far more than a remarkable military and political exploit; that it was also one of the greatest attempts the world has seen to make Christian precepts prevail in the relations between peoples. This attempt became basically a spirited defense of the rights of the Indians, which rested on two of the most fundamental assumptions a Christian can make: namely, that all men are equal before God, and that a Christian has a responsibility for the welfare of his brothers no matter how alien or lowly they may be.

In the written history of America the undeniable courage and spectacular daring of the conquistadores have hitherto been emphasized, as well as the impressive stability of the far-flung empire which Spain brought within the orbit of European civilization and ruled for over three hundred years. There is more, however, to Spain's contribution to the New World,

From Lewis Hanke, *The Spanish Struggle for Justice in the Conquest of America.* (Philadelphia: University of Pennsylvania Press, 1949), pp. 1–13. Reprinted by permission of the publisher.

noteworthy as these aspects of her work will always be. Other nations sent out bold explorers and established empires. But no other European people, before or since the conquest of America, plunged into such a struggle for justice as developed among Spaniards shortly after the discovery of America and persisted throughout the sixteenth century. This study attempts to examine this unique quality of Spanish effort and to show how it influenced Spanish action in America.

The struggle occurred because of the widespread concern felt by soldiers, ecclesiastics, and the crown that all Spain's laws and actions in America be just. What constituted justice and how it could be achieved were questions raised with every important step Spaniards took in the discovery, colonization, and administration of their new dominions. This concern for justice, which can only be understood in relation to the political and spiritual climate of opinion in sixteenth-century Spain, to be described later, led to sharp and basic controversies on a variety of particular issues.

What political and economic rights should Spain enjoy from her overlordship there? Were the Indians rational beings and, if so, what were their rights? How should the faith be preached to them; under what circumstances could they be made to work for Spaniards; and when could war be justly waged against them? All these and other questions were asked and heatedly debated throughout the sixteenth century in both Spain and America and by all classes and manner of men.

The papal bulls of Alexander VI and Julius II conferred upon the crown of Spain even greater power to direct the administration of church affairs in America than that enjoyed by the crown in Spain. The acceptance by the crown of the obligation to provide for the Christianization of the Indians led to a theory of empire and colonial policy in which ecclesiastics, who had always been important in royal councils, became trusted advisers to the crown and to the Council of the Indies, the principal administrative body for ruling America. Although the ecclesiastics never agreed on a united policy and were frequently in direct conflict with the conquistadores and royal officials, their influence was felt in all quarters and ensured that every basic decision made during the conquest be scrutinized from the point of view of Christian justice. The kings of Spain, one after another, were confused and troubled by the multitude of differing voices raised at home and half a world away to advise them on the proper way to discharge their temporal and spiritual responsibilities.

The crown, faced with enormous administrative problems and surrounded by strident champions of widely varying solutions, decided to experiment. This volume describes four extraordinary attempts, made during the critical first half-century with the full approval of the crown, to test certain daring theories put forward by ecclesiastics as solutions for the pressing problems of the New World. Could the Indians learn to live like Spaniards? Was it possible to colonize the new lands peacefully with Spanish farmers? Could the Indians be won over to Christianity by peaceful means alone? Could the *encomienda* system, by which some Spaniards were supported by Indians, be abolished?

Some influential Spaniards believed strongly that the answers would all be "yes," but the experiments or quasi-experiments failed to convince the crown and resulted in no fundamental change in royal policy. Hotly debated at the time, they never really had a chance to succeed in the hostile environment of the New World. The experiments appear to us today, from the vantage point of four hundred years, as tragic comedies enacted on doomed little islands around which the ocean of the conquest boiled and thundered until it overwhelmed them. But it is an important fact that the experiments were conducted at all and that many loyal Spaniards gave years of their lives trying to prove the validity of their conviction that the conquest of a new world, conducted by the nation whose military force was probably the greatest in Europe, could be achieved without trampling on the rights of the relatively defenseless natives.

The struggle for justice continued during the second half of the sixteenth century and spread from the islands of the Caribbean to Mexico, Peru, and even to the distant Philippines. Wherever Spaniards carried their banners in the New World opened up by their energy and daring, there also they carried the ideas and concern for justice which led inevitably to those bitter controversies which endow the Spanish experience in America with original characteristics. The eighteenth-century Scottish historian William Robertson realized this truth when he wrote: "The Spanish monarchs, having acquired a species of dominion formerly unknown, formed a plan for exercising it to which nothing similar occurs in the history of human affairs. . . ."

SPIRIT OF THIS STUDY

A historian writing today cannot be certain that he has presented the facts of this mighty sixteenth-century struggle accurately. Even now some of the essential facts are not known and the clarification of some problems must await further archival investigation. Interpretation of the available facts is even more difficult. Learned controversies have long raged, and their fires are not yet quenched, over many of the men and events discussed in this book.

Besides the usual doubts and disagreements that spring up among historians, no matter what the subject, those who write the history of Spain in America have often been subject to the special hazard of strong religious or political bias. On this account the struggle for justice has been one of the topics in Spanish history most vulnerable to partisan treatment.

Historians, especially those writing in English, even when they have recognized the existence of Spanish theories dealing with Spain's American problems, have usually confined themselves to pointing the finger of scorn to show how far Spanish practice in America departed from the theory elaborated by the crown in Spain. The Spaniards' concern to work out a policy which they could justify to their own consciences has been dismissed as hypocritical religiosity akin to the spirit of the walrus in *Alice's Adventures in Wonderland,* who shed such bitter tears while busily assisting the carpenter to consume so many oysters. Thorstein Veblen faithfully represented a large body of opinion — outside Spain at least — when he asserted: "The Spanish enterprise in colonization was an enterprise in pillage, inflamed and inflated by religious fanaticism and martial vanity."

Spanish "revisionists," eager to justify their ancestors' ways and to combat the "black legend" of Spanish cruelty and oppression in America, have replied to these critics by quoting long extracts from the humanitarian laws of the Indies with intent to prove the just and enlightened nature of the Spanish conquest and colonial system. Or they point out that other European nations were at least as cruel as the Spaniards, a characteristic defense which appeared most recently in the volume entitled *The Rise of the Spanish American Empire,* by the brilliant Spanish controversialist Salvador de Madariaga.

A completely objective attitude toward the historical controversies centering around a people as vital and as complex as the Spaniards is, of course, impossible to attain. But, allowing for my long-standing and incurable predilection for all things Spanish, my effort has been to be both accurate and honest and to exemplify the spirit so well described by Samuel Purchas over three hundred years ago as he presented an English translation of the writings of the Dominican friar Bartolomé de Las Casas to his countrymen. Las Casas, a loud champion of the Indians, had bitterly accused his fellow Spaniards of horrible cruelty in America. Purchas, explaining his publication of the writings of this partisan figure, prefaced his translation with these words:

And if any thinke that I publish this in disgrace of that Nation (Spain); I answere, Every Nation (We see it at home) hath many evill men, many Devillmen. Againe, I ask whether the Authour (himself a Spaniard and Divine) intended not the honour and good of his Country thereby. . . . For my part I honour vertue in a Spaniard, in a Frier, in a Jesuite. . . . And so farre am I from delighting to thrust my fingers in sores

(which yet I doe on necessitie even with the English also) that I have left out many invectives and bitter Epithetes of this Authour, abridging him after my wont, and lopping off such superfluities which rather were the fruit of his zeale, than the flowre of his History.

My ideal has been to follow the counsel of Fernando de los Rios, whose writings first led me to enquire into this subject. He urged: "Let us judge the Spanish colonial activities, not as Catholics or Protestants, but as observers with the objectivity necessary to one who proposes to study a problem of great significance in history."

The Climate of Opinion in Sixteenth-Century Spain

The almost incredible story of the amusing, curious, and tragic episodes which took place when the theories decided upon in Spain were put into practice in America cannot be understood except in relation to the climate of opinion prevailing in sixteenth-century Spain.

It was an age of theologians who believed that their "duties and functions extended over a field so vast that no argument and no discussion seemed alien to the practice and purpose of theology." Their importance was so widely recognized in that century that even frontier officials in Florida felt the need of a theologian in their midst and requested the crown to send them one.

Religiosity was an integral and vital part of Spanish life. Captains of slaving ships promulgated and enforced strict laws against blasphemy and card playing. Even while Sir Francis Drake was raiding the Spanish coast, Philip II took time to consider how the sailors on the Armada could be kept from swearing. Another example of the strength of religious formalism has been well described by Alonso de Ercilla in his great epic poem La Araucana (1569) on the conquest of Chile. The Araucanian chief Caupolicán had been captured and was about to be put to death when he

expressed a desire to be baptized and become a Christian. "This caused pity and great comment among the Castilians who stood around," according to Ercilla, and Caupolicán was baptized "with great solemnity, and instructed in the true faith as well as possible in the short time available." After this, the Spaniards made him sit on a sharp stake and shot him through and through with arrows.

Sixteenth-century Spaniards were thoroughly saturated also with the spirit of legal formalism, and the New World offered many opportunities for the exercise of juridical formalities. The Requirement or proclamation to be read to the Indians before warring against them, which will be discussed later, was probably the best single example, but many others could be cited. Spaniards were so accustomed to certifying every action they took that notaries were as indispensable to their expeditions as friars and gunpowder. The extraordinary concern for legality of even the Spanish soldier of the period reveals itself in the account given by the foot soldier Bernal Díaz of the encounter between his captain Hernán Cortés and the Indians at Cholula. Cortés explained that "he had been sent to these countries to give them warning and to command them not to worship idols, nor sacrifice human beings or eat their flesh, or practice sodomy or other uncleanness" and urged the Indians to render obedience to the king of Spain. The Indians refused to give up their idols but "as to rendering obedience to our king, they were content to do so. And thus they pledged their word, but it was not done before a notary."

But it was not done before a notary! Would a pikeman of any other European nation have noticed, let alone recorded, such a fact? And one cutthroat conquistador, Lope de Aguirre, even took the trouble to rebel against his king in a legal way, drawing up while deep in the Amazonian jungle a manifesto which announced to the crown that he no longer considered himself subject to Spanish law.

The element of Spanish character which most deeply affected the struggle for justice in America is what Spanish and foreign interpreters alike have termed its "tendency toward polarization, a native passion for extremes." All the great figures of the conquest were moved by one or the other of two dominant and diametrically opposed motives.

The conquistador Francisco Pizarro once replied to an ecclesiastic in his company who was protesting the despoilment of Indians in Peru and urging upon him that God and the faith ought rather to be made known to them: "I have not come for any such reasons. I have come to take away from them their gold."

There it is in its stark simplicity, the oldest and most familiar motive, the lust for material wealth. But it is deeply significant that the incident showing this motive cannot even be recounted without involving the second one, best set forth in a statement made by Friar Bartolomé de Las Casas, who cried:

The aim which Christ and the Pope seek and ought to seek in the Indies — and which the Christian Kings of Castile should likewise strive for — is that the natives of those regions shall hear the faith preached in order that they may be saved. And the means to

effect this end are not to rob, to scandalize, to capture or destroy them, or to lay waste their lands, for this would cause the infidels to abominate our faith.

Here the other face of sixteenth-century Spanish character looks boldly at us, and the second motive compelling Spaniards during the conquest reveals itself: the missionary urge to carry to far places and hitherto unknown men the great message from Christendom — the faith.

Between the two poles — the thirst for gold and the winning of souls, not for Spain but for the glory of God — a variety of mixed motives appeared. Some conquistadores were at times as missionary-minded as the most devoted friars. A few ecclesiastics were as worldly as Pizarro in their search for wealth and a life of ease in America. Many Spaniards, however, exemplified both motives. As the classic statement by Bernal Díaz put it: "We came here to serve God, and also to get rich."

The motives of men are usually complicated and we must avoid undue simplification. But as the conquest proceeded there developed two conflicting interpretations of justice and how to achieve it. One group regarded Indian conversion as important, but secondary, and its members devoted themselves to justifying to the royal conscience the virtual enslavement of the Indians as a means to develop the resources of the New World for the benefit of the crown and for the glory of Spaniards and of Spain. The other group placed primary emphasis on Indian conversion and on the welfare of the Indians, relegating to an inferior place the material development of the continent. Both groups sought political power as the indispensable force required to make their views prevail, the ecclesiastics just as energetically as the conquistadores. Indeed, one writer today suggests that "behind all the discussion of the rights of the crown to the conquered lands lies the plan, very natural in Spain, to erect a spiritual power, over against that of the state. The self-assurance and anti-imperialistic aggressiveness of Las Casas . . . hide a desire for ecclesiastical and utopian imperialism."

However the various motives may be interpreted, the fundamental divergence represented by the quotations from Las Casas and Pizarro remains, nevertheless, one of the abiding truths.

FREE SPEECH IN SPAIN AND AMERICA

The historian today would know much less about the struggle for justice if the Spaniards had not discussed their American problems so freely and so frankly. In the Archive of the Indies in Seville lie thousands of letters and reports advising, admonishing, exhorting, and even threatening the mightiest monarchs of the time in Europe. Ferdinand and Isabella, Charles V, and Philip II were powerful rulers who usually brooked little opposition. From the very beginning of the conquest and throughout the sixteenth century, however, ecclesiastics, conquistadores, colonists, Indians, and a multitude of royal officials from all the far corners of Spain's New World empire sent personal messages to their kings, explaining what and who was wrong and describing the measures required to remedy the situation. The great distances lying between the various regions of the Indies and the court, the royal policy of playing off one group against another, and the responsibility of the crown for both the spiritual and temporal welfare of Indians as well as Spaniards all tended to stimulate the vast flow of correspondence between America and Spain.

The king's loyal subjects did not sugarcoat the pill of their criticism. Nor did ideas and complaints remain hidden in correspondence, for they often achieved the permanence of print. No one from the king downward was exempt from criticism and no subject seems to have been too small or correspondent too humble for the highest authorities in Spain to lend an ear. Nor was any part of the empire too far away to command the attention of the king. When the Bishop of Manila, the vigorous Dominican Domingo de Salazar, insisted on making the Chinese converts to Christianity in the Philippines cut off their pigtails as a visible symbol of their emancipation from heathenish customs, the opponents of this extreme measure carried their protest to Philip II and won. No problem was too important to touch upon, for the kings allowed and even encouraged at times the discussion of such a tender issue as the justice of their own right to rule the New World.

Always the basic conflict of approaches to American problems impelled Spaniards to speak out and to communicate by letter and messenger with the directing power in Spain. Men of action, men of thought, men eager to consolidate the expanding empire or to govern it, men burning to advance the spiritual conquest by their various plans and devices — all carried their claims and grievances to the crown or Council. Each correspondent or messenger was intent on moving the great machinery at home to the uses he or his faction considered paramount and felt that the success of the whole Spanish enterprise hung in the balance while he struggled to convince the lawmakers at the seat of power.

What makes the freedom of speech enjoyed in sixteenth-century America so notable is that the Spanish rulers not only permitted but encouraged it. As early as August 14, 1509, King Ferdinand ordered that "no official should prevent anyone from sending to the king or anyone else letters and other information which concern the welfare of the Indies," and in 1521 a standard instruction was issued which read:

We order and emphatically maintain that now and henceforth at all times when each and every Royal Official and all other persons who are citizens and residents and inhabitants of the Indies, Islands and Tierra Firme of the Ocean Sea wish to write and give an account of everything that appears to them to be convenient to our service or if they wish to send messengers or come themselves, they shall be allowed to do these things and no one (including Captains, pilots and sailors) is to be permitted to place any restriction or hindrance or obstacle, whether directly or indirectly, under penalty of losing all favors, privileges, and positions granted by Us and loss of all property and under pain of Our displeasure.

Freedom of speech was, of course, subject to restrictions in certain fields such as religion. Nor was the press wholly free as the prohibition against some books, particularly after 1550, indicates. Some of the writings of the opponents of Las Casas, for example, were never allowed to be printed in the sixteenth century although he was able to distribute — all too freely in the opinion of some of his contemporaries such as the venerable Franciscan Toribio de Motolinía — his published and unpublished tracts throughout Spain and the New World. On the other hand, those who challenged Las Casas wrote steadily and extensively to the crown against what they considered his exaggerations and falsehoods. Never during the sixteenth century did the crown attempt to stop the flow of news — good and bad — from the New World to Spain. The historian who digs away today in Spanish archives becomes painfully aware of the results of this policy, for literally tons of reports and letters of the most controversial and divergent nature have been preserved there on every topic of colonial administration.

The crown did not merely provide that mail should be free to move to Spain without censorship. It also encouraged discussion of practically every American problem before the regular and special tribunals that were set up in Spain and America to carry on the vast imperial enterprise. Established institutions, such as universities, were also drawn into these disputes although the royal patience was strained at least once, for the records show that Charles V rebuked the professors and friars of Salamanca on one occasion when he considered they had presumed too far in their consideration of Spain's title to the New World.

What was the real meaning of this freedom of speech? Was it merely a device by which Spaniards of all degrees were encouraged to bear tales simply to keep the crown informed, a sort of Hapsburg intelligence service? Certainly the crown deliberately utilized the material resulting from this freedom of speech in the administration of the Indies toward the end that it might retain its dominance in all things. In common with every other fundamental aspect of Spanish thought and character, the degree of freedom of speech which flourished in the sixteenth century can be and has been interpreted variously. My own interpretation is that it was not merely a carefully calculated administrative device and not merely a lack of postal censorship. The fostering of discussion on American problems also reveals, it seems to me, both the highly developed individualism of the Spaniards and a deliberate, imaginative, and courageous attempt by the crown and the Spanish people to shoulder the heavy burdens placed on Spain by her political and ecclesiastical dominion in America. The period in which Spaniards expressed their views most freely coincided with the greatest age Spain has ever known, and some Spaniards well understood that this was no accidental relationship. The plain speaking of sixteenth-century Spaniards must be considered — along with their legal formalism, religiosity, devotion to theology, and passion for extremes — as an important element in the climate of opinion which prevailed during the momentous epoch which Spaniards considered the eighth wonder of the world — the discovery and conquest of America.

THE NATURE OF THE INDIANS

Spaniards not only spoke freely on American problems, they also wrote extensively and heatedly on American history as they were making it. One great topic touched upon by every historian or free-speaking Spaniard was the true nature of the Indians. No other controversy so universally embroiled Spaniards during the sixteenth century or so well illustrates the climate of opinion.

From the very beginning of the conquest, opinion was sharply divided concerning the nature of the Indians — particularly their capacity to live according to the ways of Spaniards and their ability to receive the Christian faith. As the discovery and colonization proceeded, the treatment of the Indians became an issue of prime importance, for the proper treatment to be accorded the Indians, the proper laws to be devised to govern them, depended to a large degree on their nature or at least upon the Spaniards' concept of their nature.

Though more subtle, more moderate, and more realistic theories were eventually developed, the majority of the Spaniards in the Indies during the first half-century of the conquest tended to look upon the natives either as "noble Indians" or as "dirty dogs."

Bartolomé de Las Casas may be taken as an extreme example of the "noble Indian" group when he cried:

God created these simple people without evil and without guile. They are most obedient and faithful to their natural lords and to the Christians whom they serve. They are most submissive, patient, peaceful and virtuous. Nor are they quarrelsome, rancorous, querulous or vengeful. Moreover, they are more delicate than princes and die easily from work or illness. They neither possess nor desire to possess worldly wealth. Surely these people would be the most blessed in the world if only they worshipped the true God.

Gonzalo Fernández de Oviedo, official historian and sworn foe of Las Casas, was one of the most prominent among the rival school. He considered the Indians

naturally lazy and vicious, melancholic, cowardly, and in general a lying, shiftless people. Their marriages are not a sacrament but a sacrilege. They are idolatrous, libidinous and commit sodomy. Their chief desire is to eat, drink, worship heathen idols, and commit bestial obscenities. What could one expect from a people whose skulls are so thick and

hard that the Spaniards had to take care in fighting not to strike on the head lest their swords be blunted?

Thus began the inevitable conflict, which continued throughout the sixteenth century. Practically every important figure in the New World and many in Spain delivered a judgment on the capacity of the Indians. Humble friars and renowned theologians, such as Francisco de Vitoria at the ancient University of Salamanca, arose to defend the Indians from the charge of irrationality. One of the greatest battles on the nature of the Indians, which will be described later in the book, took place in Valladolid in 1550 and 1551 when Juan Ginés de Sepúlveda and Las Casas fought bitterly over the question whether the Aristotelian theory that some men are by nature slaves was applicable to the Indians.

As indicative of the bitter and open conflict that raged on the subject, a conflict which still divides historians and influences their history, may be cited the deathbed retraction by Friar Domingo de Betanzos of his previous opinion that the Indians were beasts. This Dominican had been instrumental in persuading Las Casas to become a friar, had later reproved Las Casas for his "indiscreet zeal," had labored in the Indies for thirty-five years, and now in 1549 returned to Spain on his way to die in the Holy Land. After going on foot from Seville to Valladolid, he stopped at the San Pablo monastery where death overtook him. But before this occurred, a solemn and impressive drama was enacted.

Surrounded by his Dominican brothers, Betanzos repudiated the idea that the Indians were beasts. In the words of the notary who was called to witness this event and whose formal record of it was discovered not long ago in a Bolivian monastery:

In the very noble city of Valladolid on September 13, in the year of Our Lord 1549, before me Antonio Canseco, notary public of Your Majesties, being in the monastery of San Pablo of the Order of Preachers, in a room in that monastery there was an old man with head and beard shaven, lying in bed apparently ill but in his right mind, called Friar Domingo de Betanzos. And he handed over to me, the aforesaid notary public, a sheet of paper on which he told me he had written and declared certain matters, which concerned his conscience, and which related especially to the affairs of the Indies, which manuscript and declaration he delivered to me.

This declaration referred to a written memorial Betanzos had presented to the Council of the Indies some years before in which he had declared that the Indians were beasts (*bestias*), that they had sinned, that God had condemned them, and that all of them would perish. Now on his deathbed he believed that he had erred "through not knowing their language or because of some other ignorance" and formally retracted the statements in the memorial.

A few days after signing this declaration, Betanzos died. For him the struggle was resolved. His Dominican brothers, who doubtless were largely responsible for the whole episode, hastened to make sure that his final statement was made public and that the Council of the Indies received a duly certified copy.

But the issue was not resolved for the King, the Council of the Indies, and all those concerned with the administration of the New World. One of the ablest administrators Spain sent to America, Antonia de Mendoza, the first viceroy of New Spain, arrived at what seems to us today a common sense conclusion on the question. Writing a formal memorial of advice to his successor, about the time that the friar Betanzos made his retraction in Valladolid, Mendoza recommended that neither those Spaniards who considered the Indians simple, industrious, humble, without malice or evil, or those who held the contrary view should be believed. "Treat the Indians like any other people," he urged, "and do not make special rules and regulations for them. There are few persons in these parts who are not motivated, in their opinion of the Indians, by some interest, whether temporal or spiritual, or by some passion or ambition, good or bad."

Some Spaniards in America followed this counsel of moderation, but most did not and all continued to grapple with the problem which was directly or indirectly related to practically every event in the history of the struggle for justice.

IV. THE MEANING
OF EUROPEAN EXPANSION

America and the Wider World

SILVIO ZAVALA

Dr. Zavala is a distinguished Mexican historian with a long career of scholarship, public service, and international teaching. Born in 1909 and educated in Mexico and in Spain, he was secretary of the Museo Nacional de México in 1937–38; is the founder and director of the *Revista de Historia de América;* president of the historical commission of the Pan-American Institute of Geography and History; vice-president of the International Council of Philosophy and Humanities; and, since 1963 president of the Colegio de México. He has also served as permanent delegate to UNESCO, a member of its executive council, and is now vice-president. As a visiting professor in many of the colleges and universities of Latin America, the United States and Europe, he has become conversant with the problems and issues of an international scope. Some of his many written works on Spanish colonization and New World history are indicated in the bibliography.

I F ON ONE SIDE the life of America was formed, after the Columbian discovery, by the influx of immigrants and culture traits from Europe, Africa, Asia, and Oceania, on the other it exercised an influence of its own upon those other continents by the way of the communications established by the European navigators and the colonizers of the New World. The connections of the European colonies in America with their mother-countries were, of course, preponderant; but the connections of the new continent with other parts of the earth acquired great importance in certain cases and certain regions.

It is to be noted that six years after the discovery of the New World by Columbus the Portuguese Vasco da Gama found the maritime route to Asia. Two decades later, Magellan began and Elcano completed the circumnavigation of the globe. This series of great voyages, which were accompanied by other ramifications, inaugurated the transoceanic ties between the various continents.

The history of the influence of America falls within this world perspective of communications. For the first time in history there had been formed the genuinely world-wide network of relationships that characterizes the modern era and differentiates it from all preceding times, not only with regard to America, but, also with regard to all the other continents, although in a variety of degrees and forms in the case of each continent.

The influence of America on the economic life of Europe has been considerable. Between the sixteenth and eighteenth centuries great quantities of metals and

From Silvio Zavala, "America in the New, World-Wide Relationships," *Journal of World History,* IV, 3 (1958), pp. 753–59. Issued under the auspices of the International Commission for a History of the Scientific and Cultural Development of Mankind by Les Editions de la Baconnière, Boudry, Neuchâtel, Switzerland. Reprinted by permission.

precious stones came to Europe from the Iberian possessions. These treasures gave added impulse to the formation of European capitalism, altered prices and standards of living, and caused an influx into the Iberian Peninsula of merchants from Italy, Flanders, and Germany, notably under the rule of Charles V, and reinforced substantial streams of foreign commerce, such as the English trade with Portugal and the French trade with Spain. Similarly, these circumstances facilitated commercial exchanges between Europe and the Orient.

The exploitation of silver in the New World favored the European export of mercury, since it was used so extensively in the extraction of the silver. The Fugger agents in Seville in 1558 observed that the price per quintal of mercury in New Spain had risen from sixty ducats to 150; this fact gave new impetus to the mining of mercury, in Almadén and Idria.

Besides the precious metals, we have already noted that many American plants were incorporated into the agriculture of Europe—notably maize and the potato. Other articles of American production, such as fish from Newfoundland, fine skins from Canada, tobacco and sugar from the English colonies, dye-woods from Brazil, and hides from the great plains in various parts of the New World, as also, medicinal products such as sarsaparilla, quinine, cocaine. Some of these products were re-exported from the mother-countries to Northern Europe and the eastern Mediterranean.

The American colonies consumed great quantities of European manufactures, and thereby augmented the commercial exchange and the development of an international credit system among the European states. For the conduct of trade with Portugal and Spain and their colonies, groups of foreign merchants established themselves in Portugal (Lisbon) and Spain (Cadiz). On the other hand, the export of American goods to other European states and the import from them into Spain and Portugal of commodities for re-export to America contributed to the increase of commercial relations with the northern cities like Antwerp.

In proportion as the treasures and products of America penetrated into the economies of Spain and Portugal, those economies, and especially the fiscal systems, came to count upon their regular importation; by the same token, other countries felt an increasing interest in this same American connection.

Stimulated by the knowledge of the vast profits made by Spain and Portugal from their colonies, the merchants of England, France and Holland entered into the international competition for colonies, and with the support of their governments organized great companies for promoting their transoceanic enterprises in the "two Indies," i.e., the western and eastern "New World."

A later example of the influence of America in European finance was the position that Louisiana occupied in the projects of John Law (1717–1720). When Adam Smith wrote his *Wealth of Nations* (1776), the products and commerce of America merited his attention and entered into his proposals for loosening the colonial monopolies of the great European powers in the interest of greater freedom of international trade.

In sum, the treasures, products, and consumption of the transatlantic possessions of the European states expanded European economic activity and multiplied the transactions between the states of that continent, despite their frequent political rivalries. Thus may be followed the destiny and the influence of the ultramarine products once they had entered into the network of properly European circulation. This study shows that America occupied a significant place in the prosperity of the companies, the mercantile houses, and the states of Europe and in the evolution of mercantile thought and institutions.

Certain ports and regions of Europe presently came to be specialized in direct relationships with America. Such was the case, in the Iberian Peninsula, of Cadiz and Seville, Lisbon and Oporto, in France, of Honfleur, La Rochelle, Dieppe, St. Malo, Bordeaux and Nantes. The overseas trade of Holland passed chiefly through Amsterdam; in England the chief ports of entry for American commerce were London, Plymouth, Bristol, and Liverpool.

The movements of emigrants from Europe toward America affected various regions, including some in the interior. The mother-countries began to be worried over the possible social consequences of the emigration. The fear of a scarcity of labor in England, for example, induced at given moments a policy of attracting to the colonies emigrants from the European continent rather than encouraging Englishmen to emigrate.

The fluctuations in these movements of emigration, their relationships to the social situation in each of the regions of Europe from whence they came (economic crises, wars, famines, epidemics), the eventual return of some emigrants, the diffusion of illnesses along the lines of the new relations between continents — all these constitute a chapter in the social history of Europe that has been studied especially by the historians of the United States; these studies, however, do not embrace the entire movement, but only the important streams that flowed toward North America.

The traces of American influence in the politics, diplomacy, and wars of Europe are easy to perceive. The resources of the New World aided the Iberian powers to sustain their European struggles, while they invited attack by the rivals of these states. Overseas commerce, and in particular the slave trade, figure largely in the European treaties of the colonial era.

European rivalries over the treasures of the New World became more and more significant in the colonial centuries, producing repercussions in world events, in peace and war, and in colonial matters in the War of the Spanish Succession: in 1709 Louis XIV said that the principal object of that war was the trade of the Indies and the wealth it produced. On the other hand, the opposition of Austria, England, and Holland was based on the fear that "a union of the French and the Spanish might soon become so formidable that they might easily reduce the whole of Europe to submission to their imperial authority." For his part, the French ambassador in Spain in 1708 saw the other side of the problem, foreseeing that if the League (against France) should find itself strengthened by the adherence of Spain, if the English and the Dutch became masters of the riches of the Indies, directed this great group of states and energized it with the silver of Mexico and Peru, it was quite clear that France would have more to fear."

It is not strange that, the riches of America having become one of the great factors in the competition between the European powers, the French Mesnager should have proposed the establishment in Cadiz of an international consular tribunal, with Spanish, French, English, Portuguese, Italian and Dutch representatives and that a guard of Swiss Catholics be constituted to watch over the commerce of the Indies. In the negotiations for peace, the French negotiators inclined toward the position that Spanish America should be considered "as the common patrimony of all of Europe, to supply it with the gold and silver; that it would not be proper for any one state to possess anything thus in exclusive right, but that Spain should be, as it had always been, the trustee."

During the War of the Spanish Succession, the English attitude toward the commerce of Spain with the Indies found expression in these instructions: to procure the diminution of tariffs upon English goods entering Spain; to obtain freedom of export of the gold and silver of the Indies from Spain; to secure for English merchants the privilege of shipping English goods in the galeons without paying any higher imports than the Spanish merchants paid; and, if possible, to obtain authorization to send English ships and merchandise to the American colonies of Spain directly from England. By contrast, in the negotiations there also appeared the general fear that England, given its enterprising nature, might be hiding political ambitions behind its demand for commercial concessions.

In the Treaties of Utrecht the navigation and commerce of the Spanish Indies were finally put in the condition in which they stood in the time of Charles II, that is to say, the *status quo ante bellum.* Yet England succeeded in getting the *asiento* for thirty years and a "permission ship" of 500 tons.

In the wars between the colonizing powers in the eighteenth century there was customarily opened an American front, as occurred in the Seven Years War; on the other hand, the rivalry in America over possession of territory exacerbated the traditional political contests of the European nations. Similarly, the independence of America was an important factor in the international balance of power in Europe.

For the administration of its overseas territories each mother-country established either state institutions or commercial companies; the agents and representatives of the colonies at times had considerable influence with the home governments; all the home governments formed colonial archives, often monumental in size; in each country there appeared a whole set of financial arrangements relative to the colonies — imports, monopolies, fiscal bureaucracies, et cetera; the home governments created fortifications, armies, and fleets for the conservation of the overseas possessions. The states of Europe were more complex, more extensive, more powerful, in large measure by reason of the products and the changes of overseas expansion.

Similarly, the papacy, the metropolitan churches, and the religious orders created organs, adopted policies, and trained personnel for the administration and extension of their overseas activities. The expansion of Christianity in so much new land gave the missionary activities a very broad range, and it came to be thought that the discoveries had opened a second apostolate which had for its grand object the carrying of the message of Christ to the parts of the earth that had hitherto remained ignorant of this ecumenical faith. The overseas activities of the Jesuits exemplified the development that a number of such European ecclesiastical organizations attained — empires within empires, as it was said in the eighteenth century.

America also exercised a powerful influence on the development of European culture.

The discovery of America very early produced repercussions in the intellectual climates of Europe. The return of Columbus from his first voyage was observed with immense interest in the courts of Portugal and Spain. The first letters, chronicles of discovery, and foreign news were received with curiosity, and some of them were published, commented upon, and translated in other countries.

The return of conquerors with the fame of Hernán Cortés, surrounded with treasures and Indians, always created a stir in the court of Charles V. This was also true in the other European courts.

A vast new world had been opened before the intellectual curiosity of the Europeans; they, for their part, assimilated, in the realms of geography, botany, zoology, and ethnography, varied data hitherto unknown. More significant, the Europeans were compelled to revise their old concepts of the world and form new ones, more in accord with the realities revealed by the age of discovery.

The American experience raised doubts as to the validity of the ancient natural and human sciences. New questions were raised as to the origin of man in the new continent; the ancient geographers had to be corrected; European knowledge of peoples, religions, and customs was vastly multiplied. These germs of the ideological revolution that followed the Columbian discovery grew in the cultural climate of Europe until they flowered in the literature of the eighteenth century, which was so intimately related with European, American, and world-wide problems.

The interest in the natural phenomena of America and the progress of medicine there had produced some notable studies by the last half of the sixteenth century. In the Enlightenment, many European scientists visited the New World. Their writings constituted a highly significant enrichment of European scientific knowledge.

Along with the European studies of American natural phenomena, should be noted statistical and social studies, from those of Lopez de Velasco in the sixteenth century and of von Humboldt early in the nineteenth. Critical essays were written on the indigenes of America and their culture, as well as histories — religious and secular — of European expansion in the New World.

At the same time, American plants and animals appeared in the botanical and zoological gardens of the European nations, and American artifacts came to form part of the collections of antiquities. Many maps of America were printed in Europe.

The appearance of educated Americans in Europe, along with their works and their contacts with Europeans, contributed to the growth of European interest in America. This in effect is to be noted, for example, in the presence in Europe of the Jesuits expelled from the American possessions of Portugal and Spain, of Anglo-American painters in London, and of such writers as Franklin and Jefferson.

The revision of theological, moral, political, social, and juridical ideas that stemmed from European expansion in the New World was especially rich.

The Spanish felt the necessity for justifying their conquest and rule of the native Americans. Medieval theories as to relations between Christians and infidels served as the first solution to the problem; the classical Greek theories of natural superiority of some men over others were revived by the men of the Renaissance. But all of these older theories emerged from the debate over America considerably modified. Other repercussions of the debate appeared in international law, in theories relative to the freedom of the seas, the right to the occupation of new territories, et cetera.

The expansion of European religion in America raised certain questions that had to be resolved by the thinkers of Europe, particularly in problems touching upon the conversion of Indians and Negroes; these problems and policies invite comparative studies of the methods of evangelization of the Spanish, Portuguese and French, in one area of missionary activity, and of those of the English and the Dutch in another. The syncretism of European Catholicism and the native religions of the Indians and the Negroes, which marked the development of religion in Latin America, constituted another aspect of this vast missionary effort or second apostolate. In close association with Catholic evangelization appeared philological development (as to catechism, doctrines, arts, grammars or vocabularies in native and European languages, et cetera), and the first ethnographical investigations of the religious workers who sought to discover the secrets of the native cultures and souls. The consequences of this expansion of Christianity and its contacts with a great variety of exotic native religions are to be seen in the philosophical position of the eighteenth century, particularly in the ideas of "natural religion."

The discovery of the New World had already influenced Renaissance utopias such as that of Thomas More, which in its turn inspired some of the actual contacts with the Indians of New Spain. The philosophical literature of the eighteenth century admired the republicanism of the young United States, exalted the innocence of the "noble savage," and supported the cause of the abolition of slavery. This literature was especially critical of the

Spanish conquest, the commercial monopoly, and the Inquisition in the Spanish colonies; the European writers of philosophical spirit awaited impatiently the moment when the New World would break the political ties that still bound it to the Iberian Peninsula. Among these themes life overseas was linked with European political preoccupations, which envisaged the transformation of the European societies of the Old Regime.

In the *belles lettres* and art of Europe, America also left its mark. The Spanish theatre introduced to the stage the *"Indiano"* or *"Perulero,"* who interested Lope de Vega. The Portuguese expansion inspired Camoëns. Montaigne wrote of the cannibals. Franz Post caught the Brazilian landscape in his canvases. Albert Eckhout painted the Indian, the Mulatto, and the Negro, against a background of Brazilian tropical nature. In the Jesuit literature, and in the exotic literature of the eighteenth century, there are sketches of the Indians of French Canada, of Angloamerica, of Hispanoamerica, and of Brazil.

American resources contributed, in turn, material support for certain manifestations of European artistic splendor: for example, the building of the Escorial by Philip II and the rebuilding of Lisbon after the earthquake of 1755.

The transformation of European customs was related, in certain cases, with overseas expansion. The potato appeared in European cuisine, chocolate appeared among the drinks, and the use of tobacco became general. Exotic decorative themes appeared in apparel — such as parrots, monkeys, and some applications of American Indian feather-work. Among European dances there appeared the Spanish-American *chaconne* and the Brazilian *modinha;* the latter was popular among the aristocrats and the people of Portugal in the eighteenth century.

In Africa, the procurement of Negroes for the American slave-trade was one aspect of both war and commerce and affected the life of the continent, if only by reason of the diminution of the population in the slave-trading areas. The rum and tobacco from America figured among the commodities introduced into Africa in exchange for slaves; maize, peanuts and manioc were among the American plants that became important elements in the African economy.

Some emancipated Negroes from the United States and Brazil went to Africa; there they caused diffusion of certain linguistic and cultural influences from America.

The principal American contribution to the life of Asia lay in the precious metals sent there to pay for oriental products brought to Europe and America. Asiatic products and immigrants went to the Philippines; they also came to America. But those movements of population into the New World did not attain great numbers in the colonial period; it was in the nineteenth century that they became really significant.

The American potato and tobacco found their way into Asia by the routes of commerce.

The independence of Hispanoamerica and the retention of the Philippines by Spain through the nineteenth century interrupted the communication between America and Asia constituted by the line of galeons between Acapulco and Manila; the independence of Brazil interrupted the old contacts between that country and Asia by way of Portugal. Later, the independent United States, which until the end of the eighteenth century had not participated in them, dominated American contacts with the Orient.

It is clear that, as a consequence of the expansion that followed the great discoveries, Europe passed through a series of significant new experiences. The modern life of that continent was extended to far-flung territories overseas, extracted from its ancient channels, and spread over a vast new world. Europe's intellectual horizon was extended to include new geographical knowledge, new political experiences and ideas, new economic resources and relations, broadened religious fields, and a vast enrichment of its cultural life.

The relations between the continents of the world evolved, during the modern centuries, with a significant shifting of the equilibrium of their relative positions in the whole scheme of things. The dynamism of this evolution can only be perceived clearly if seen in a chronological perspective that begins in 1492. Certainly between the end of the fifteenth century and the beginning of the nineteenth, the first important beginnings of this evolution may be seen in the rise in importance of the colonies that culminated in American independence. At the end of the colonial period, similarly, there may be seen the emergence of an American culture that could already present its first fruits to Europe, as one shall see. But the political, economic, and cultural preponderance of the old world was still evident. Afterwards, great transformations contributed to invigorate the position of the New World and to give to it a different position in world affairs.

The Great Frontier

WALTER PRESCOTT WEBB

In Arnold Toynbee's words, "Walter Prescott Webb [1888–1963] became an historian of a kind that is not very common in our time. He managed to combine mastery of a special area of history [the American West] with a vision of the total history of the world." Webb began teaching at the University of Texas in 1918, fourteen years before he received his Ph.D. from that same university. During the next forty-five years he became almost an institution, and his popular frontier seminar attracted some of the finest students of the country. His wider fame rests largely on his trilogy: *The Great Plains* (1931), *The Texas Rangers* (1936), and *The Great Frontier* (1952). He was honored by his professional colleagues in 1953 as president of the Mississippi Valley Historical Association, and in 1958 as president of the American Historical Association. The essay below is the substance of his opening chapter of *The Great Frontier*.

WHAT HAPPENED in America was but a detail in a much greater phenomenon, the interaction between European civilization and the vast raw lands into which it moved. An effort will be made here to portray the whole frontier, to suggest how it affected the life and institutions of Western civilization throughout the modern period; and as a basis for this exposition four propositions are submitted for consideration:

(1) Europe had a frontier more than a century before the United States was settled.

(2) Europe's frontier was much greater than that of the United States, or of any other one nation; it was the greatest of all time.

From Walter Prescott Webb, "Ended: 400 Year Boom: Reflections on the Age of the Frontier," *Harper's Magazine,* CCIII (October, 1951), pp. 27–33. Reprinted by permission of Mrs. Walter Prescott Webb.

(3) The frontier of Europe was almost, if not quite, as important in determining the life and institutions of modern Europe as the frontier of America was in shaping the course of American history. Without the frontier modern Europe would have been so different from what it became that it could hardly be considered modern at all. This is almost equivalent to saying that the frontier made Europe modern.

(4) The close of the Great Frontier may mark the end of an epoch in Western civilization just as the close of the American frontier is often said to have marked the end of the first phase of American history. If the close of the Great Frontier does mark the end of an age, the modern age, then the institutions designed to function in a society dominated largely by frontier forces will find themselves under severe strain.

If we conceive of western Europe as a unified, densely populated region with a common culture and civilization — which it has long had basically — and if we see the frontier also as a unit, a vast and vacant land without culture, we are in position to view the interaction between the two as a simple but gigantic operation extending over more than four centuries, a process that may appear to be the drama of modern civilization.

To emphasize the unity of western Europe, and at the same time set it off in sharp contrast to its opposite, the frontier, we may call it the Metropolis. Metropolis is a good name, implying what Europe really was, a cultural center holding within it everything pertaining to Western civilization. Prior to 1500 the Metropolis comprised all the "known" world save Asia, which was but vaguely known. Its area was approximately 3,750,000 square miles, and its population is estimated to have been about 100 million people.

There is no need to elaborate the conditions under which these people lived, but it should be remembered that by modern standards the society was a static one with well-defined classes. The population pressed hard on the means of subsistence. There was not much food, practically no money, and very little freedom. What is more important, there was practically no means of escape for those people living in this closed world. The idea of progress had not been born. Heaven alone, which could be reached only through the portals of death, offered any hope to the masses of the Metropolis.

Then came the miracle that was to change everything, the emancipator bearing rich gifts of land and more land, of gold and silver, of new foods for every empty belly and new clothing stuffs for every half-naked back. Europe, the Metropolis, knocked on the door of the Great Frontier, and when the door was opened it was seen to be golden, for within there was undreamed-of treasure, enough to make the whole Metropolis rich. The long quest of a half-starved people had at last been rewarded with success beyond comprehension.

Columbus has been accepted as the symbol, as the key that unlocked the golden door to a new world, but we know that he was only one of a group of curious investigators, Portuguese, Spanish, English, Dutch, and Scandinavian, men of the Metropolis and not of one country. Within a brief period, as history is told, Columbus and his prying associates pulled back the curtains of ignorance and revealed to the Metropolis three new continents, a large part of a fourth, and thousands of islands in oceans hitherto hardly known. They brought all of these — continents, oceans, and islands — and deposited them as a free gift at the feet of the impoverished Metropolis.

The Metropolis had a new piece of property and the frontier had a new owner. The Metropolitans were naturally curious about their property, and quite naturally began to ask questions about it. How big is it? Who lives on it? What is its inherent worth? What can *I* get out of it? They

learned that the frontier had an area five
or six times that of Europe; that it was
practically vacant, occupied by a few primitive inhabitants whose rights need not be
respected; that its inherent worth could
only be guessed at. As to what can *I* get
out of it?, the answer came in time clear
and strong: You can get everything you
want from gold and silver to furs and
foods, and in any quantity you want, provided only that you are willing to venture
and work! And more faintly came the small
voice, hardly audible: Something all of
you can get as a by-product is some measure of freedom.

The Metropolitans decided to accept the
gifts. Instantly the divisions in Europe
were projected into the frontier as each
little European power that could man a
ship seized a section of the frontier bigger
than itself and tried to fight all the others
off. Each nation wanted it all. The result
was a series of wars lasting from 1689 to
1763 and from these wars England,
France, and Spain emerged as chief owners of the frontier world. Their success was
more apparent than real, for a spirit of freedom had been nurtured in the distant
lands, and in less than fifty years England
had lost her chief prize while Spain and
France had lost practically everything.

But their loss, like their previous gain,
was more apparent than real. True, by
1820 the Metropolis had lost title to most
of the new land, but it had not lost something more precious than title — namely,
the beneficent effects that the frontier exerted on the older countries. The political
separation of most of North and South
America relieved the Metropolis of responsibility and onerous obligations, but it did
not cut off the abundance of profits. Europe continued to share in the riches and
the opportunity that the opening of the
golden door had made visible.

What was the essential character of the
frontier? Was the direct force it exerted
spiritual, intellectual, or was it material?

The frontier was basically a vast body of
wealth without proprietors. It was an
empty land more than five times the size
of western Europe, a land whose resources
had not been exploited. Its first impact was
mainly economic. Bathed in and invigo-
rated by a flood of wealth, the Metropolis
began to seethe with economic excitement.

With all the ships coming and going,
the wharves of Europe were piled high
with strange goods, the tables were set
with exotic foods of delightful flavors, and
new-minted coins of gold and silver rattled
in the coffers of the market place. The
boom began when Columbus returned
from his first voyage, and it continued at
an ever-accelerating pace until the frontier
that fed it was no more. Assuming that the
frontier closed about 1890, it may be said
that the boom lasted approximately four
hundred years. It lasted so long that it
came to be considered the normal state, a
fallacious assumption for any boom. It is
conceivable that this boom has given the
peculiar character to modern history, to
what we call Western civilization.

Assuming that there was such a boom
and that it lasted four hundred years, it
follows that a set of institutions, economic,
political, and social, would in that time
evolve to meet the needs of the world in
boom. Insofar as they were designed to
meet peculiar conditions, these institutions
would be specialized boomward. It is accepted that a set of institutions has developed since 1500, and we speak of them as
modern to distinguish them from medieval
institutions. Therefore we may well in-
quire whether our modern institutions —
economic, political, and social, constituting
the superstructure of Western civilization
— are founded on boom conditions.

The factors involved, though of gigantic
magnitude, are simple in nature and in
their relation one to another. They are the
old familiar ones of population, land, and
capital. With the opening of the Great
Frontier, land and capital rose out of all
proportion to population, of those to share
it, and therefore conditions were highly

favorable to general prosperity and a boom. What we are really concerned with is an *excess* of land and an *excess* of capital for division among a relatively *fixed* number of people. The population did increase, but not until the nineteenth century did the extra population compare with the extra land and capital that had been long available.

For example, in 1500 the Metropolis had a population of 100 million people crowded into an area of 3,750,000 square miles. The population density for the entire Metropolis was 26.7 persons per square mile. For each person there was available about twenty-four acres, a ratio that changed little from 1300 to 1650. The opening of the frontier upset the whole situation by destroying the balance that had been struck between land and man. A land excess of nearly 20 million square miles became available to the same number of people, reducing population density to less than five, increasing the average area per individual to 148 acres instead of 24.

Capital may be considered in two forms, as gold and silver and as capital goods or commodities. The Metropolis was short of both forms of wealth throughout the medieval period, and the dearth of coin prior to the discoveries was most critical. It has been estimated that the total amount of gold and silver in Europe in 1492 was less than 200 million dollars, less than two dollars per person. Certainly there was not enough to serve the needs of exchange, which was carried on by barter, or to give rise to erudite theories of money economy. Then very suddenly the whole money situation changed.

By 1500 the Spaniards had cracked the treasure houses of the Great Frontier and set a stream of gold and silver flowing into the Metropolis, a stream that continued without abatement for 150 years, and that still continues. This flood of precious metals changed all the relations existing between man and money, between gold and a bushel of wheat or a *fanega* of barley. That changed relationship wrought the price revolution because temporarily — so fast did the metals come — there was more money than things, and so prices rose to the modern level. This new money was a powerful stimulus to the quest for more, and set the whole Metropolis into the frenzy of daring and adventure which gave character to the modern age.

Since our concern here is with the excess of wealth over population, we may examine with interest the rise in the quantity of gold and silver. Taking the 200 million dollars of 1492 as a base, we find that by 1600 the amount had increased eightfold, by 1700 it had risen nearly twentyfold, by 1800 it stood at thirty-sevenfold, and by 1900 at a hundred-and-fourfold over what was on hand when the frontier was opened. Obviously this increase of precious metals was out of all proportion to the increase in population. If we grant that an excess of money makes a boom, then here in this new treasure was the stuff a boom needed. It is safe to say that out of each $100 worth of precious metals produced in the world since 1493, not less than $85 have been supplied by the frontier countries and not more than $15 by the Metropolis, including Asia. The bearing of these facts on the rise of a money economy, of modern capitalism, is something for the economists to think about.

The spectacular influx of precious metals should not obscure the fact that they constituted but the initial wave of wealth rolling into the Metropolis from the Great Frontier. Wave followed wave in endless succession in the form of material things, and each deposit left the Metropolis richer than before. Unfortunately the quantity of material goods cannot be measured, but we know it was enormous. South America sent coffee; Africa, cocoa; and the West Indies sent sugar to sweeten them. Strange and flavorsome fruits came from the tropics. From primeval forests came ship timbers, pitch, and tar with which to build the fleets for merchants and warriors. North America sent furs for the rich and cotton for the poor so that all could have more than one garment. The potato, adapted to the Metropolis, became second to bread as the staff of life. The New World gave Indian corn or maize, and the rich lands on which to grow it, and in time hides and beef came from the plains and pampas of two continents. Everywhere in Europe from the royal palace to the humble cottage men smoked American tobacco and under its soothing influence dreamed of far countries, wealth, and adventure. Scientists brought home strange plants and herbs and made plant experiment stations in scores of European gardens. In South America they found the bark of a tree from which quinine was derived to cure malaria and another plant which they sent to the East Indies to establish the rubber industry. No, it is not possible to measure the amount of goods flowing into Europe, but it can be said that the Great Frontier hung for centuries like the horn of plenty over the Metropolis and emptied out on it an avalanche of wealth.

At this point let us turn to the growth of population, the number of people who in a rough sense shared the excess of land and of precious metals. As stated above the population in 1500 stood at about 100 million, and it did not increase appreciably before 1650. All the people of European origin, whether in the Metropolis or in the Great Frontier, had a little more than doubled by 1800. Not until the nineteenth century was the increase rapid. By 1850 the increase was more than threefold, by 1900 more than fivefold, but in 1940 population had increased eightfold over that of 1500. The significant fact is that between 1500 and 1850 the quantity of both land and capital stood high out of all proportion to the quantity of population. Equally significant, and somewhat disturbing, is the fact that the excess of land incident to opening the frontier disappeared in the world census of 1930. By 1940 the enlarged Western world was more crowded than the small world of Europe was in 1500. It was the observation of this fact which led Dean Inge to remark in 1938 that "the house is full." Much earlier William Graham Sumner commented on the man-land ratio: "It is this ratio of population to land which determines what are the possibilities of human development or the limits of what man can attain in civilization and comfort." To put the matter in another way, if the boom rested on a four-century excess of land over population, the land base of the boom disappeared in 1930.

The boom hypothesis of modern history may be summed up by stating that with the tapping of the resources of the Great Frontier there came into the possession of the Metropolis a body of wealth consisting of land, precious metals, and commodities out of all proportion to the number of people. . . .

If the opening of the Great Frontier did precipitate a boom in Western civilization, the effects on human ideas and institutions must have been profound and far-reaching. In general such a boom would hasten the passing away of the ideas and institutions of a static culture and the sure appearance of others adapted to a dynamic and prospering society. There is no doubt that medieval society was breaking up at the time of the discoveries, that men's minds had been sharpened by their intellectual exercises, and that their spirits had been stirred by doubt. The thinkers were restless and inquiring, but what they lacked was room in which to try out their innovations, and a fresh and uncluttered soil in which some of their new ideas could take hold and grow. Their desires had to be matched with opportunity before they could realize on their aspirations, however laudable. The frontier offered them the room and the opportunity. It did not necessarily originate ideas, but it acted as a relentless sifter, letting some pass and rejecting others. Those that the frontier favored prospered, and finally matured into institutions; those it did not favor became recessive, dormant, and many institutions based on these ideas withered away. Feudal tenure, serfdom, barter, primogeniture, and the notion that the world was a no-good place in which to live are examples of things untenable in the presence of the frontier.

Since we are dealing with the modern age, it would be very helpful if we could discover what it emphasized most. Where was the chief accent of modernity? What has been its focus? *Who* has held the spotlight on the stage of history since 1500? There can be little doubt, though there may be enough to start an argument, that the answer to all these questions is: the Individual. It is he who has been emphasized, accented; it is on him that the spotlight has focused; it is his importance that has been magnified. He is — or was — the common denominator of modern times, and an examination of any strictly modern institution such as democracy or capitalism will reveal an individual at the core, trying to rule himself in one case and make some money in the other. Not God nor the devil nor the state, but the ordinary man has been the favorite child of modern history.

Did the Great Frontier, which was his contemporary, have any part in giving the individual his main chance, the triple opportunity of ruling himself, enriching himself, and saving his own soul on his own hook? These three freedoms were institutionalized in Protestantism, capitalism, and democracy — whose basic assumption is that they exist for the individual, and that the individual must be free in order to make them work. The desire for freedom men surely have always had, but in the old Metropolis conditions prevailed which made freedom impossible. Everywhere in Europe the individual was surrounded by institutions which, whether by design or not, kept him unfree. He was walled in by man-made regulations which controlled him from baptism to extreme unction.

Then the golden door of the Great Frontier opened, and a way of escape lay before him. He moved out from the Metropolis to land on a distant shore, in America, Australia, South Africa. Here in the wild and empty land there was not a single institution; man had left them, albeit temporarily, far behind. Regardless of what befell him later, for an instant he was free of all the restrictions that society had put upon him. In short, he had escaped his human masters only to find himself in the presence of another, a less picayunish one.

The character of the new master, before whom he stood stripped of his institutions, was so in contrast with that of the old one as to defy comparison. Man stood naked in the presence of nature. On this subject, Alexander von Humbolt said, "In the Old World, nations and the distinction of their civilization form the principal point in the picture; in the New World, man and his production almost disappear amidst the stupendous display of wild and gigantic nature." The outstanding qualities of wild and gigantic nature are its impersonality and impassiveness. Nature broods over man, casts its mysterious spells, but it never intervenes for or against him. It gives no orders, issues no proclamations, has no prisons, no privileges; it knows nothing of vengeance or mercy. Before nature all men are free and equal.

The important point is that the abstract man we have been following did not have to *win* his freedom. It was imposed upon him and he could not escape it. Being caught in the trap of freedom, his task was to adjust himself to it and to devise procedures which would be more convenient for living in such a state. His first task was to govern himself, for self-government is what freedom imposes.

Of course there was not just one man on the frontier. In a short time the woods were full of them, all trained in the same school. As the years went by, they formed the habits of freedom, cherished it; and when a distant government tried to take from them that to which they had grown accustomed, they resisted, and their resistance was called the American Revolution. The American frontiersmen did not fight England to gain freedom, but to preserve it and have it officially recognized by the Metropolis. "Your nation," wrote Herman Melville, "enjoyed no little independence before your declaration declared it." Whence came this independence? Not from parliaments or kings or legislative assemblies, but from the conditions, the room, the space, and the natural wealth amidst which they lived. "The land was ours," writes Robert Frost, "before we were the land's."

The other institution that magnified the importance of the individual was capitalism, an economic system under which each person undertakes to enrich himself by his own effort. It is only in the presence of great abundance that such a free-for-all system of wealth-getting can long operate. There must be present enough wealth to go around to make such an economy practicable. We have seen that the tapping of the frontier furnished just this condition, a superabundance of land, of gold and silver, and of commodities which made the principle of *laissez faire* tenable. In the frontier the embryonic capitalists of the sixteenth and seventeenth centuries hit a magnificent windfall which set them up in business by demonstrating that the game of wealth-getting was both interesting and profitable. For four hundred years, to paraphrase Bernard DeVoto, "men stumbled over fortunes looking for cows." Free homesteads in Kansas, free gold claims in California, and free grass on the Great Plains are examples of windfalls coming at the tag end of the frontier period, windfalls which come no more. In the larger sense the Great Frontier was a windfall for Europe.

There is an unpleasant logic inherent in the frontier boom hypothesis of modern history. We come to it with the reluctance that men always have when they come to the end of a boom. They look back on the grand opportunities they had, they remember the excitement and adventure of it, they tot up their accounts and hope for another chance. Western civilization today stands facing a closed frontier, and in this sense it faces a unique situation in modern times.

If we grant the boom, we must concede that the institutions we have, such as democracy and capitalism, were boom-born; we must also admit that the individual, this cherished darling of modern history, attained his glory in an abnormal period when there was enough room to give him freedom and enough wealth to give him independence. The future of the individual, of democracy and capitalism, and of many other modern institutions is deeply involved in this logic, and the lights are burning late in the capitals of the Western world where grave men are trying to determine what that future will be.

Meantime less thoughtful people speak of new frontiers, though nothing comparable to the Great Frontier has yet been found. The business man sees a business frontier in the customers he has not yet reached; the missionary sees a religious frontier among the souls he has not yet saved; the social worker sees a human frontier among the suffering people whose woes he has not yet alleviated; the educator of a sort sees the ignorance he is trying to dispel as a frontier to be taken; and the scientists permit us to believe that they are uncovering the real thing in a scientific frontier. But as yet no Columbus has come in from these voyages and announced: "Gentlemen, there is your frontier!" The best they do is to say that it is out beyond, that if you work hard enough and have faith enough, and put in a little money, you will surely find it. If you watch these peddlers of substitute frontiers, you will find that nearly every one wants you to buy something, give something, or believe in something. They want you to be a frontier for them. Unlike Columbus, they bring no continents and no oceans, no gold or silver or grass or forest to you.

I should like to make it clear that mankind is really searching for a new frontier which we once had and did not prize, and the longer we had it, the less we valued it;

but now that we have lost it, we have a great pain in the heart, and we are always trying to get it back again. It seems to me that historians and all thoughtful persons are bound by their obligation to say that there is no new frontier in sight comparable in magnitude or importance to the one that is lost. They should point out the diversity and heterogeneity, not to say the absurdity, of so-called new frontiers. They are all fallacies, these new frontiers, and they are pernicious in proportion to their plausibility and respectability. The scientists themselves should join in disabusing the public as to what science can be ex-

pected to do. It can do much, but, to paraphrase Isaiah Bowman, it is not likely soon to find a new world or make the one we have much bigger than it is. If the frontier is gone, we should have the courage and honesty to recognize the fact, cease to cry for what we have lost, and devote our energy to finding the solutions to the problems now facing a frontierless society. And when the age we now call modern is modern no longer, and requires a new name, we may appropriately call it the Age of the Frontier, and leave it to its place in history.

Europe and the Wider World

GEOFFREY BARRACLOUGH

Geoffrey Barraclough is well known in the field of historical scholarship. Fellow of St. John's College, Cambridge, honorary member of the Austrian Institute of Historical Research, and vice-president of the Historical Association, he has been recognized in many ways from a scholar at the British School at Rome in 1931 to research professor of international history at the University of London (1956–62). Barraclough was born in 1908, educated at Oriel College, Oxford, and the University of Munich. He has been a Fellow of Merton College, Oxford; university lecturer at Cambridge; and professor of medieval history at the University of Liverpool (1945–56). His best-known writings have been in the field of early German history, where he has produced *Mediaeval Germany* (1938); *The Origins of Modern Germany* (1946); and *The Mediaeval Empire* (1950). Interested also in the philosophy of history, he is author of *History in a Changing World* (1955).

E VER SINCE THE END of the war a change has come over our conceptions of modern history. We no longer feel that we stand four square in a continuous tradition, and the view of history we have inherited, the history which has western Europe at its centre, seems to have little relevance to our current problems and our

current needs. In the Second World War "the collapse of the traditional European system became an irrevocable fact," and "what is called the 'historic Europe' is dead and beyond resurrection." [1] "The old Europe of the years between 1789, the

[1] H. Holborn, *The Political Collapse of Europe* (1951), x.

World Copyright: The Past and Present Society, Corpus Christi College, Oxford. This article is reprinted with the permission of the Society and the author from *Past and Present, A journal of historical studies*, No. 5 (May 1954), pp. 77–90.

year of the French Revolution, and 1939, the year of Hitler's War, has gone for ever." [2]

This fundamental change is bound to have repercussions upon the writing of modern history, in particular upon the inescapable assumptions of historians. There is still, for those who lived through the period beginning with the great depression of 1929, a morbid interest in the *post mortem* type of history, of which Sir Lewis Namier has made himself the master; but such history avails little as orientation among the dilemmas which face us in the post-war constellation of world-affairs, and it is natural and inevitable that a younger generation of historians should turn away from the old preoccupions, which no longer correspond to a living need, and attempt to hammer out a new vision of the course of modern history, to replace the world-picture which the war has torn to shreds. [3] In some cases this has taken the form of a critique of the assumptions which had become the unquestioned foundations of western historiography — in particular, the assumption, which nineteenth-century economic developments seemed to prove, that Europe was destined to transform all other civilisations and carry over into the hemispheres the system of a balance and concert of powers, by which it was loosely integrated. [4] The illusory nature of these assumptions is already common knowledge. [5] European predominance in Asia is seen today as a temporary phase — almost as a breach in historical continuity — that has now passed. [6] In European history itself the old tendency to exaggerate the rôle of

the "historic core," springing from the empire of Charlemagne, has given way to a better appreciation of the significance for us all of the enduring factors in Russian history — not merely its impact on the western world from the days of Peter the Great, but the importance of the period from the end of the eleventh to the middle of the sixteenth centuries in which the essential features of Russian culture, distinguishing it from western Europe, took shape. [7] We realize better that historic Europe includes not only the Germanic peoples looking to Rome, but the Slavonic peoples looking to Byzantium and later to Moscow, the "Third Rome." [8] And instead of emphasizing the impact of Europe on the New World, historians today are giving greater attention to the impact of the New World on Europe, or are at least seeking to treat their history not as that of separate continents but as directly related elements in the history of a world which, since the Industrial Revolution, has become ever more closely integrated. [9]

Underlying this change of orientation is not so much new knowledge as a new vision playing on old facts, and a realization of the inadequacy of old formulations in a new situation. The older historiography, with its myopic concentration on Europe and the European powers and — where it looked further afield — its independent treatment of the history of America and the overseas territories as distinct units or spheres moving in a separate axis, had discredited history and denuded it of sense and significance; it seemed to be lost in a world of nationalities which has dis-

[2] A. Bullock, *Hitler: A Study in Tyranny* (1952), 738.
[3] Some of these views I attempted to summarize in *The Listener* (1953), 384–387.
[4] Cf. L. Dehio, "Ranke und der deutsche Imperialismus," *Hist. Zeitschrift* CLXX (1950), 307–328; also *ibid.* CLXXIII (1952), 77–94, and CLXXIV (1952), 479–502.
[5] Cf. A. J. Toynbee, *The World and the West* (1953).
[6] K. M. Pannikar, *Asia and Western Dominance* (1953).

[7] Cf. W. Philipp, *Hist. Zeitschrift* CLXXVI (1953), 590.
[8] H. F. Schmid, "Eastern Europe in the light of world history," *Eastern Review*, I (1948), 7–23; S. H. Gross, *Slavic Civilisation through the Ages* (1948); H. Ludat, "Die Slaven und das Mittelalter," *Die Welt als Geschichte* XII (1952), 69–84; O. Halecki, *Borderlands of Western Civilisation. A History of East Central Europe* (1952).
[9] Cf. M. Silberschmidt, "Wirtschaftshistorische Aspekte der neueren Geschichte," *Hist. Zeitschrift* CLXXI (1951), 245–261.

integrated visibly before our eyes. The effort of the newer writers is therefore directed to blasting a way through the blank wall, against which our previous historiography had come to a halt; to opening a path for the historian into the future; and to restoring the connexion between past and present, between history and life, which had perished.

Two main postulates underlie the new view. The first is the realization that what has been called "the European age," which may be dated roughly from 1492 to 1914, was not a steady culmination, but a phase with its beginning and its end, lying between the preceding "Mediterranean" and the succeeding "Atlantic" ages.[10] The second is that the history of this age cannot profitably be studied in isolation, particularly for us who stand outside its limits, and are interested as practical persons above all else in the establishment, during the "European age," of the foundations of the period which, after the wars of 1914–18 and 1939–45, was to succeed it; that, in particular, the distinction between European and American history, as though they were two trams running simultaneously down parallel tramlines, is as unreal and deceptive as would be the attempt today to draw a dividing-line between the economic and political problems of the European and the American continents. There have, of course, from Tocqueville onwards, always been historians who have perceived the temporal limitations of the "European age," and were acutely conscious that it was running to its close; but they remained eccentric and exceptional, and exerted no clear influence over the tradition of historical writing. Today it is different. The failure of the old historiography to provide reliable guidance — for example, in regard to the rise of Russia to the rank of a world-power — its extraordinary capacity, which has bred widespread

scepticism as to the "use" of history, to get the portents wrong, because it failed (if, indeed, it did not often deliberately refuse) to take a wider view, have cleared the decks; and what we may call "the Tocqueville tradition" is at length coming into its own. Much of the writing today, naturally enough, is still tentative, a groping after new formulations, and he who attempts a new synthesis does so at his peril. But already we have from a German historian a challenging re-examination of the whole course of international relations for the five centuries following the fall of Constantinople — a reappraisal which has placed the political history of modern Europe in an entirely new light by setting it in an extra-European context[11] — and here is evidence that this work will not stop short at the political level. Equally important is the economic impact of the outer world on European affairs and its transforming effects upon the whole superstructure of ideas and institutions in the modern world. And precisely this is the field which the American historian, Walter Prescott Webb, has chosen to investigate anew. For Webb, the opening of the frontier lands of the western hemisphere to a static European society in 1492 is the beginning of a new epoch in the story of mankind. Thereafter "in the history of western civilisation the two are inseparable," and "the interaction between the two," a "gigantic process extending over more than four centuries," is for him the essential "drama of modern history."[12] Whatever reservations we may have to formulate as to its positive results, *The Great Frontier* deserves every recognition, as a bold attempt to re-examine along new lines the fundamental postulates of modern history; even where, we may think, it fails to convince, it helps us to clarify the issues,

---

[10] O. Halecki, *The Limits and Divisions of European History* (1950), 29, 61.

[11] L. Dehio, *Gleichgewicht oder Hegemonie. Betrachtungen über ein Grund. problem der neueren Staatengeschichte* (1948).

[12] W. P. Webb, *The Great Frontier* (1952), viii, 8, 11.

and, above all else to see the present not as a continuation of, but as a break with past development.

*   *   *

The conventional starting-points of modern history, for historians in western Europe, are the Renaissance and the Reformation. Walter Prescott Webb takes another view. There had been other renaissances, a long series reaching back to the time of Charlemagne; there had been reformers without number before Luther. But the earlier reforms had withered, the earlier renaissances had failed to produce a decisive turning in the human mind. Why was it that the sixteenth century registered a permanent advance, where other centuries had experienced only a transient stimulus? Webb's answer is clear and categorical. The supreme architect of the modern world, for him, was Christopher Columbus; the decisive event was the discovery of the New World in 1492, and the series of voyages, explorations and discoveries which followed in its wake. Decisive, because the vast accretion of new territory, "of gold and silver, of new foods for every empty belly and new clothing-stuffs for every half-naked back," opened up possibilities no previous society had known. Down to 1492, for all its political upheavals, society had been static in essential things. The rise of empires, Persian or Roman or Carolingian, did not add to wealth, but simply transferred it to other hands. Apart from insignificant increments, due to the slow recovery of forest and marsh, "the land area available to Europeans" remained substantially unchanging; and the consequence was that population, pressing hard on the means of subsistence, was stable too. The idea of progress had not been born; "heaven alone, which could be reached only through the portals of death, offered hope to the masses." [13]

[13] *Ibid.*, 9, 143.

The discovery of the New World completely altered this situation. It added to the old inhabited areas — the "closed world" of the Metropolis — the whole "frontier" zone, the unexploited habitable regions revealed by the explorations of the fifteenth, sixteenth and seventeenth centuries — "three new continents, a large part of a fourth, and thousands of islands in oceans hitherto hardly known." What this signified figures best make clear. The population of the "Metropolis" in 1500, about 100 millions, was crowded into an area of three and three-quarter million square miles, giving an average density of 26.7 persons per square mile. But now "to the 100 million people of the Metropolis was suddenly made available" — in addition to the exportable wealth, gold and silver, timber, furs — "nearly 20 million square miles of fabulously rich land practically devoid of population, an area more than five times as great as all Europe." The result was that "the population density was reduced to less than five persons per square mile, and each individual could have an average of 148 acres instead of 24." In addition, however — and far more immediately effective — there was the impact on the Metropolis of the wealth of the New World. It was American treasure, and American treasure alone, "that reversed the long descent of prices and sent them slanting upwards to such heights as to constitute a revolution." It was the "windfalls" of the frontier — those commodities which fell into the hands of explorers and adventurers almost for the taking — that brought about the capital accumulation which made the Industrial Revolution possible. As Webb says, "it is inconceivable" that the people of Europe in 1500, confined to their original area, "could by any stretch of their genius or by any invention they might make produce the wealth and create the boom which they enjoyed during the following four centuries." The frontier was "the matrix of the modern world." "Without its frontier modern Europe would be so different from what it is that it could hardly be considered modern at all." [14]

Modern history is therefore the drama of the impact of the Metropolis on the frontier and of the frontier on the Metropolis. If western Europe — the Metropolis — is considered alone, its history does not make sense. It was through contact with the frontier in the New World that the institutions handed down from the Middle Ages disintegrated; and "the character of the modern age is due in large measure to the fact that it had a frontier setting, that it grew up in an economic boom induced by the appropriation and use of frontier resources, and that its institutions were designed and modified to meet the needs of a booming society." In 1500 "wherever man turned, some guardian was telling him what to do, what to believe, what to think. All around he was walled in by authority, which saw to it that he moved in a prescribed groove." The frontier was "the fifth column of liberty." It put a premium on the individual, made possible "his temporary supremacy over institutions." "Democracy," says Webb, "is a frontier institution, so far as the modern world is concerned." On the frontier the old-world "baggage" of "ideas about rank, status and relative position" was jettisoned, because it was useless; and instead there arose a new creed of equality. The institutions of the old corporate class-conditioned European society of the *ancien régime* "wore themselves out against the abrasive frontier grindstone." And in their place — spreading back to the Metropolis — arose the characteristic institutions and outlook of a frontier society: individualism, equality, democracy, the "religion of work," "un-

bridled optimism," "rude manners," the profit-motive — a mixed bag, indeed, for the frontier "ruthlessly crushed out many fine qualities which human beings derive from leisure," but a mixture without which modern civilisation, in the Metropolis as well as in the New World, would be unrecognizable.[15]

It is easy to take these changes for granted "as merely another logical step in the orderly progress of an endowed people." To do so is to miss the essential point. In reality, the whole substructure and the whole superstructure of modern civilisation rest upon a "windfall." "The modern age," in other words, "was an abnormal age and not a progressive orderly development which mankind was destined to make anyway." "The institutions developed in this exceptional period were exceptional institutions . . . quite different from what might be expected in the course of human affairs." Like the ideas that went with them — ideas, for example, about the relations of the individual and government — they were "highly specialized to meet boom conditions," and as such bound to undergo violent change as soon as "boom conditions" passed away "and history returned to normal." And precisely that is what has happened. The "Age of the Frontiers" is an age which has passed. Between 1890 and 1910 the frontier closed. As we have seen, the ratio of population to land in 1500 was about 27 to the square mile; by 1900 it was again approaching that mark; by 1930 it has passed it; a decade later it was touching 35. There was a "pause" lasting about a generation, from 1900 to 1930; but "by 1940 the big house was much fuller than the little house was in 1500." [16]

Just as the opening of the "frontier" marked the beginning of a new era, so the closing of the "frontier" marks its passing. The repercussions are already being felt all along the line. "Frontier individualism

---

[14] *Ibid.*, 7, 10, 16, 17, 144, 174. As instances of the "windfalls" of the frontier Webb cites the examples of the gold and silver brought back by Drake in the *Golden Hind* — which provided the capital behind the Levant and East India Companies — and the dividend paid in 1687 by Sir William Phipps — "what is probably the biggest dividend in business history, 10,000 per cent. as against a paltry 4,700 per cent. paid by Drake about a century earlier" (*ibid.*, 197, 201).

[15] *Ibid.*, 5, 11, 30, 31, 34, 35, 49 sqq., 55, 140, 265, 303.
[16] *Ibid.*, 14, 15, 18, 107, 141, 160, 413.

is now old, a thing of history," something
to look back on, representing the "goal of
an extinct period"; and the modern individual, "caught between the closing frontier
and the expanding production of the machine," feels himself "useless, baffled and
defeated." He sees the economic system he
knew in process of falling about his ears;
"and the case is not much different in our
attitude toward democracy." Even if scientific discovery and technology can maintain the abundance which "made the profit-
motive tenable" and carried society "along
the road to capitalism," it will still "bring
with it a new set of needs" and "it will be
necessary to specialize in another direction
determined largely by . . . whatever force
dominates society." "We should not be so
obtuse as to believe that the means of man-
agement are the same as those of conquest,
or that frontier institutions will necessarily
serve a metropolitan society." Obsessed by
the idea of guarding against the limitations
they had escaped, in the form of absolutism
and mercantilism, people failed to see that
out of their new condition, out of "abundance and freedom," "new institutions as
menacing as the old ones" were arising.
None was more important than the business corporation, "the pattern maker of
institutionalized modern life." "Corporate-
ness is now the primary fact and the dominant force." "Curbed on all sides by corporations or government agencies or labour
unions, or associations," the individual is
"approaching anonymity in the modern corporate culture"; "the chief choice left to
him is a choice of curbers." "It is not that
people are no longer willing to take risks,
but rather that they are overborne by a
sense of futility in striving for what seems
unattainable." Nevertheless the result is
a situation "which makes it possible for
the corporate organizations . . . to gather
their recruits," and "gives the few bold
leaders their opportunity . . . to command an army more noted for its docility
than for its courage." Above all else, it is
a situation "favourable to the dictator,"

who rises from "the cemeteries of dead
hopes and aspirations." [17]

This is the new age upon which we are
entering; and of necessity our entry into
it "will be accompanied by basic changes in
the nature of the institutions which grew
up in the earlier one" — particularly in
"those institutions which best fulfilled the
needs of a frontier society." In the end men
looking back will see "the Age of the
Frontier" and all its ideas and institutions
as "an aberration, a temporary departure
from the normal, a strange historical de-
tour." [18]

*   *   *

The force of Webb's argument is due to
the fact that it is based not on chance observation of contemporary trends but upon
a rigorous historical analysis which, if true,
is inexorable. Few of his arguments are
new in themselves. His debt to Turner's
famous "frontier concept" is obvious;[19] and
scarcely less marked, in his analysis of
boom conditions, is his debt to Keynes and
to Earl Hamilton, the historian of the sixteenth-century price revolution.[20] His own
contribution is to bring familiar concepts
and arguments within the fold of an en-
compassing vision which illuminates them
afresh. Nor is it a serious criticism that
his narrative — in common with many
other great simplifying visions — is sometimes crudely expressed and marred by
error in detail. It should nevertheless be
noted that he does not hold "that the frontier originated ideas or institutions, but
only that it altered them, often in a spectacular manner," he does not claim that it
was the only factor, but simply that it was
the formative factor, which provided the

[17] *Ibid.*, 71, 78, 101, 103, 107–109, 113, 118,
119, 128, 131, 414, 418.
[18] *Ibid.*, 414–415.
[19] F. J. Turner, *The Frontier in American History* (1920).
[20] Cf. J. M. Keynes, *A Treatise on Money* II
(1930), 148 sqq.; Earl J. Hamilton, "American
Treasure and the Rise of Capitalism," *Economica*
(1929).

impetus otherwise lacking.[21] It might be argued that he exaggerates the rôle of the "frontier" and pays too little attention to economic developments within Europe since the Industrial Revolution, to the coal of South Wales and the Ruhr and the development of the iron and steel industries, as factors in the creation of modern industrial civilisation. To this criticism his answer would be that the capital accumulation and the economic milieu favourable to technical progress, which were preconditions of the Industrial Revolution, owed their existence to "frontier exploitation"; that, however formidable in themselves, they were secondary consequences, and the "frontier," which "increased manifold the room over which European people could move, and the body of wealth which they could acquire," was primary.[22] It is, no doubt, true that the "fertilization of industry by commercial capital" derived ultimately from the frontier was a less straightforward process than Webb appears to suggest;[23] but whatever nuances might be introduced, it would be difficult to write off his generalization as unfounded. Undoubtedly the historical situation at every stage was more complicated than he indicates; but this fact does not in itself impair the force of his argument, and we are still entitled to ask, what is its validity, not at this or that particular point, but as a comprehensive view of the course of world-history since the age of Columbus.

To this fundamental question — all criticism in detail apart — the answer must be that Webb illuminates part of the scene, but does not illuminate the whole scene because his vision — though wider than that of the average western European historian — is still not worldwide. His study, he says, "is confined to the empty lands of North and South America, Australia, and that portion of the Dark Continent comprised in the Union of South Africa"; Asia "has no part" in his "exposition."[24] The limitation is arbitrary; for it rules out a phase in the relations of Frontier and Metropolis comparable in scale to, and no less heavy in consequences than those with which he deals: the history of the Russian frontier. It may be true that, relatively, the extent of European colonisation, beginning in the Middle Ages — in Prussia, for example, and other trans-Elbean lands — is too small to set beside that of the New World, though the repopulation of the Hungarian plain in the eighteenth century, after the expulsion of the Turks, was so vast a movement that Hungary at that time has been compared with America.[25] But all historians are agreed that in Russian history the "frontier," moving across Asia to the Pacific, has been as important a factor as it was in that of the United States; and in excluding Russia and Russian expansion from his scheme, Webb not only violates the unity of history, but also vitiates his own conclusions. The elementary geo-political facts are sufficient to demonstrate this. The Soviet Union is as large both in extent and numbers as the whole of the North American continent; it is four times the size of Europe, and yet has less than half its population.[26] This itself implies a ratio of land and population radically different from that upon which Webb's whole argument rests. In fact, where Webb establishes for 1940 a figure of approximately 35 inhabitants per square mile, the figure for the Soviet empire is no more than 22 — a figure, significantly, still be-

[21] *The Great Frontier*, 239; cf. pp. 15, 101, 143, 173, 174, 258.
[22] "The early stages of the Industrial Revolution were the middle stages of the frontier revolution"; *The Great Frontier*, 129. Cf. *ibid.*, 75, 101, 238, 410. Cf. M. Dobb, *Studies in the Development of Capitalism* (1946), 207 sqq.
[23] Cf., for example, Dobb, *op. cit.*, 195.

[24] *The Great Frontier*, 9.
[25] Nevertheless we should remember that two-fifths of modern Germany — estimated by its pre-war frontiers — was added by colonisation in little over two centuries, between 1125 and 1346; cf. G. Barraclough, *The Origins of Modern Germany* (1946), 251.
[26] B. H. Sumner, *Survey of Russian History* (1944), 9; "throughout Russian history," he adds, "one dominating theme has been the frontier."

low the European ratio of 1500.[27] In addition we may take into account — by contrast with the "ruinously rapid rate of soil exploitation in North America" — the slow tempo of Russian colonisation in Asia, which only got going on a major scale after 1891.[28] If we accept Webb's postulates, only one conclusion is possible: namely, that the turn of the wheel which he claims to have been completed by about 1910 in the western hemisphere, has not yet occurred in the Soviet Union, that the Soviet frontier is not yet "closed," and therefore that the decline, the "devolution and retrogression," that set in the west with the closing of the frontier, does not apply in the Russian orbit.

It is, however, another question whether we can accept Webb's postulates, and in particular the statistical basis upon which he works. To throw together the land area and population of Europe and the New World, as he does, may illuminate certain facts in their relations, but it obscures others. Even if "the influence of the frontier on the Metropolis was indivisible," if "it exerted its influence on non-owners as well as on the proprietors" — if, for example, "Spanish gold prospered England and Holland and France," and we should not allow "the concept of colonies and empires" to "obscure its common characteristics and the unity of the force it exerted" [29] — the fact remains that its impact was uneven. It is certainly worth emphasizing that the wealth of the New World was not canalized by political frontiers; but that does not mean that political frontiers counted for nothing. When, for example, Webb states that the discoveries "made available nearly 20 million square miles" for the inhabitants of the Metropolis,[30] it is fair to point out that this availability was largely

theoretical, and that in many directions it became illusory when political action in the form of immigration laws checked and even halted the flow of population. When Hitler in 1939 drew President Roosevelt's attention to the fact that the United States, with a population scarcely one-third greater than that of Germany, possessed more than fifteen times as much living space,[31] he unerringly put his finger on the inherent weakness of any argument comprising the European metropolis and the New World in one formula. To treat either the New World or the Metropolis as a "unity," as Webb postulates, is itself of dubious validity; but it will suffice for present purposes to emphasize the broad distinction between the two "colonial" regions, the Asian and the American, and Europe. The only safe course, for the purpose of analysis, is to treat each area separately.

This fact becomes even clearer if we turn to the political and institutional developments, which Webb associates with the influence of the frontier. It is a plausible (though by no means new) argument that the values of individualism were born on the frontier and "that democracy is a frontier institution so far as the modern world is concerned"; but a finer analysis — particularly if, unlike Webb's, it is extended to include Russia — will not stop at this point. Democracy, as a descriptive term, has been used from the time of Aristotle to denote a variety of ills, a number of different political systems; and it is important — not in order to make moral judgements, to castigate the one or the other as merely "a semblance of democratic forms," [32] but simply in order to secure a sound basis for historical analysis — to distinguish between the democracy of the frontier lands, of Russia and the United States, and that of Europe. There are adequate reasons, if we so wish, for describing all three forms of

---

[27] Assuming a population of 192 millions; cf. A. Mousset, *Le monde slave* (1946), 8. The figure of the 1939 Soviet census is 170 millions, but this covers an area smaller than the Russian empire; cf. Sumner, *op. cit.*, 391.
[28] Cf. Sumner, *op. cit.*, 17, 55.
[29] *The Great Frontier*, 11, 21, 410.
[30] *Ibid.*, 17.

[31] *Documents on International Affairs*, 1939–1946, I (1951), 255. "In this state," he had already remarked, "there are roughly 140 people to each square kilometer — not 15, as in America" (p. 254).
[32] *The Great Frontier*, 161, 165.

government as democratic, provided that we realize that such a description does not imply identity between them, or even identity between any two. Neither Russian nor American democracy — despite obvious interconnexions and cross-influences — is the type of democracy we know as a historical fact in western Europe, if only for the reason that they are products of a totally different environment. For Webb the class structure of modern Europe, the privileges of groups and local communities, the corporations which existed to bolster and defend these privileges, constitute both restraints on liberty and the antithesis of democracy. For the European historian who is in a position to compare both the United States and Russia, they are on the contrary the very core and kernel of European democratic institutions. Whether we like it or not, Cromwell's famous dictum: "Where is there any bound or limitt sett, if . . . men that have noe interest butt the interest of breathing shall have a voice in elections?",[33] is an essential ingredient of European democratic practice; and "liberty" and "privilege" in European political tradition are historically not antitheses but co-ordinates, at some periods even synonyms.[34] In western European experience democratic practice has resulted from the action of estates and — on the continent, if not in England — of provincial groupings, fighting for their "rights";[35] it is for that reason and in that sense that it has so often been described as "empirical" or "pragmatic," the product of historical circumstance rather than of systematic

theory.[36] We do not need to nourish any illusions about the limitations of democracy of this type, still less — as is now so common in Germany — to entertain nostalgic longings on its behalf; but it would be blindness to ignore the historical force of the traditions upon which it rests.[37]

From this point of view the historian in western Europe is more likely to contrast Europe with America and Russia, the two societies of the great open spaces, than to range Europe and the United States together as one type, in contrast to Russia.[38] In America, the dismantling of the corporative structure introduced by the early settlers — the collapse of guild-organisation and apprenticeship, the destruction of the village-community, the disestablishment of the church, and the introduction of a free system of land-tenure in place of entail and primogeniture — had occurred before the end of the eighteenth century.[39] In Russia, except perhaps on the western frontiers, such a social structure had never existed.[40] As in America, the open spaces, the moving frontier, the flow of population, stood in the way of the formation of stable social and regional groups comparable to those of the west; even the provincial and district

---

[33] Cf. C. H. Firth, *The Clarke Papers I* (1891), 309. I have cut out the double negative of Cromwell's statement in the defective copy of the shorthand notes. The text is reprinted in A.S.P. Woodhouse, *Puritanism and Liberty* (1938), 59.
[34] Cf. G. Tellenbach, *Church, State and Christian Society at the time of the Investiture Contest* (1940), 16 sqq. — an important statement of the relations of *privilegium* and *libertas* which, no doubt because of the special context in which it is found, has not received the general attention that it deserves.
[35] It is sufficient to refer to Mill's classic statement in the historical introduction to his essay *On Liberty* (Everyman's Library edition, 66).

[36] Cf. G. H. Sabine, *A History of Political Theory* (1938), 665; M. Oakeshott, *The Social and Political Doctrines of Contemporary Europe* (1939), xviii; C. E. M. Joad, *Guide to the Philosophy of Morals and Politics* (1938), 770, 788; T. D. Weldon, *The Vocabulary of Politics* (1953), 87. — it will be evident, with regard to the last-mentioned, that I accept neither his argument for "stealing" the word "democracy" from the communists, nor his attempt (p. 86) to identify the democracy of the United States with that of western Europe. Such arguments may be possible for the political philosopher, but the historian cannot ignore the differentiating influence of historical circumstance.
[37] Cf. for the whole of the above paragraph and for what follows, D. Gerhard's impressive study, "Regionalismus und ständisches Wesen als ein Grundthema europäischer Geschichte," *Hist. Zeitschrift* CLXXIV (1952), 307–337.
[38] Cf. M. Beloff, "Is there an Anglo-American political tradition?" *History* XXXVI (1951), 77, and *passim*.
[39] Cf. Gerhard, *op. cit.*, 327–328; for primogeniture and entail, cf. Webb, *op. cit.*, 259–268.
[40] Cf. Gerhard, *op. cit.*, 312.

assemblies of the nobility were weak.[41] And, as in America, the open frontier and the existence of free land created possibilities for the sudden rise of the individual, which find their parallels in America rather than in western Europe.[42] Indeed, in Russia, as in America, the open frontier has been the source of liberties — the history of the Cossacks is the best evidence of that[43] — but these liberties were never incorporated in fixed institutions in such a way as to withstand the extension of state power and the transformation of the structure of frontier society.[44] Hence it may be argued that "the democracy of the frontier," for Webb the only true democracy, is a fragile growth precisely because it lacks the support of ingrained institutions, because it is related to a theoretical structure of individual rights and based on the atomized individual standing alone in society, whereas western democracy has its roots in groups and associations which effectively bind individuals together as a counterpoise to the power of Leviathan. "Take away corporations and communities," wrote Bodin, "and you ruin the State and transform it into a barbaric tyranny." [45] Not the least significant feature in the situation in Germany leading to the rise of Hitler was the undermining, by economic and other factors, of the old-standing corporative associations, from the *Länder* to the trade unions and the Christian churches. We may well think that Russian history is evidence of the fragile nature of "frontier democracy," that the weakness of local institutions and the mobility of the population go far to explain the triumph of autocracy. And if that is so, we may attach particular importance to Webb's chance remark, that "if totalitarianism comes, it will come hardest among the people who made the most of individualism, the Americans of the United States." [46] In spite of contemporary political and ideological divergencies, there may well, in short, be fundamentally more affinity between the two extremes than between either extreme and the mean.

*   *   *

The foregoing reflections, summary as they are, may serve to throw into relief some of the main limitations of *The Great Frontier,* as a comprehensive picture of the development of modern society. They indicate three main reasons why Webb's thesis fails to convince, although it helps to illuminate certain aspects of modern history. The first is that he exaggerates the influence of frontier institutions; even in the United States there are good reasons to think that the frontier was not the sole or even the main factor in the evolution of political and social democracy,[47] while it still has to be satisfactorily explained why, if decisive, it failed to produce parallel results in South and Latin America.[48] Secondly, he fails to perceive that, in the Metropolis, what we may call "frontier values" have never been accepted as the norm of human existence, and that their influence has been limited historically by counter-currents coming from the heart of western society. European historians are accustomed to see this reaction — with its ideal of an organically articulated society, built up of groups and associations, in contrast to the ideal of a uniform egalitarian society — as finding its outlet in the Romantic movement after 1815; indeed, many would regard it as the essence of the Romantic movement, and it is of the deepest historical significance, that, whereas European rationalism of the eighteenth century

[41] Sumner, *op. cit.,* 76.
[42] Cf. Gerhard, *op. cit.,* 329–333.
[43] Cf. Sumner, *op. cit.,* 49 sqq.
[44] Cf. A. von Schelting, *Russland und Europa im russischen Geschichtsdenken* (1948), 274–278.
[45] J. Bodin, *Les six livres de la république* (Geneva, 1629), 502 (bk. iii, cap. 7); cf. Gerhard, *op. cit.,* 329.

[46] *The Great Frontier,* 122.
[47] As Gerhard points out, *op. cit.,* 326 n. 2, referring to authorities such as A. H. Schlesinger, *The Age of Jackson* (1945).
[48] Webb's summary treatment of this problem (pp. 87–89), in which he emphasizes exclusively the "rigidity and stability of the Catholic Church," as a differentiating factor, is inadequate and unsatisfactory.

had powerful repercussions in America and in the Russia of Catherine the Great, the Romantic movement remained, in its political aspects, a western European phenomenon, affecting Russia only in so far as it was diverted into Slavophile channels, and thereby sharply differentiating the temper of European thought from that of Russia and of America alike.[49] We may, if we like, call this temper conservative, provided we realize it is not the conservatism of political parties; and it is again of the deepest historical significance — wherever our personal sympathies may lie — that the force of this conservatism in Europe, as events since 1945 have demonstrated, is not spent, and that it still exists as a powerful check to the levelling and atomizing influence of "frontier civilization," though in what direction its influence will be exerted no one can foretell. But Webb does not merely exaggerate the influence of the frontier and underestimate the strength of contrary forces. His third major error is to misinterpret the rôle of frontier institutions, which historically have weakened the safeguards of individual rights and so have marked a dilution rather than an advance of the democratic tradition which Europe inherits from its Middle Ages. It is another question whether the new "democracy" is, except in the most indirect way, a product, as Webb supposes, of the frontier; whether it is not more simply the result of the growth of an amorphous urban proletariat which, inadequately represented by the older political associations, gave rise to a new political machinery to cope with its requirements and implement its aspirations. In either case, no one would deny the force of the institutions and ideas which Webb identifies with the frontier. But to admit their force does not imply that we must welcome their advance as progress. On the one side, we can see all too plainly — for all the obstacles have been torn down — the wide road leading from "frontier de-

mocracy" to totalitarianism. On the other side, we can assert with a good deal of conviction that diversity, regional differentiation and stability — the very things that the levelling force of the frontier attacked — are part and parcel of the indispensable foundations of civilisation.[50]

It remains true that Webb is right in emphasizing the importance of the closing of the frontier, the cessation of the boundless opportunities for the individual which it betokened, and the problems of a frontierless society. Even in Russia the time cannot be far distant when the frontier will have closed. But whereas Soviet Russia claims to have its own answer to the problems of a frontierless society, western society, in Europe and in America, is still entangled in the "philosophy of a free and unfettered world," still "trying to harness the dreams of yesterday . . . to the machines of today and tomorrow," and searching among the débris of the old for new or "substitute" frontiers.[51] On these "unreal images of new frontiers" Webb is caustic and astringent; in particular, he is sceptical of the common assumption that the problems of a frontierless society can be circumvented by science which, in place of the open frontier that has gone, can give us the infinite possibilities of a "scientific frontier" stretching indefinitely ahead, and a new abundance produced by scientific means.[52] Science, he insists, cannot create abundance; it may "speed up the rate at which resources already in existence" can be "utilized," but its end-effect is destructive. Indeed, by fostering "a population that is expanding with explosive force all over the world," it is more likely to add to our problems than to solve them. The solution to these problems, if they are to be solved, can only come on the political level. But this solution is complicated by the fact — to which Webb scarcely refers — that the conquest of the frontier, for good

---

[49] Cf. for example G. Ritter, "Ursprung und Wesen der Menschenrechte," *Hist. Zeitschrift* CLXIX (1949), 233–263.

[50] Cf. Gerhard, *op. cit.*, 337, and Oakeshott, *op. cit.*, xix.
[51] *The Great Frontier*, 121, 133.
[52] *Ibid.*, 280–302.

or for evil, has made the whole world one. There is no "overspill" area left, no outlet for surplus population, not even room for manoeuvre. Precisely because the unification of the world — in every sense save the political sense — is something unique in history, it has created a situation without parallel in the past.[53] The question today is whether we can devise new means of coping with this new world-situation. One of the virtues of Webb's analysis is that — parting company from most of his compatriots — he realizes that the newness of our situation leaves no room for the classical individualistic remedies, and makes no attempt to fob us off with the empty clichés — "the middle way," "constitutional co-operation," "spiritual rebirth," and the like[54]

[53] Cf. A. J. Toynbee, "The Unification of the World and the Change in Historical Perspective," *Civilization on Trial* (1948), 62–96.
[54] Toynbee, *op. cit.*, 27, 39, 40, 142, and *passim.*

— of threadbare liberalism. It is a cardinal weakness, on the other hand, that he ignores the achievement of Communism and the fact that Communism — whether we like it or not — provides the only alternative to date, which has not lost constructive force and imaginative grip; it offers at least a plausible solution for the countless millions of "under-privileged" in Asia and Africa as well as in Europe, to the problems of a frontierless society. But there is another way out, of which Hitler has given us a foretaste, — the conquest of "living-space" at the expense of others. It is the classical solution and probably the line of least resistance in a world of contending powers, with a resurgent Asia looming ever larger in the background; but it is a solution which entails famine, bloodshed, want, destruction, and its result can only be the survival of the least fit, the crudest, earthiest and least civilized.

SUGGESTIONS FOR ADDITIONAL READING

Among the many books on the expansion of Europe, students will find the following both informative and stimulating. Although somewhat dated, the standard general accounts of geographical expansion are still J. N. L. Baker, *A History of Geographical Discovery and Exploration* (London, 1931), and J. E. Gillespie, *A History of Geographical Discovery, 1400–1800* (New York, 1933). The *Histoire de l'expansion coloniale des peuples européens* (Brussels, 1907), by Charles de Lannoy and Herman Vander Linden, is also basic, concentrating more on the impact of Portuguese and Spanish colonization than on geographical discovery alone. More popular and very readable narratives are Sir Percy Sykes, *A History of Exploration* (London, 1949), Joachim G. Leithäuser, *Worlds Beyond the Horizon* (New York, 1955) and Paul Herrmann, *The Great Age of Discovery* (New York, 1958). For a more detailed treatment of the early expansion see vol. 3 of Sir Raymond Beazley's monumental *The Dawn of Modern Geography* (Oxford, 1906), and Arthur P. Newton (ed.), *Travel and Travellers of the Middle Ages* (London, 1930). The latter's *The Great Age of Discovery* (London, 1932), also merits attention. A new four-volume series, called *Histoire universelle des explorations,* published by Louis-Henri Parias and others, is an outstanding addition to the literature of expansion. The texts are expertly written by capable scholars, and the maps and illustrations are of exceptional quality.

Charles E. Nowell's *The Great Discoveries and the First Colonial Empires* (Ithaca, 1954), although very brief, is a handy summary of the first two centuries of expansion, as is J. H. Parry's *Europe and a Wider World, 1415–1715* (London, 1949), republished in the Harper Torchbook series (1961) with the title *The Establishment of the European Hegemony.* Parry's latest book, *The Age of Reconnaissance: Discovery, Exploration and Settlement, 1450 to 1650* (London, 1963) is now the best single-volume study of the expansion of Europe, in all of its diversity and excitement. Had he used a little less technical jargon in his chapters on ships and navigation he might have made an even greater contribution. A close second to Parry is Boies Penrose, *Travel and Discovery in the Renaissance, 1420–1620* (Cambridge, 1952), which contains outstanding chapters on navigation, cartography, and geographical literature as well as a good narrative of Portuguese, Spanish, English, French, and Dutch discovery and exploration, and an excellent bibliography. Paperback editions (1964) of both Penrose and Parry are now available.

Several recent articles covering the specific as well as broad aspects of expansion should be read by anyone interested in the meaning and impact of this phenomenon; among these are: Frédéric Mauro, "Towards an Intercontinental Model: European Overseas Expansion between 1500 and 1800," *Economic History Review,* XIV (1961), 1–17, which is good, but technical; E. E. Rich, "Expansion as a Concern of All Europe," *New Cambridge Modern History,* I, 445–69; Carlos Seco Serrano, "El siglo de los grandes descubrimientos geograficos," *Cahiers d'Histoire Mondiale,* IV (1958), 553–81, an excellent survey of European expansion through Magellan. On Italian influences see Roberto Almagià, "The Contribution of Italian Navigators to the Politico-Commercial Expansion of the XVIth Century," *Ibid.,* VII (1963), 285–97, and Ruth Pike, "The Genoese in Seville and the Opening of the New World," *Journal of Economic History,* XXII (1962), 348–78. An earlier but still highly provocative series of articles by William R. Shepherd, "The Expansion of Europe," *Political Science Quarterly,* XXXIV (1919), 43–60,

210–25, 392–412, has been the starting-point for countless students of European expansion. Some enlightening critiques of Webb's thesis may be found in "The Great Frontier Concept," in *The New World Looks at Its History*, ed. by A. R. Lewis and T. F. McGann (Austin, 1963), 133–69, which includes articles by four historians, also in Peter Marshall, "The Great Frontier," *Past & Present*, VII (1955), 55–62.

On some of the technological aspects of navigation and exploration, see Armando Cortesão, "Nautical Science and the Renaissance," in *Science, Medicine, and History*, ed. by E. A. Underwood (Oxford, 1953), 303–16; Frederick C. Lane, "The Economic Meaning of the Invention of the Compass," *AHR*, LXVIII (1963), 605–17 [Many of his articles are now easily available in the commemorative volume entitled *Venice and History* (Baltimore, 1966)]; G. S. L. Clowes, *Sailing Ships* (London, 1932); Quirino da Fonseca, *A caravela portuguesa* (Coimbra, 1934); R. Morton Nance, "The Ship of the Renaissance," *Mariner's Mirror*, XLI (1955), 180–92, 281–98; Guilleux la Roërie, "More About the Ship of the Renaissance," *Ibid.*, XLIII (1957), 179–93; E. G. R. Taylor, *The Haven-Finding Art* [navigation] (London, 1956); Edward L. Stevenson, *Portolan Charts* (New York, 1911); and especially R. A. Skelton, *Explorers' Maps* (London, 1958). The Hakluyt Society's publications are indispensable sources and early narratives of European exploration and travel.

The most active modern interpreter of Portuguese expansion is Charles R. Boxer, of London University. His books and articles are numerous, among them: *Four Centuries of Portuguese Expansion, 1415–1825* (Johannesburg, 1961); *Race Relations in the Portuguese Colonial Empire* (Oxford, 1963); *Fidalgos in the Far East, 1550–1770* (the Hague, 1948); *The Christian Century in Japan, 1549–1650* (Berkeley, 1951); *The Great Ships from Amacon* (Lisbon, 1959); *Fort Jesus and the Portuguese in Mombasa* (London, 1960);

"From the Maghgreb to the Moluccas, 1415–1521," *History Today*, XI (1961), 38–47, and many others. Edgar Prestage's *The Portuguese Pioneers* (London, 1933) is a standard work on the Portuguese expansion. Other valuable more recent studies are: Bailey Diffie, *Prelude to Empire: Portugal Overseas before Henry the Navigator* (Lincoln, 1960); T. O. Marcondes de Souza, *Novas achegas à história dos descobrimentos marítimos* (São Paulo, 1963); Gilbert Renault, *The Caravels of Christ* (New York, 1959); and Antonia Silvia Rego, *Portuguese Colonization in the Sixteenth Century* (Johannesburg, 1959). H. V. Livermore's brief "Portuguese Expansion," in the *New Cambridge Modern History*, I, 420–30, is a handy introduction. Elaine Sanceau's *The Land of Prester John: A Chronicle of Portuguese Exploration* (New York, 1944), is readable and exciting. For more on the mysterious Prester John, see Vsevolod Slessarev, *Prester John: The Letter and the Legend* (Minneapolis, 1959), and Alastair Lamb, "Prester John," *History Today*, VII (1957), 313–21.

There is a great deal of interesting literature on Henry the Navigator and the Portuguese expansion around Africa. The standard works are Sir Raymond Beazley, *Prince Henry the Navigator* (New York, 1895), and the more controversial J. P. Oliveira Martins, *The Golden Age of Prince Henry the Navigator* (London, 1914). In a lighter vein, but still suggestive, are Ernle Bradford, *A Wind from the North: The Life of Henry the Navigator* (New York, 1960) [British edition entitled *Southward the Caravels*]; and Elaine Sanceau, *Henry the Navigator* (New York, 1947). A number of recent articles shed additional light on Prince Henry. See in particular, Eric Axelson, "Prince Henry the Navigator and the Discovery of the Sea Route to India," *Geographical Journal*, CXXVII (1961), 145–55; M. N. Dias, "O Infante D. Henrique e sua época," *Revista de Historia*, XX (1960), 5–22; and Yves Renouard, "L'Infant Henri le Navigateur dans l'histoire de l'Occident," *Revue d'His-*

toire *Economique et Sociale,* XL (1962), 5–14. On the continued Portuguese explorations of Africa see John W. Blake, *European Beginnings in West Africa, 1454–1578* (London, 1937); and Eric Axelson, *Portuguese in South-East Africa* (Johannesburg, 1960), covering the seventeenth century.

In addition to the previously cited writings of C. R. Boxer on the Portuguese in the East, see Frederick C. Danvers, *The Portuguese in India,* 2 vols. (London, 1894); Henry H. Hart, *Sea Road to the Indies* (New York, 1950); K. G. Jayne, *Vasco da Gama and his Successors, 1460–1580* (London, 1910); Edgar Prestage, *Afonso de Albuquerque, Governor of India* (Watford, 1929); I. A. Macgregor, "Europe and the East," *New Cambridge Modern History,* II, 591–614; Kiichi Matsuda, "Influencia de los Portugueses en la cultura japonesa de los siglos XVI y XVII," *Boletim da Sociedade de Geografia de Lisboa,* LXVIII (1960), 309–26; and especially *Asia in the Making of Europe,* by Donald F. Lach. Volume I, books one and two (covering the sixteenth century) of this valuable and detailed work have already appeared (Chicago and London, 1965), and five more are promised. For the labors of missionaries in the Far East, see Vincent Cronin, *The Wise Man from the West* (New York, 1955), about Matteo Ricci; Arnold H. Rowbotham, *Missionary and Mandarin: The Jesuits at the Court of China* (Berkeley, 1942); C. R. Boxer, "'Christians and Spices': Portuguese Missionary Methods in Ceylon," *History Today,* VIII (1958), 346–54; and James Broderick, *Saint Francis Xavier* (Garden City, 1957).

The following are helpful in understanding the Portuguese expansion into Brazil: T. O. Marcondes de Souza, *O descobrimento do Brasil* (São Paulo, 1956); Samuel Eliot Morison, *Portuguese Voyages to America in the Fifteenth Century* (Cambridge, 1940); Frederick J. Pohl, *Atlantic Crossings before Columbus* (New York, 1961); Alexander Marchant, *From Barter to Slavery: The Economic Relations of Portuguese and Indians in the Settlement of Brazil* (Baltimore, 1942); Gilberto Freyre, "Impact of the Portuguese on the American Tropics," *Cahiers d'Histoire Mondiale,* IV (1958), 582–602; and "The Indian Policy of Portugal in America," *The Americas,* V (1948–49), 131–71, 439–53, by Mathias C. Kiemen.

Modern Columbiana and the Discovery of America are vast fields from which only a few titles can be mentioned here. Antonio Ballesteros' *Cristóbal Colón y el descubrimiento de América,* 2 vols. (Buenos Aires & Barcelona, 1945), is a very helpful guide to the subject. Rodolfo Baron Castro, *Palos y la Rábida en el descubrimiento de América* (Madrid, 1947), and "The Discovery of America and the Geographical and Historical Integration of the World," *Cahiers d'Histoire Mondiale,* VI (1961), 809–32, emphasize the spiritual environment of the monastery of Santa María de la Rábida and its effects on Columbus. Salvador de Madariaga has attempted, in his *Christopher Columbus* (New York, 1940) to make Columbus a Spanish Jew. Although not convincing, the argument is interesting and the book is valuable. Jean Merrien's *Christopher Columbus: The Mariner and the Man* (London, 1958), is a good recent biography, but Samuel Eliot Morison's *Admiral of the Ocean Sea: A Life of Christopher Columbus* (Boston, 1942) still remains the most readable and the most reliable study of the discoverer to date. Cecil Jane's publication of *The Journal of Christopher Columbus* (New York, 1960) makes fascinating reading, as does Morison's *Journals and Other Documents on the Life and Voyages of Christopher Columbus* (New York, 1963). Another "must" is the *Life of the Admiral Christopher Columbus,* by his son Ferdinand (New Brunswick, 1959). This edition by Benjamin Keen is the first complete and adequate English translation of the book, first published in Italian in 1570, though originally written in Spanish. Also compare Emiliano Jos, "Fernando Colón y su historia del Almirante," *Revista de Historia de América,* X (1940), 5–29. For other interesting documents see John Langdon-Davie (ed.) *Columbus and the Discovery of America* (London, 1964).

Vespucci literature, though not as vast as that of Columbus, is nonetheless extensive and very contradictory. Among the most valuable are: Henry Vignaud, *Americ Vespuce, 1451–1512, sa biographie, sa vie, ses documents* (Paris, 1917), old but still suggestive; Alberto Magnaghi, *Amerigo Vespucci,* 2 vols. (Rome, 1924), the book that revolutionized the Vespucci controversy; Roberto Levillier, *América la bien llamada,* 2 vols. (Buenos Aires, 1948); and R. Almagià, *Amerigo Vespucci* (Rome, 1954). Frederich J. Pohl's *Amerigo Vespucci, Pilot Major* (New York, 1944), is another important contribution to the Vespucci rehabilitation. Some recent periodical literature has focused on other important aspects of Vespucci's achievements, among these are: Roberto Levillier, "Vespucio, descubridor del Plata, en su V centanario," *Revista de Indias,* XII (1953), 515–25; "Las cartas e viagens de Vespúcio, sugundo Magnaghi," *Revista de História,* V (1954), 407–81; "New Light on Vespucci's Third Voyage," *Imago Mundi,* XI (1955), 37–46; Giuseppe Caraci, "Amerigo Vespucci e um moderno critico argentino," *Revista de Historia,* III (1952), 311–51, which responds to Levillier; and Germán Arciniegas, "Vespucci, una vida malhadada," *Boletín de Historia y Antiguedades,* XLI (1959), 12–36.

Interesting narratives of other discoverers and discoveries are: J. A. Williamson, *The Cabot Voyages and Bristol Discovery under Henry VII* (New York, 1962); L. A. Vigneras, "New Light on the 1497 Cabot Voyage to America," *Hispanic American Historical Review* [hereafter cited *HAHR*], XXXVI (1956), 503–09; Charles L. G. Anderson, *Life and Letters of Vasco Núñez de Balboa* (New York, 1941); Kathleen Romoli, *Balboa, conquistador du Pacifique* (Paris, 1961). On Magellan compare Diego Barros Arana, *Vida y viaje de don Fernando*

de Magallanes (Santiago, 1954), and Leonce Peillard, *Magellan et le premier tour du monde de la 'victoriax'* (Brussels, 1961), with Stefan Zweig, *Magellan: Pioneer of the Pacific* (London, 1938) [American edition entitled, *Conqueror of the Seas: The Story of Magellan*], a very readable popular account. Of great interest also is the recent English edition of Antonio Pigafetta's classic, *Magellan's Voyage Around the World* (Evanston, 1962). For the exciting story of the first man to actually sail around the world, Juan Sebastián del Cano, read Martin Mitchell, *Elcano, the First Circumnavigator* (London, 1958). North American explorations are well told in John B. Brebner, *The Explorers of North America* (New York, 1933); Theodore Maynard, *De Soto and the Conquistadores* (London, 1930); Morris Bishop, *The Odyssey of Cabeza de Vaca* (New York, 1933); and Herbert E. Bolton, *Coronado, Knight of Pueblos and Plains* (New York, 1949).

Useful general accounts of the Spanish conquest and of the conquistadores include Sir Arthur Helps, *The Spanish Conquest in America,* 4 vols. (London & New York, 1900–04); and Bernard Moses, *Spain Overseas* (New York, 1929). The work of Silvio Zavala in this field is indispensable, particularly his *New Viewpoints on the Spanish Colonization of America* (Philadelphia, 1943); *Las institutiones jurídicas en la conquista de América* (Madrid, 1935); and *Ensayos sobre la colonización española en América* (Buenos Aires, 1944). The best book on the conquistadores is F. A. Kirkpatrick, *The Spanish Conquistadores* (London, 1946). Rufino Blanco-Fombona's *El conquistador español del siglo XVI* (Madrid, 1922; Caracas, 1956), is a vigorous defense, while Jean Descola's *The Conquistadores* (London, 1957) is a less laudatory evaluation. Several articles, in a variety of periodicals, contribute a great deal to our knowledge of the conquistadores and to many aspects of the conquest. See in particular, Roger Howell, "Conquerors and Conquered in the New World, Part II:

The Spaniards and the Conflict of Ideas," *History Today*, XIV (1964), 202–12; J. H. Parry, "Spaniards in the New World," *New Cambridge Modern History*, I, 430–44; William Lytle Schurz's perceptive chapter on the conquistadores in his *This New World* (New York, 1954), 109–59; Javier Malagón-Barceló, "The Role of the Letrado in the Colonization of America," *The Americas*, XVIII (1961), 1–17, showing the importance of law and legal procedure to the sixteenth-century Spaniards; and Dorothy McMahon, "Sidelights on the Spanish Conquest of America," *Ibid.*, 19–31.

On Cortés and the conquest of Mexico see Ernesto Barrios Berumen, *La conquista española: Hernán Cortés y su obra* (Mexico, 1954); Francis A. McNutt, *Fernando Cortés and the Conquest of Mexico* (New York, 1909); Salvador de Madariaga, *Hernán Cortéz, Conqueror of Mexico* (New York, 1941); and, of course, William H. Prescott, *The History of the Conquest of Mexico* (many editions). Ursula Lamb, "Religious Conflicts in the Conquest of Mexico," *Journal of the History of Ideas*, XVII (1956), 526–39, is also of considerable interest, but rather involved. On Cortés' companions, see Herbert Cerwin, *Bernal Diaz, Historian of the Conquest* (Norman, 1963); John E. Kelly, *Pedro de Alvarado, Conquistador* (Princeton, 1932); and Marvin E. Butterfield, *Jerónimo de Aguilar, Conquistador* (Tuscaloosa, 1955),

For Peru and South America, see Philip A. Means, *Fall of the Inca Empire and the Spanish Rule in Peru* (New York, 1932); William H. Prescott, *History of the Conquest of Peru* (many editions); Germán Arciniegas, *Knight of El Dorado* (New York, 1942), on Jiménez de Quesada; and *Germans in the Conquest of America* (New York, 1943), concerning the settlement of Venezuela; R. B. Cuninghame Graham, *The Conquest of New Granada* (London, 1922); *The Conquest of the River Plate* (London, 1924); Pedro de Valdivia, *Conqueror of Chile* (London, 1926); and José Toribio Medina, *The Discovery of the Amazon* (New York, 1934). For horse lovers, and those interested in another fascinating aspect of the conquest, see Cunninghame Graham's *The Horses of the Conquest* (Norman, 1949).

The Indian problem was crucial in the conquest and has been treated in many ways by historians. The best modern studies of the Black Legend are Sverker Arnoldsson, *La leyenda negra: estudios sobre sus orígenes* (Göteborg, 1960); and Rómulo D. Carbia, *Historia de la leyenda negra hispanoamericana* (Madrid, 1944). Among Juan Friede's many books and articles on the Indians and Spanish-Indian relations, *Los indios del Alto Magdalena* (Bogotá, 1943); and *El indio en lucha por la tierra* (Bogotá, 1944), are very useful. By far the most prolific, and in many ways the most penetrating, writer on Spanish-Indian relations in the conquest is Lewis Hanke, of Columbia University. His first notable contribution in this field was *The First Social Experiments in America: A Study in the Development of Spanish Indian Policy in the 16th Century* (Cambridge, 1935), and his most recent is *Aristotle and the American Indians* (London, 1959). Between these two have come scores of books and articles examining many aspects of the subject, including "Francisco Toledo and the Just Titles of Spain to the Inca Empire," *The Americas*, III (1946), 3–19; "Pope Paul and the American Indians," *Harvard Theological Review*, XXX (1950), 65–102; and "Free Speech in Sixteenth-Century America," *HAHR*, XXVI (1946), 135–49. Compare Edmundo O'Gorman's "Sobre la naturaleza bestial del indio americano," *Filosofía y Letras*, no. 1 (1941), 141–58; no. 2, 303–15; and J. M. Ots Capdequi, *El Estado español en las Indias* (Mexico, 3rd ed. 1957). The best studies of the *encomienda* and other colonial institutions are Lesley B. Simpson, *The Encomienda in New Spain* (Berkeley, 1929); *Studies in the Administration of the Indians in New Spain* (Berkeley, 1934); Silvio Zavala, *La encomienda indiana* (Madrid, 1935), and especially his *De encomienda y propiedad territorial* (Mexico, 1940), which clarifies many misunderstood points; Howard F. Cline, "Civil Congregation of the Indians in New Spain," *HAHR*, XXIX (1949), 349–69; and M. M. Lacas' important "The Encomienda in Latin-American History: A Reappraisal," *The Americas*, VIII (1952), 259–87. David L. Wiedner's "Forced Labor in Colonial Peru," *Ibid.*, XVI (1959–60), 357–84, is also valuable.

The literature on Las Casas is voluminous, and growing yearly. Many of the older studies, such as George E. Ellis, "Las Casas, and the Relations of the Spaniards to the Indians," in *Narrative and Critical History of America*, ed. by Justin Winsor (Boston, 1884), II, 299–342, are still useful, but new dimensions have been added by Marcel Brion, *Bartolomé de las Casas, padre de los Indios* (Mexico, 1953); Manuel María Martínez, *Fray Bartolomé de las Casas, el gran calumniado* (Madrid, 1955), which is very hostile; and numerous articles by Marcel Bataillon. The most persistent work on Las Casas has been done by Lewis Hanke, whose sympathetic, though rather repetitious treatments of the "champion of the Indians" have given him new meaning and importance to English readers. In particular see Hanke's *Bartolomé de las Casas: An Interpretation of His Life and Writings* (The Hague, 1951); *Bartolomé de las Casas: Bookman, Scholar, Propagandist* (Philadelphia, 1952); *Bartolomé de las Casas, Historian* (Gainsville, 1952); "Bartolomé de las Casas: An Essay in Hagiography and Historiography," *HAHR*, XXXIII (1953), 136–51, in which he challenges O'Gorman's contention that Las Casas' preaching in Vera Paz was like a "scientific experiment." O'Gorman's answer to Hanke is found in "El método histórico de Lewis Hanke on the Spanish Struggle for Justice in the Conquest of America," *HAHR*, XXIX (1949), 563–71, where he agrees with Hanke's overall view of Spanish justice but disagrees with his interpretation of Las Casas. See also Venancio Diego y Carro, "Bartolomé de Las Casas y las controversias teológico-jurídicas de

Indias," *Boletín de la Real Academia de la Historia*, CXXII (1953), 231–68; Juan Friede, "Las Casas y el movimiento indigenista en España y América en la primera mitad del siglo XVI," *Revista de Historia de América*, XXXIV (1952), 339–411; "Fray Bartolomé de las Casas, exponente del movimiento indigenista español del siglo XVI," *Revista de Indias*, XIII (1953), 25–55; and Fernando Ortiz, "La leyenda negra contra Fray Bartolomé," *Cuadernos Americanos*, XI (1943), 146–84. A convenient collection of a few of Las Casas' writings may be found in Francis A. MacNutt, *Bartholomew de Las Casas, His Life, His Apostolate, and His Writings* (New York & London, 1909).

On other facets of the Indian question, see Carlos E. Castañeda, "Fray Juan de Zumárraga and Indian Policy in New Spain," *The Americas*, V (1948–49), 296–310, and Charles Gibson, *The Aztecs under Spanish Rule, 1519–1810* (Stanford, 1964). For the impact of the Indian controversy on the origins and development of international law see Arilio dell' Oro Maini, *La conquista de América, y el descubrimiento del moderno derecho internacional* (Buenos Aires, 1951); Luciano Pereña Vicente, *Misión de España en América, 1540–60* (Madrid, 1956), an excellent study of the Indian question in international relations theory; José Antonio Maravall, "El descubrimiento de América en la historia del pensamiento político," *Revista de Estudios Políticos*, XLIII (1952), 229–48; James B. Scott, *The Spanish Origin of International Law* (Oxford, 1934); Marcel Bataillon, "Charles-Quint, Las Casas et Vitoria," in *Charles-Quint et son temps* (Paris, 1959), 77–91; and Ramón Menéndez Pidal, *El Padre Las Casas y Vitoria, con otros temas de los siglos XVI y XVII* (Madrid, 1958).

Several aspects of Spanish policy and administration may be studied in Clarence H. Haring, *Trade and Navigation between Spain and the Indies in the Time of the Hapsburgs* (Cambridge, 1918); *The Spanish Empire in America* (New York, 1947), which contains a valuable bibliography; Earl J. Hamilton, "Spanish Mercantilism before 1700," in *Facts and Factors in Economic History* (Cambridge, 1932); *American Treasure and the Price Revolution in Spain, 1501–1650* (Cambridge, 1934); André Sayous, "Partnerships in the Trade between Spain and America and also in the Spanish Colonies in the Sixteenth Century," *Ibid.*, 283–301; Ruth Pike, "Seville in the Sixteenth Century," *HAHR*, LXI (1961), 1–30; and A. P. Usher, "Spanish Ships and Shipping in the Sixteenth and Seventeenth Centuries," *Ibid.*, 189–213. J. H. Parry, *The Spanish Theory of Empire in the Sixteenth Century* (Cambridge, 1940); *The Audience of New Galicia in the Sixteenth Century* (Cambridge, 1948); Fernando de los Ríos, *Religion y estado en la España del siglo XVI* (Mexico, 1957); and Antonio Tovar, "L'incorporation du nouveau monde a la culture occidentale," *Cahiers d'Histoire Mondiale*, VI (1961), 833–56.

The participation and rivalry of other nations in the New World can be seen in Arthur P. Newton, *The European Nations in the West Indies* (London, 1933); Philip Means, *The Spanish Main: Focus of Envy, 1492–1700* (New York, 1935); Garrett Mattingly, "No Peace Beyond What Line?" *Transactions of the Royal Historical Society*, 5th Ser., XXIII (1963), 145–62; Henry Folmer, *Franco-Spanish Rivalry in North America, 1524–1763* (Glendale, 1953); Francis Parkman, *Pioneers of France in the New World* (Boston, 1900); E. K. Chatterton, *English Seamen and the Colonization of America* (London, 1930); Franklin T. McCann, *English Discovery of America to 1585* (New York, 1952); A. L. Rowse, *The Expansion of Elizabethan England* (London, 1955); J. A. Williamson, *The Age of Drake* (London, 1952); David B. Quinn, "Some Spanish Reactions to Elizabethan Colonial Enterprises, *Transactions of the Royal Historical Society*, 5th Ser., I (1951), 1–24; Kenneth R. Andrews, *Elizabethan Privateering* (London, 1964). The great source collection on English voyages is Richard Hakluyt's *Principal Navigations*, 12 vols. (Glasgow, 1903–15). Engel Sluiter, "Dutch-Spanish Rivalry in the Caribbean Area, 1594–1609," *HAHR*, XXVIII (1948), 165–96; C. R. Boxer, *The Dutch in Brazil, 1624–54* (Oxford, 1957); *Salvador de Sá and the Struggle for Brazil and Angola* (London, 1952); and Frédéric Mauro, *Le Portugal et l'Atlantique au XVIIe siècle, 1570–1670* (Paris, 1960).

1 2 3 4 5 6 7 8 9 0